ɟore t
ɐ ɹǝɔ.ɯ by persoɾ... applɩɕ
reɾ.ɐw give the date due anɑ
Fines are charged on ɔνǝ·
rred ɪ·

Baghdad's Spy

ABOUT THE AUTHOR

An expert on Britain's commercial lobbying industry, Corinne Souza wrote the first industry exposé, published by Politico's in 1998. She followed up with its first directory, also published by Politico's, in 2000. She prepared four research papers for the Committee on Standards in Public Life, 1998 and 1999, and was a witness before Lord Justice Neill, the Committee's then chairman, in 2000.

A contributor to espionage journal *Lobster* since 2000, she is the only writer to have brought into the public domain the impact that espionage can have on children and family. A graduate of the School of Oriental and African Studies (SOAS), London University, she is the daughter of a decorated businessman-spy, who at one time was the Secret Intelligence Services foremost authority on Iraq.

A Personal Memoir of Espionage and Intrigue
from Iraq to London

BAGHDAD'S SPY

CORINNE SOUZA

MAINSTREAM
PUBLISHING
EDINBURGH AND LONDON

In Memory of Sheila

First published in Great Britain in 2003 by
MAINSTREAM PUBLISHING COMPANY (EDINBURGH) LTD
7 Albany Street
Edinburgh EH1 3UG

ISBN 1 84018 703 4

A catalogue record for this book is available from the British Library

Typeset in Allise and Garamond
Printed and bound in Great Britain by
Mackays of Chatham plc

CONTENTS

THREE: INHERITING ESPIONAGE, 1980–2001

ACKNOWLEDGEMENTS

I acknowledge the kindness of the SIS officer responsible for my family's pastoral care in 1986.[1] He called himself 'Adrian Firbeck' while having different initials on his briefcase. He was a compassionate and decent man and I am very pleased to have this opportunity to thank him for his assistance.

I am grateful to publisher Bill Campbell for 'backing a hunch'; Will Mackie and Graeme Blaikie for the finished product; Tina Hudson for the cover design; and publicist Sharon Atherton. Particular thanks go to international relations specialist Richard Moir and espionage authority Robin Ramsay, who made factual contributions and kindly read earlier drafts of the text. Robin, as editor of *Lobster*, also generously provided me with an espionage profile. I commend his magazine to any reader interested in para-politics and intelligence affairs.[2]

Special acknowledgement goes to espionage author and investigative journalist Mark Hollingsworth. Over 15 years, his integrity and loyalty has seen me through some difficult times. He also introduced me to Bill Campbell and edited my book.

Finally, I thank my mother, Julia, and Richard, whose life I have been privileged to share for many years. There is no second of any day when I do not give thanks for them and for everything they mean to me.

Corinne Souza
March 2003

NOTES

[1] Secret Intelligence Services (SIS) also known as MI6. I use the abbreviation 'SIS' throughout the book because this is how the Foreign Office referred to itself in correspondence.

[2] *Lobster*; details: robin@lobster.karoo.co.uk

Introduction

OPEN LETTER TO SIR RICHARD DEARLOVE

Director General

'The Chief'

Secret Intelligence Services

London,
19 October 2002

Dear Sir Richard,

This book is about a spy, his daughter and sorrow. The spy was my father, Lawrence de Souza. He was the best of men. The sorrow is mine. If you read my story, you will understand why.

I have several objectives in writing it. I hope to draw attention to the impact that espionage can have on a spy's family and children; assist those considering a career in espionage to make an informed choice about some of the moral confusions; and raise the profile of our country's spies and the Crown's treatment of them. I believe that the Crown has sabotaged the reputation of our spies in order to boost that of the staff, principally SIS diplomats and Whitehall civil servants. In so doing it has denied espionage-families their histories and pride in their relatives.

As you will know, my decorated businessman father served our country for nearly two decades, retiring from the SIS in 1978. He died in 1986. His last act of service, when he was terminally ill, was to put in place the arrangements for the handling of anticipated intelligence after his death. These arrangements became relevant shortly before Iraq invaded Kuwait in 1990. As a result, I have a four-decade view of espionage.

Staff retire. Spies do not. Even when they are dead.

My father's expertise pertaining to the Middle East and specifically Iraq was unrivalled. As a businessman, he was a dual-career civilian with diplomatic rank equivalent to First Secretary. Had Britain been at war, he would have gone into uniform as a full colonel. He was responsible for the recruitment of Iraqi and

Kurdish contacts and additionally specialised in countering Arab terrorism.

Because of his cosmopolitanism, discipline, languages and skin colour – above all, a knowledge of and respect for other faiths – he was able to access the networks so essential to our security. As a result, he could enrol and run reputable sources and contacts, whether locally based in volatile countries or from key communities outside of them.

Despite his operational excellence, he was driven out of the SIS by the incompetence, appalling personnel management and racism of many of its staff, as well as the organisation's lack-of-safety culture. This, I believe, explains why the Crown has been unable to replace people like him, or nurture a confident, select cadre of Arabic specialists who were, above all, British patriots as well as experienced spies.

These were not SIS diplomats or civil servants but dual-career civilians with the seniority to alert our government to possible economic problems, military developments, political upheaval or terrorist strikes. In addition, they could recruit the necessary sources and informants. This ability, while being one of espionage's most highly prized skills, is also one of the most dangerous.

The spy, operating overseas without diplomatic immunity, is at his most vulnerable when he is seeking to secure the services of a collaborator, because in doing so, he has to expose his non-civilian identity, and, crucially, country of allegiance, which might not have been suspected. He does so knowing that if he gets caught, he is not protected by the equivalent of a 'Vienna Convention'.

Some spies are ruthless – it is a punishing profession. They make no apology for themselves or what they do . . .

My father's clandestine life dominated mine. His colleagues were a seamless carpet of SIS diplomats, SIS Whitehall civil servants, SIS businessmen and insurance brokers and finally SIS 'No Names' – young intelligence officers who used aliases. Nevertheless, the last time I met your organisation's Foreign Office representatives, in July 1994, they tried to claim I 'was not there'.

It is an easy mistake for staff to make. This is because they are not aware that all over the world espionage is predicated on the suburban home.

While the staff have Whitehall offices, limousines or embassies to inhabit, spies do not base themselves in their offices, whether or not they own the company, because their colleagues or employees do not know what they do. Their clandestine work is directed from their (usually) suburban houses or family cars, whether in Baghdad or presumably today Kabul, or back in London. These (usually) contain children. They go with espionage's territory.

It is a suburban occupation.

Unlike you, the reader will know nothing about my father. He was born in Baghdad in 1921. His mother was half-Kurdish and half-Iraqi; his father, from whom he acquired his British papers without citizenship rights, an Indian. As with many of his generation from the British Commonwealth, he was passionate about the Crown. He served it first in his native Iraq, and subsequently in what he called 'the Mother Country' – the United Kingdom – from which he travelled frequently overseas.

He met my English mother in London in 1949. After a whirlwind romance, they married within three weeks of meeting. They came from a different class, culture, faith and race to each other, and, having no money, their union could have been doomed to failure. Instead, it lasted a lifetime. Fearless, taking incredible risks, they were quiet people who led an amazing life.

Their heroism purchased, as something my father's modest SIS salary was able to provide, my private education. In addition, a one-off bonus was my British passport. (In those days British nationality could not be inherited from an English mother.)

My parents raised their children in Iraq before sending them to boarding school in England. My turn came in 1965, when I was ten. Although I returned to Baghdad in the school holidays, for the most part, picnics under the ancient Lion of Babylon or on the banks of the Tigris gave way to hockey and cold baths.

My father was a businessman, an imperialist, a right-wing Tory, a monarchist and a Roman Catholic who, unusually, was also a freemason. He believed Britain was an example to the world, including what he called the 'Free World'. He also thought Iraq, once under British mandate, was part of the Commonwealth and that 'the Mother Country' would always have its best interests at heart. A fervent anti-Communist, he thought SIS was on the front-line of the Cold War, protecting citizens all over the world from totalitarianism. He believed that SIS had an honourable agenda.

Many years later, as a seasoned spy with considerable authority, he could, for enormous financial reward – there has always been a great deal of money sloshing around in espionage – have gone to another Western power. He did not do so. As you know from his files, he was not for sale. When he was dying, he told me: 'I would rather have been a subaltern in the Queen's army, than a general in the most powerful army in the world that did not serve my Queen.'

I clashed with many of his opinions – the Almighty has a keen sense of humour – and had difficulty with various aspects of his work. We disagreed repeatedly on his politics, British policy in the Middle East, Zionism and his belief in the arms trade. However, I have absolutely no doubt that the views he held, and the way he conducted his dual commercial–espionage career, were as sincere as they were upright.

My mother did not approve of my father's decision to serve SIS, believing, first, it was too dangerous for a family man, and second, that he would be treated badly because of the colour of his skin. Once, however, the decision had been taken, she supported him throughout. In espionage, a wife's contribution cannot be overestimated.

She demurred twice. First in 1968, after she and my father decided to leave Iraq when SIS requested my father defect to Moscow. Well known for stingy salaries, the Crown asked him to name his price. My father, although keen, did not go – because my mother refused to accompany him.

Her refusal, although she did not know it at the time, was to save his life since, as careful reading of *The Mitrokhin Archive* shows, the Soviets were already onto him but at this stage had not identified him.[1] Neither my mother nor I have any illusions about what would have happened had he been caught. After the Soviets had finished with him, they would have passed what was left of him to the Iraqis. . .

Many forget that the Soviets were brutal – they are encouraged to do so by retired Soviet spies anxious to imply that they were 'gentlemen'. This is rubbish. No state espionage service, including SIS, conducts itself well, although individuals within it can and do.

My mother also made one condition for supporting my father's intelligence career – their children must never become similarly involved in it. He accepted wholeheartedly. To protect my brother and myself from becoming targets, he did not teach us Arabic, telling friends we were English and had no requirement for the Arabic language.

My mother describes how, standing by my cot when I was an infant, while an Iraqi dust-storm turned the sky outside orange, my father promised, 'Our children will be as free as the seagulls on the White Cliffs of Dover and as beautiful as the flowers in St James's Park.'

He did not know then that an infant born into SIS – particularly one who owed her British passport to it – was born into controversy. As a result, in all his married life it was the one promise, to his very great distress, he was unable to keep. Over 20 years later his career was to haunt mine when, employed as a Westminster lobbyist (1980–85), I refused to work for the intelligence services or spy on Labour politicians.

My parents left Iraq in 1968, a few weeks before the first of the two July revolutions which brought the Ba'aths to power again. Saddam Hussein was one of the young officers involved. My parents never returned to Baghdad, although my father continued to specialise in the country, as well as other Middle Eastern states, on behalf of SIS for the following ten years. In addition, as a bona fide businessman, he traded with Iraq and other parts of the Arab world.

He adored both his professions. Although he was never part of a global network of friends and contacts in what was to become the intertwined world of international finance and politics, he was well known and had extensive business contacts in the Middle East, in particular his native Iraq. This made life fun.

Espionage, although usually dangerous, is fantastically interesting. Its excitement gives a family its private identity. It was, and is, a career and a lifestyle.

It is therefore a shock when, for whatever reason, that career collapses.

In my family's case, it did so because some years before my father retired he became a fierce internal critic of much SIS conduct, including individual staff, language skills, and competence in, and knowledge of, the modern Middle East.

His SIS reports should still be in his file, if you care to read them. These he passed to the Crown via those I knew well. At no time did he break the Official Secrets Act. Nor would he have thought of doing so.

He criticised as a Crown servant and was not aware that criticism in itself was regarded as treachery. Nor did he know that instead of considering the constructive advice he offered, SIS would unleash a vicious spite machine against him. This was executed by a cabal of urbane noxious troubadours strutting their stuff, seemingly launching themselves from a playpen of narcissism. They turned SIS's one-time internationalism on its head, plunging it headlong into white supremacism.

Their onslaught ruined the last years of my father's service, destroyed his peace of mind during his retirement and ultimately enveloped me. As a result, and through no fault of his own, he could not keep the promise he made to my mother. I was sucked into SIS's mayhem. It broke his heart.

It is easy to force a retired spy to conform. All you have to do is ensnare his child. This has two advantages. First, it destroys the father and, very nearly, wrecks his marriage. Second, it makes the child responsible for the father's destruction and sole heir to the human debris of espionage.

I will always be sad that the fine spirit in which my father and his original SIS diplomat colleagues served the Crown soured so badly. I recognise that they were not responsible for what happened to my father in the '70s and '80s; nor to me in the '90s. It was their successors, whose conduct has such serious consequences today, who shame their memory.

My mother, of course, speaks constantly of my father and of Iraq. Like him, she believed the country was part of the British Commonwealth in all but name. It never occurred to her that Britain would take up arms against the Iraqi people, nor, for so many years, sustain Saddam Hussein. It was not for this that my father served the Crown.

Until the end of his days, he remained in love with two countries. His tragedy was that in serving one, he believed he served the other.

His life was dominated by three women: his wife, his daughter and his Queen. Despite all that happened, he remained Her Majesty's devoted servant. He had no regrets. Neither did my mother. They said, 'We would do it all again. It was our duty.' The young man who perfected his English by listening to what he called the 'wireless', and dreamed that one day he would bring his family to 'the Mother Country', remained in love with Britain and his monarch for the rest of his life.

I am not a royalist. However, out of respect for my parents, I ask Her Majesty, through you, to consider a memorial without religious connotation, in a place of beauty, in honour of all our spies, particularly those from the Commonwealth. I acknowledge with gratitude Her Majesty's commitment to the Commonwealth, and contrast it with the 18-year rule of the Conservatives, who treated it with disdain. In so doing, they discarded the goodwill of the Commonwealth's multiethnic and multi-faith diaspora, in the process confirming the Crown's racism and diminishing SIS's capabilities, geographical reach and multi-focus. I regret that, despite the Commonwealth's diversity, and the crucial relevance of this today, Prime Minister Blair omitted all mention of it in his detailed speech on the new world order. I expected greater sophistication from a Labour leader who has been in government for over five years.

As for whether my father would have approved of my book, the answer is 'No'. He believed that he had a lifelong duty of confidentiality to the Crown. He would have found it unforgivable that the daughter he trusted implicitly in her youth could embarrass the Crown in maturity. However, this would be to ask the wrong question.

If, instead, you were to query whether he would have approved of my right to write this book, his answer would have been 'Yes'. This is why he sent me to a free country. If, having read it, I have persuaded some to acknowledge the legitimacy of my objectives I will not have wasted my time. I will, however, always be disappointed by the Crown's attempts to silence me.

I have one further request which I express at the end of my book, in my concluding letter.

My memoir contains no secrets. It is merely a domestic time capsule of British espionage from 1958 to 2001. I offer it as part of our historical record which has long been denied. It begins in 1960s Baghdad. You will only understand what SIS has thrown away if you see through my child's eye the Iraqi people, their hopes and the pride of my then-young parents in the Crown they served.

Yours sincerely,

Corinne

NOTES

[1] Andrew, C. and Mitrokhin, V. (2000) *The Mitrokhin Archive: The KGB in Europe and the West.* Allen Lane: London.

ONE

An SIS Childhood

BAGHDAD, IRAQ
1958–68

1

RECRUITING A BRITISH SPY

In 1958, the Boy King of Iraq was murdered and the monarchy overthrown. President Qassem declared the Iraqi Republic. The collapse of the monarchy confirmed the continued diminution of British power in the Middle East and exacerbated fears that President Nasser of Egypt would 'export' Arab nationalism throughout the area. This posed a threat to British oil companies. BP, for example, was frantic that SIS defend its interests against such nationalism and, as importantly, protect it from American rivals.

Despite constant attempted coups, President Qassem remained in power for five years, 1958–63. In 1960 he gave the Iraqi Communists the upper hand. Eighteen months later he claimed Kuwait. In addition, he struck at British and American oil companies. About this time, the Kurds in the North of Iraq went into armed revolt, and British and American ships steamed up the Gulf to protect their oil investments.

In 1963, President Qassem was overthrown by the pro-Nasser President Abd al Salam Aref and his Ba'athist Prime Minister Ahmad Hasan al Bakr. Thousands of Communists, and those suspected of Communism, were killed. The new president renounced Iraq's claim to Kuwait. Also that year, there was a coup in Damascus, Syria, with the result that the Ba'athis became top dogs in Baghdad and Damascus.

SIS pleasure at the toppling of President Qassem was soon muted when President Aref began a nationalisation programme. Two years later, there was a further coup but the attempt failed. President Aref died in a helicopter crash in 1966. He was succeeded by his brother, who made peace with the Kurds. Later that summer the new president dismissed his civilian prime minister. There followed an endless procession of military governments which went out of their way to co-operate with foreign companies competing for commercial favours in Iraq.

17

In 1967 Iraqi airfields were attacked by Israel during the Six Day War. To the consternation of the American business community, which demanded that the US government stop backing Israel, American and British diplomatic relations in Egypt and Iraq were broken off. The following year, in July 1968, there were two coups in Iraq. The first saw off the president; the second secured the position of Ba'ath army officers. The future President Saddam Hussein was one of those Ba'ath officers.

This was the political background to my father's first decade as a British spy.

My father's idyllic Baghdad childhood was shattered in 1933 when, aged 12, he witnessed his millionaire Indian father go bankrupt. As a result, my father was unable to complete his education beyond high school. For a brilliant scholar at the American Jesuit College, it was a personal tragedy.

Aged 18, my father was briefly interned because of his British papers by the anti-British Iraqi Prime Minister Rashid Ali. Many years later he commented wryly: 'I was interned because I was British. Nevertheless, my "Mother Country" refused to recognise my children as British. How can a man be interned for his "Britishness" when his "Mother Country" refuses to recognise it or allow him to pass it to his son?'

In the summer of 1941, he became an English–Arabic translator at the British embassy, where he remained until the end of the Second World War. Still a teenager, he heard endless complaints about the embassy's arrogance. Many locals were particularly offended that it misspelt the word 'Baghdad' – as 'Bagdad' – on its official notepaper and refused to correct the mistake.

He visited London for the first time in 1949, where he met and married my mother. My father was 27; my mother 25. 'For as long as I could remember,' he recalled, 'I was in love with the idea of Britain. I was always British. When I married your mother, I became more so. I admired her and the country that created her.'

His future wife had never heard of Iraq. Nevertheless, it became her home for nearly two decades. 'I spent the happiest years of my life in Baghdad, with my husband and Iraqi people,' my mother says today. She speaks of a blend of Christian, Jew and Muslim and the vibrancy of lifelong friendships; of Nimrud and Nineveh, desert and snow, Tigris and Euphrates to explain the beauty of Iraq's ancient land and proud, diverse people.

Following her marriage, she left with my father for Iraq. They went by various boats to Beirut and continued their journey overland to Baghdad on a wooden bus. A year later, my brother was born. Anxious to establish their baby's nationality, my father had the birth registered at the British embassy. This conferred no nationality rights. However, he believed that 'it would make the paperwork look better in the future'.

Although constantly short of money, they enjoyed their life to the full. Their mixed marriage was not unusual – many Iraqis were marrying European and

American girls at the time – and they had many friends. Some of these friends were Communists.

Recalling the party at the British embassy held to celebrate the Queen's coronation in 1953, my father said, 'Those of us with English wives were all invited. One couple in our group were staunch Communists. We all thought this a great joke. Of course, we had no idea that a few years later the Iraqi monarchy would be over and the husband of the Communist couple, who remained our very dear friends, would become important.'

Joining ICI as senior salesman, my father soon began to prosper. He and my mother were often spotted at the smartest cocktail parties. Their only worry continued to be my brother's nationality. The British Consul was brutally frank about this, informing them in a letter in 1954: 'The children of British subjects without citizenship rights do not inherit their father's national status. It therefore follows that your son, if he does not possess any other nationality, must be stateless [. . .]'.

Born in Baghdad the following year, so was I.

In 1956, my parents left for Britain to try to sort out the problem of their children's nationality from London. They drove from Iraq to the UK in a Morris Minor – 'with the roof down, except in the Alps' – with my brother and myself and all their possessions on the back seat. Before leaving, my father solicited the support of ICI, his former employers. Up until his death, he spoke of the company with great affection for the help its personnel tried to give in his quest to obtain British papers.

Six months into their stay in Britain, my parents ran out of money. Having no option but to return to Iraq, they asked ICI if it could speed up progress with the British Authorities. Despite ICI's efforts, the request was refused. My brother and I remained stateless.

Profoundly depressed, my father saw a job for a 'Senior Salesman, Iraq' advertised in *The Times*. He went for an interview with Gresham Linley Limited, of City Wall House, Finsbury Pavement. The company described itself as 'Government Stores Contractors & Exporting Agents & Purchasing Agents'. It was in business in the Middle East with a firm owned by a wealthy Armenian whom my father knew well and had worked for previously. Gresham Linley, chaired by Brigadier Crosland CBE, told my father that they would give him their reply on his return to Iraq.

Once more in their Morris Minor, my parents set off for Baghdad again. On arrival, my father heard that his application had been successful and he joined the company. Progressing rapidly, he and my mother soon resumed their enjoyable social life. Our family albums are littered with photographs of my striking parents at countless cocktail parties. My brother, meanwhile, was enrolled at the British Council school where, every sports day, the English headmaster arranged for the Iraqi crown prince to give away the prizes.

In 1958 came the Iraqi revolution and the murder of the Iraqi royal family.

The crown prince, who, only a short while before, had doled out silver cups to sports-mad small boys, was shot dead with the young king in the palace gardens. The British embassy was sacked and looted, a harrowing time for the ambassador, his colleagues and their families.

My father was able to get his wife and children on to the last flight out of Iraq to London before Baghdad airport closed, but stayed behind himself. Almost destitute, he went to live at the YMCA. He did not know when he would see his family again, nor how he would support them financially when he did.

Some months later he was contacted by a charismatic Scottish aristocrat called Sandy Goschen.[1] My father was aged 36, Goschen 7 years older. Today, Goschen would be called an intelligence officer operating under diplomatic cover. My father understood him to be a diplomat.

My father never asked Goschen how SIS first talent-spotted him. He believed that my Indian grandfather, prior to his bankruptcy, had been a British source and espionage can pass from one generation to the next. My father's school records (always significant when recruiting a spy) would have been acceptable, confirming that he was anti-Communist. These would have been passed to London when he applied for British passports.

My mother would also have been acceptable to SIS, which was always on the lookout for good-looking prospective husband-and-wife teams.

She had served throughout the London Blitz in the fire service with my grandfather, who was disabled and too old to be at the front. As a 16 year old she watched London burn as the Thames was set alight. Meanwhile, her two brothers were away fighting. One was seriously wounded in the North African desert, while the other was a pilot in the Battle of Britain. Prior to her marriage in 1949, she was a telephonist at the Board of Trade.

My father was an ideal SIS candidate because SIS had very few Arabists, and those it did have were based in Beirut. These people were not universally respected. More importantly, my father knew some of the junior army officers – some of whom had British wives – in the new Iraqi republican regime. (While my father was always saddened by the manner of the Boy King's death, he was not an Iraqi monarchist. He was the first to admit that had the monarchy not been swept aside, SIS would not have recruited him. It did so because it hoped that as his friends rose in rank, he would retain their friendship and rise with them, which he did.)

My father jumped at the opportunity to 'work for the Crown', as Goschen suggested. So far as I am aware, no money exchanged hands. Instead, my father asked for British passports. Six months later, in the spring of 1959, he had them. 'Meeting Sandy [Goschen] was a dream come true,' my father said. 'He honoured all his promises to me.'

My father dated the start of his Crown service from Sandy Goschen's first approach in 1958. However, SIS date it from 1961 when it first made regular, tax-free payments into my father's London bank account.[2] I do not blame SIS for this discrepancy – paper records, for obvious reasons, were notoriously unreliable – although it was later to have implications for my father's pension. Certainly he considered himself in Crown service from the earlier time.

Following my mother's return to Iraq, my father waited one week before he told her that he had been recruited by SIS. He recalled, 'Your mother was very upset. Very against it. She believed I would not have agreed to work with Sandy had she not been in England. She begged me to change my mind. I told her it was better for us and better for our children.

'The next time I met Sandy, I told him about my wife's reservations. He understood immediately and found them sensible. As soon as he could, he made arrangements for us to meet his wife. They were both wonderful, charismatic people. We adored them. In all my life, I never once regretted meeting Sandy. He was fearless. A wonderful man.'

My mother remembers the couple with equal affection. In particular, she recalls Goschen's pride in showing her a photograph of his Scottish castle. 'The joke was,' she said, 'because of his surname, everybody thought he was either Jewish or a German fleeing the Third Reich.' When Goschen left Iraq, he gave her a valuable cigarette lighter which had enormous sentimental value to my parents. Regrettably, it was subsequently stolen in London.

NOTES

[1] Sandy Goschen OBE MC joined the Foreign Office from the Special Operations Executive in 1954. He served in Vienna, Berlin, Mogadishu, Baghdad, Lagos, Malta. My parents last had news of him when he was working for SIS in Nigeria in the 1970s. Source: 'A Who's Who of the British Secret State', *Lobster* special (1989).

[2] These disbursements paid for my brother's school fees and subsequently my own.

2

ENTERTAINING SPIES

My father was never an 'agent of influence'. Instead, he was expected to rise in Baghdad society and gather intelligence on people, armaments and commercial contracts. SIS's goals in the Middle East were to combat the 'Nasser effect' – the rise of Arab nationalism following the Suez War of 1956 – prevent the Soviets from increasing their influence and stop oil supplies shifting to the American oil companies.

One of my father's key successes was the recruitment of a source from within an important Iraqi ministry. Substantial sums of money were paid to the source by my father on behalf of the Crown. Eventually, an overseas bank account was established. Payment was made directly, in sterling.

Today, not least because of the Internet and other communications, information is easy to come by. In the 1960s this was not the case. In addition, very little was known about the Soviet Union and the emerging Middle East. Therefore, to find a spy who considered himself British, whose friends, some of whom were Communists, were part of the emerging new order, was a real find. My father recalled, 'Sandy said that I was a gem.'

In addition to Sandy Goschen, my father served in Baghdad with SIS diplomat Keith Womersley[1] and SIS diplomat 'Frank Tay' (not his real name). My parents, the Goschens and the 'Tays' were members of the same social club – the Alwiyah – one of the two most prestigious in Baghdad.

Another SIS diplomat based at the British embassy was Guy Bowden.[2] My father recalled, 'Guy asked me to obtain the serial numbers of a Soviet aircraft the Soviet embassy had invited me to inspect. I was very happy to agree. However "Frank" objected and was very cool, telling Guy to find his own sources.

'I liked Guy and felt embarrassed for him. I could not understand why there was a problem since we were all working for the Crown. This was when I realised that there were other branches of the Crown and each branch had its own spies.

There must have been dozens of us in Baghdad. "Frank's" objections seemed silly. As I say, we were all working for the same country.'

The new spy developed into a bold collector of information. Suave and charming, with enormous social confidence, my father had a talent for friendship. This enabled him to mix freely in Iraqi society and in the diplomatic community, especially with diplomats from the Soviet embassy and satellite countries. He provided profiles of Iraqi military and political personalities, many of whom were his friends, as well as intelligence on their plans, and relationships with the Soviets and Arab countries.

By 1962, his commercial life had prospered sufficiently for him to set up his own company. Although SIS did not assist with its financing, my father said, it 'Strongly encouraged me to go into business on my own.' The firm my father established was modest. According to his notepaper, it had limited liability in Iraqi dinars equivalent to £20,000 sterling and had branch offices in three Iraqi towns – Baghdad, Kirkuk and Mosul. He had a Muslim partner and a Jewish broker. Neither man was aware of my father's spying activities. Both subsequently left for the United States.

My father acquired much of his intelligence on the social round. He could reach parts SIS could not. For example, he was invited to foreign embassies that were out of bounds for SIS and could circulate beyond those embassies' immediate orbit. In this work he was ably assisted by my mother. She had very little formal education but ran on instinct.

'She developed a sixth sense,' said my father, continuing, 'I relied on her intuition all the time. She could read faces. She always knew if someone was lying.'

My father – but not my mother – had a blind respect for a secret service about which little was known. However, he was not dazzled by the British, nor by their diplomats. He believed the embassy had been hopeless prior to the Boy King's murder, had been rightly condemned for arrogance and racism, and had failed to provide an intelligence warning of the 1958 revolution.[3]

SIS did not give my parents any formal training. For the most part, it relied on the innate talents of its spies. My father said, 'On countless occasions "Frank Tay" assured me I need have no worries about your mother. He said she had a "poker face" and nobody ever knew what she was thinking. He wished all the others were like her. He was very complimentary about your mother.

'Because your mother was so beautiful, invitations to all the best parties rolled in all the time. I have always said that to do his job properly, a spy requires a beautiful and honourable wife. I was the proudest man alive as I led your mother onto the dance floor.

'All spies and their wives must know how to dance well, which we did. In particular, a spy had to know how to dance the tango. The British only knew how to waltz so they were at a disadvantage. The best dancers were the Soviets. They were superb. They all knew how to dance the tango.

'The attention your mother got never turned her head, nor made her vain. In our early years, we did not have the money to buy her expensive dresses or fine jewellery. It did not matter a jot. She was so beautiful that she outshone them all. She drank "White Lady", the same cocktail she drank when I courted her in London, and that is what she was.'

As a local, my father was valuable to SIS because he had a different focus to that of his colleagues. This was useful when, say, he attended receptions at the Afghan, Pakistan or Indian embassies. 'The Soviets constantly milled around these,' he said, 'for this reason, SIS was very pleased that I was going to them as well. It was too self-conscious to be much use itself. It could not accept that India had gone. This coloured its view on everything.'

According to my father, SIS did not see Afghanistan, Pakistan or India in any terms other than Empire. 'I remember telling Sandy Goschen that my father, an Indian nationalist, had locked himself in his room for three days at the time of Partition and Sandy colouring with grief,' recalled my father. Goschen's family had close connections with India.

My parents hosted wonderful receptions themselves. Such was their success, uniquely, that at one of their cocktail parties at the height of the Cold War, the British, American, West German and Soviet ambassadors were all present at the same time, albeit in different corners of the room.

Mixing with important locals required a less urbane approach.

My father said, 'As a party trick, I became adept at reading coffee cups and palms. As a result, the wives of countless Iraqis begged me to tell their fortunes. Sometimes, their husbands did too – Iraqis are very superstitious. However, they were more discreet than their wives. They always invited me to their private offices or houses for such a session. I picked up incredible intelligence this way, not least because of the answers they were hoping to find in the cups, which meant posing the questions.

'It was a remarkably successful way of building intimacy. I have always suggested that those wanting to be spies should learn how to read coffee cups if this is part of the culture of the countries in which they are working. It would not work in, say, New York. However, there are rules. If you can, read a family member's coffee cup – always when other family members are present – before you read your target's. The family group allows for teasing, which creates an atmosphere of trust and good humour.

'The ideal family member, in Iraq at any rate, can be the target's mother. Once she is relaxed, you can make a "prediction" that will encourage her, unwittingly, to reveal something interesting. A useful starting point could be, for example, "health" such as, "The cups are telling me you are worried about the health of someone close to you . . ." On one occasion, I was rewarded with chapter and verse on my target's physical health and, more importantly, when he was going to be out of the country for medical treatment. London was absolutely chuffed to have the dates. Next, I was told to which country he was going. This was also helpful since it confirmed hitherto suspected bias. It was all exceedingly useful.'

Sandy Goschen loved the idea that 'while the Soviets were going around clicking their heels and kissing the tips of ladies' fingers, his spy was reading coffee cups!'

Both my parents were highly disciplined and had strong nerves. As a result, my father was able to swing with the various political shifts. For example, during the Qassem regime, many believed him to be a Communist, which he was not. He never actually said he was one, but was able to give this impression. When the Communists began to lose sway, he switched allegiance again. This did not cause comment: Baghdad was essentially a merchant town and the commercial community, both local and international, were expected to be pragmatists.

Although working for the Crown was dangerous, not least because of the highly unstable political situation, my father found it exhilarating. 'I had a wildly exciting time,' he said. 'Your mother, on the other hand, never found espionage exciting.'

'She wanted us to do our duty by the Crown, but she did not want me to be a spy. She was always against it. She said it would change us. She was right, it did. For example, we had to avoid my elderly parents and other relatives as much as possible so as not to "contaminate" them if I was discovered. Therefore, they thought we were snubbing them.'

My mother particularly hated making new girlfriends because she knew my father would always be interested in what their husbands did for a living, which he was. 'We had terrible rows about me trying to use her friendships,' he admitted.

One of the most successful sources he recruited came via my mother's friendship with the man's wife. SIS was so pleased that after my father had run him for a number of years, it was decided that it was too dangerous for them to continue together. SIS did not want them both getting caught – always an occupational hazard.

As a result, my father and his source had to drop each other and not be seen in the same company. This was very difficult because it meant their respective wives had to do the same. 'It caused enormous problems – not least because my source's wife did not know that her husband was working for me. Your mother was very upset,' said my father.

In the end, while my mother knew everybody, she stopped making friends. She had no confidante. Within the space of ten years, she went from being a merry English Rose to becoming the other half of a spy. No one from her old or new life knew anything about her.

She was particularly worried about the impact my father's work would have on my brother and myself, believing that young children were born knowing there are things they must not see or hear.[4] 'Children absorb espionage through their skin,' said my father. 'A spy's life is a lot easier once they have been sent to boarding school. Everything can be organised before the school holidays bringing them home on what was then called the "Lollipop Special" [the affectionate name for the British Overseas Airways Corporation – BOAC – scheduled flights which, at the end of term, reunited children with their parents who were overseas].'

My brother went to boarding school immediately after the 1958 revolution. I returned with my mother to Baghdad and did not join him in England until 1965. As a result, my parents had to train themselves not to let me see anything – and train me not to say anything if I did.

Despite all the precautions, I still managed to compromise them. For example, I found the Boy King's flag, long after his murder, and carried it in to my parents when they were entertaining Republican army officers and their wives. I can still remember the resulting tension. As a result, I always knew that there was 'something' going on. I still have the 6 in. by 4 in. flag that I had discovered, neatly ironed, in my father's handkerchief drawer.

I also knew that other people were curious about my parents. For example, when our family cook was unwell, the relief cook tried to pump me for information about my mother and father. Subsequently, it was discovered that the relief cook was a police informant (and, incidentally, a paedophile). He was never employed again. A short while later his body was found in the Tigris. My parents never found out who killed him. (Iraqis adore children and are ruthless in dispensing justice to those who harm them.)

On another occasion, I noticed a 'bag switch', although I did not actually see it take place. I knew the bag my mother carried into the Alwiyah Club when she took me on the swings, although identical, was not the same bag she put in the car when we left. I remember mentioning this to her and her denying it.[5]

I also remember being 'punished'– when I had done nothing wrong – when I was not allowed to accompany my father to a stamp shop in Old Baghdad. This was a surprise since up until then I had accompanied him on a weekly basis and he had encouraged me to take an interest in stamp collecting, which was his passion. I never went with him again and later found out that this was due to his espionage work.[6]

It was not only in Iraq that 'funny' things happened. For instance, staying in Jordan, close to the Mandelbaum Gate which, in those days, divided Jerusalem between the Arabs and Israelis, I noticed a man talking into a walkie-talkie. When I told my father, he asked, 'Did he have skin like Daddy, darling, or did he have white skin like Mummy?' A short while later, we checked out of our hotel and left via the back door.

'For all these reasons,' said my father, 'your mother hated my career. Espionage is very hard on women with children. She went along with it for my sake.'

He was always grateful that she did because, 'I would not have been able to do my work without her. She had the English, calm temperament and nerves like steel. In dangerous situations, she was absolutely icy. However, she hated every moment of it, and went on hating it.'

My mother, who refuses to talk about my father's work, confirms he loved spying and all its dangers. Personally, I think she enjoyed some of it, but in order to restrain my father was tight-lipped about her enthusiasm.

NOTES

[1] Keith Womersley CBE joined the Foreign Office in 1946. He served in Damascus, Berlin, Vienna, Hong Kong, Baghdad, Aden, Beirut and Bonn, retiring as counsellor in 1977. My parents last met Womersley and his wife Eileen in London in the late 1970s, after Womersley's retirement.

   According to *Lobster*, Keith Womersley's service in Iraq pre-dated Sandy Goschen's. However, it was Goschen (whom *Lobster* place in Berlin at the time) who recruited my father.

   Source: 'A Who's Who of the British Secret State', *Lobster* special (1989).

[2] In his book *MI6: Fifty Years of Special Operations* (2000), published by Fourth Estate, Stephen Dorril refers to 'Col. J. Bowden' the military attaché in Baghdad when Humphrey Trevelyan was ambassador, 1958–61. I believe he means Guy Bowden.

[3] The young SIS diplomat at the embassy during the 1958 revolution became my father's case officer in London in the 1970s.

[4] This could be less of a risk today since children may have more distractions as a result of the breakdown of the family unit and increased television viewing. As a result, they may not notice as much.

[5] It is possible that children, because of their height, notice things on their eye-level an adult would not.

[6] KGB Colonel Lev Bausin, quoted in Helen Womack's *Under Cover Lives* published by Weidenfeld & Nicolson in 1998, mentions his attempts to develop similar contacts via a stamp shop in Cairo.

3

AN SIS SPY AND THE BRITISH EMBASSY

Now an established SIS spy, my father flew to London on several occasions. He had meetings in Whitehall, and was lunched in the House of Commons (1964) by SIS's oil MP at Westminster, a senior Conservative, who was also a director of a British oil company (name withheld). My father was also invited to dinner at Windsor Castle when the Queen was not in residence.

Dinner at Windsor Castle was almost a disaster because my father had not travelled with formal evening wear and had to hire his clothes. He also had to hire a shirt. On the night, his shirt sleeves were so long that his hands disappeared. He decided to see if his 'friend', whom he was introducing to HMG, had a spare one.

'Without thinking, I opened my door to make my way along the corridor to my friend's room,' he said. 'I almost had a heart attack as a sentry stood to attention and saluted. There was one outside my friend's door as well.

'He had had to hire his clothes too. Therefore, we were in the same predicament. (English people have longer arms than we do.) As a result, we sat opposite the most exquisitely attired military personnel imaginable, in our hired clothes with "bumpy" arms. It confirmed Britain's superiority.'

My father felt giddy with pride to find himself in the dining-room of the House of Commons one minute and at Windsor Castle the next. He had dragged himself up from the backstreets of Baghdad and was immensely flattered by SIS's appreciation of his work.

He believed SIS to be autonomous overseas and its diplomats more important than the ambassadors. They presented themselves as the government abroad, at the heart of British foreign policy. My father basked in the glow of working with them, believing they set the agenda in Iraq. He also thought, as they did, that this agenda was noble. 'The men I served with were honourable men. I will never allow anyone to say a word against them.'

Although SIS made it clear that if anything happened to my father, nothing could be done to rescue him, he was assured, 'Your wife and children will be looked after for the rest of their lives.'

My father said, 'I trusted the diplomats with whom I worked implicitly and have absolutely no doubt that they would have honoured my trust. We were like brothers.'

In order to protect his cover, he spent most of the time loudly denigrating Britain. This meant that, back in Baghdad, he and my mother stayed well away from the embassy. This was no great hardship since, with the exception of his SIS colleagues, my parents could not stand the embassy personnel who especially hated Englishwomen who had married a 'native'.

The racism at the embassy extended to my father's SIS case officer 'Frank Tay's' foreign-born aristocratic wife, 'Amy' (not her real name). My parents adored her and were appalled at what she went through at the hands of some of her husband's colleagues.

Up against the same snubs, my mother did not give a damn. She said that good manners and a clean heart were what made a lady. She had been through the Second World War and knew why it had been fought. 'She had such a strong identity,' said my father, 'that nobody could touch her. The fact that she had married a "foreigner", and a brown-skinned one at that, proved what a strong character she had. Naturally, those who hurt us did not know that we were working for the Crown.'

The worse culprits were some of the Britons who had been in Iraq for years. Some of these had airs and graces they would never have got away with in England. My parents called them 'limeys'.

My father was always baffled by the British class system. He could not understand why a superb British banker was not the same 'class' as a British diplomat. 'This did not handicap me,' he said, 'rather, it emboldened me. Ignorance of other people's caste system is not important when you are in your own country.

'Iraqis themselves are exceptionally snooty. However, their snootiness is based on education and profession. For example, civil engineers had high status in Iraq. It was always a surprise they did not in London. Now, even all these years later, I still do not understand why the British Council headmaster in Baghdad was socially acceptable but a highly qualified British civil engineer was not.'

My father thought that two categories of Britons did more to foster the genuine affection the Iraqi people felt for Britain than anybody else. The first of these were British bankers.

'A British banker was the finest in the world. They were honourable men. Sometimes arrogant. But honourable. They could not be bribed and were corruption-free. They believed this was their duty to Britain. They could have become millionaires if they had wanted to, but did not. The Iraqis always appreciated this. With a British banker their money was safe, and this was very good for Britain's reputation. They did far more for this [Britain's reputation] than did the embassy.'

The second group my father admired were the Scots, most of whom were working for contractors. He held them in high regard because they took the trouble to learn Arabic, loved the Iraqis, made lifelong friendships and were disgusted by drunken colonial-type Brits holding up the bar, telling jokes about 'wogs'.

The Scots – as well as the few Irish and Welsh in Iraq who were also mostly working for contractors – were not sufficiently socially acceptable to be regulars at the British embassy, where most of the staff were English. Embassy wives were particularly snooty about the Scottish contractors' families. The antipathy appeared to be mutual. This added to the steady erosion of the embassy's reputation.

When the Scots did attend functions, one or two took great pleasure in conforming to all stereotypes. This is to say, they deliberately got plastered on 'Her Majesty's booze'.

My father was very cross at the way the contractors' families were treated. 'The Irish, Scots and Welsh were my friends. I saw no reason for the embassy to be snooty with them. I have to admit, however, I did not realise many of them did not consider themselves to be British. I, inadvertently, offended them by referring to them as "English". I only learned later a few were Scottish and Welsh nationalists and [that] the Irish had their own nation. It is a bit like us with the Kurds, I suppose. This, no doubt, accounted for some of the hostility at the embassy.'

The embassy's reputation plummeted even further when its diplomats' wives refused to visit an Englishwoman dying of cancer – she had been deserted by her Iraqi husband, who had taken their young son with him. The sick woman was nursed throughout her final days by the Sisters of the French Convent.

My mother believed that the only thing the embassy wives were good for was organising the Christmas Bazaar. At one of these, she was delighted when I told one of them that I had been taken to the 'Auberge Nightclub' to see the new belly-dancer. She was even more delighted when I announced that the belly-dancer, who called herself 'Princess Amira', was English and came from Yorkshire.

The British embassy was so shocked that it did everything it could to have the lady thrown out of the country.

My father was not quite as hard on the embassy as my mother. Many years later he told me, 'I did not expect the Empire's servants, overnight, to turn into humble people. This was simply not realistic. You must remember that when many of these diplomatic families first went to Iraq, Iraqis were not even allowed into the various clubs. For example, the Alwiyah Club had a sign saying "No dogs or Indians". The Arabs were not even mentioned.

'Your mother was incensed by this because she hated anything that hurt me.

But it did not hurt me. Or if it did, it hurt her more. I found these things amusing since, firstly, I was used to them, and secondly thought it was only a matter of time before it all disappeared.'

My father did not give SIS any feedback on how the British were perceived in Iraq. He said, 'They did not ask for this, therefore I did not offer it. Besides, a lot of it was rude and I did not like being rude to my friends.'

Homosexuality was sometimes an issue for the Iraqis. For example, the British regarded the explorer Wilfred Thesiger and writer Gavin Young, who spent their lives traipsing about with the Marsh Arabs of Iraq, as great heroes. The Iraqis did not. They were shocked by Thesiger and Young's homosexuality and lack of hygiene.[1] (The latter prejudice had nothing to do with homosexuality but everything to do with the Marsh Arabs, whom Iraqi city-dwellers looked down upon.)

My father explained what he thought: 'Explorers such as Thesiger and Young did Britain's reputation no good at all. SIS, on the other hand, took pride in them and called them "eccentrics", so I kept quiet.

'SIS was never homophobic. It accepted homosexuality as a part of life. I always felt that SIS had a much wiser and more humane understanding of people than any other secret service. Certainly, when I worked in London a decade later and came across MI5's attitude to homosexuals, I was very shocked.'[2]

Another issue that my father kept quiet about was the tittle-tattle – always a problem in a small community – regarding the alleged 'boredom' of some British wives who were 'neglected' by their husbands. In effect, what the Iraqis were saying was that some British women had a 'bad' reputation. Some indeed did. The Iraqis put this down to the fault of the husband – they have a famous expression: 'A man is not a man unless he is afraid of his wife.' My father believed that the British embassy could have taken heed of this.

He also had a novel view of Britain's reputation after Suez. He would say sombrely – it took me years to realise he was joking – 'Everybody says that Britain's reputation in Iraq sunk because of Suez. This is not true. It sank because the Iraqis believed the Englishman had no interest in pleasing his wife. Sex is very important to an Iraqi. If a diplomat is not considered "manly" then neither is the country he represents. The Americans were equally poorly regarded because they could not control their women.'

When he was not having a little joke, my father spoke of the rudeness of some staff at the British embassy. This coloured many people's view of Britain. 'One highly educated Iraqi wife of one of my contacts,' he said, 'was snubbed by the wife of a British diplomat who said to her, "I do not discuss books I have not read, and have no intention of reading." The embassy thought this a great joke. The Iraqis thought it was rude and ignorant.'

Nevertheless, my father was also the first to recognise the privations that many embassy wives suffered in such an alien environment and, given the political instability, their legitimate anxieties for themselves and their families. In addition, he felt few people, least of all their husbands, gave the embassy wives credit for valiantly seeking to maintain British standards and a British way of life – sometimes against the odds.

One example of this was the 'First Baghdad Brownie pack' which met in the gardens of the British ambassador's residence. This was established by the teenage daughter of one of the British diplomats. In doing so, she and another young woman from the embassy ('Brown Owl') fought valiantly against the embassy's racism. This, originally, threatened to bar mixed-race children, including myself, as well as those from non-white Commonwealth countries.

The young embassy women won their battle.

As a result, countless little girls made the Brownie Promise every time the pack met. Standing proudly in our Brownie uniforms, with the embassy 'Wendy House' behind us; the ambassador's wife, in floral dress and straw hat, snipping roses across the grounds in front of us; we lined up to salute the Union flag, repeating solemnly, 'I promise to do my duty to God and the Queen.'

All these years later, I remain proud of those embassy girls and the barriers they tried, with great success, to punch through. Today, the scale of their achievement could be regarded as a joke. In the early '60s, when mixed-race children did not generally mix with the British diplomatic families, it was not.

The embassy children, two of whom, including the ambassador's daughter, joined the Brownie pack, were delightful. Not surprisingly, their views sometimes reflected those of their parents. Sitting in the Brownie Circle for the Brownie Pow-wow, they overheard me say I had been on a picnic to Babylon with 'Elisabeth and her parents'. Elisabeth was Polish. She had not been invited to join the Brownies.

'Aren't Polish people Communists?' asked the ambassador's daughter knowledgeably. Her friend, sitting cross-legged beside her, responded, 'They don't speak English, so they might be.' The two small girls looked at me in horror. Following the exchange, I kept quiet about my father's other Communist friends.

Soon after, Brown Owl needed something from the ambassador's residence and had to send a couple of Brownies to fetch it. To this day, I remember the ambassador's daughter's tortured little face, terrified that I, who had picnics with Communists, would be chosen to accompany her.

A diplomat's child in the early '60s trod a fine line between not wishing to give offence, while elegantly seeking to maintain barriers. All the ambassador's daughter's careful work would be undone if Brown Owl selected the wrong child.

She did not.

Soon after, there were further horrors as the sound of gunfire drifted across the Brownies' Pow-wow Ring. Many of the little girls, not yet in double figures, had heard it all before. They were seasoned veterans of the sound of indiscriminate shooting, and were more likely to wonder if birds flying overhead were safe and able to fly out of the way in time, than worry about people being killed or wounded.

Brown Owl did not have the same nonchalance. The beady eyes of half the Brownie pack watched her, certain she would over-react. She did. She gathered us all up and led us hurriedly towards the ambassador's residence.

Once safely inside, Brown Owl was presented with a further problem. The Brownie pack had been welcome in the ambassador's garden. But no one had anticipated what it would be like to have the same Brownie pack within the residency walls. Brown Owl's worries that the troop behave themselves were almost as great as her anxiety about the gunshots outside.

Soon after, news came through that the firing had only been drivers celebrating by shooting rifles in the air. We were dispatched homewards a short while later. As I left, I turned around. In the centre of the residency hall was, I think I recall correctly, a circular fountain. Brown Owl appeared to have slumped against it. Beside her was the ambassador's wife. The ambassador's wife had a bottle in her hand – it was marked 'Gordon's'.

Soon afterwards, the Brownie pack meetings were transferred to the extensive tea-gardens of the Alwiyah Club.

NOTES

[1] Iraqi society had similarly been scandalised during the Second World War by the homosexual behaviour of Stuart Pirone, the much younger husband of the SIS writer/explorer Freya Stark. Stark, to many British one of the great heroines of the Middle East, had very little following, if any, in the region. The British were regarded as decadent, not necessarily because of homosexuality but because they connived in its flaunting, and therefore insulted conservative Iraqi society. This contributed to the downfall of the Iraqi monarchy which supported the British and tolerated homosexuality.

[2] My father said that one of the biggest differences between SIS and MI5 was SIS's tolerance of homosexuality. Some believed that this was because of the public school backgrounds of many of its civil servants and diplomats. However, as my father pointed out, MI5 had its share of public schoolboys too. He believed that SIS differed to MI5 because much of its culture derived from the Special Operations Executive (SOE) men who had joined it after the Second World War.

He said, 'The SOE boys liked anybody who had fought the Fascists with them – even if they were Communists. They had fought alongside men, women, and, in some cases, children. As a result, SOE did not care what anyone was, so long as they were all on the same side. This was also the reason why SIS was not chauvinistic – chivalrous, maybe. They owed their lives to women who had hidden them across Europe. They knew what was owed to women and what women had achieved.'

4

THE AMERICANS

On the surface at least, the SIS diplomats with whom my father served in Iraq did not hold the Suez debacle against the local American community. My father said, 'Sandy [Goschen] was very very bitter about Suez, saw it in terms of India, but drew a line under it and moved on. "Frank Tay" on the other hand, whose family was also connected with India, was laid back about everything. Nothing ever seemed to perturb him.'

My father rated the Americans when it came to the Vatican's role in the Middle East. In particular, he regarded the American Jesuits, who had been in Iraq since the late nineteenth century and were respected because of their position as the Vatican's 'education wing', as an especially powerful group. 'The Americans in Baghdad understood how the Vatican worked,' he said, continuing, 'They took the Vatican seriously, especially its principal representatives in Iraq, the American Jesuits. Here, I had the advantage over my SIS colleagues because I had been educated by them. SIS was snooty about this sort of thing. An American Jesuit was not the same as an English or a Scottish one. Of course, SIS had contacts with many religious people. The Church of England was well-established and prosperous in Iraq. However, it had not accommodated the new Iraqi Republic as successfully as the Jesuits.

'This, I believe, provided the Americans with advantages. I have always assumed that they were more up to speed on the Vatican, which was anti-Israel, because American businessmen, anxious about Israel's growing influence in America which jeopardised American commerce in the rest of the Middle East, took the Vatican seriously and petitioned it.

'SIS recognised that the Vatican's role in the Middle East was to protect the Arab Christians. However, apart from this, I do not believe they appreciated how "important" the Vatican was. This, I think, was because SIS was solely focused on the superpowers and military might. SIS did not think the Vatican of consequence because it had no military. The Americans, perhaps because they had no empire, had a much better understanding of how influence worked.'

My parents moved easily within the American community. Pan Am officials were 'Quiet Americans and much liked. Absolutely wonderful people.' On the other hand, my father considered American diplomats, 'a mixed bag, sometimes let down by their wives'. He meant he disliked the way some of their wives tried to discuss politics with him.

He always protested that he did not object to women discussing politics but that his preference was for the British way to that of the Americans, where the women left such talk to the men. However, he always felt that some American wives, possibly at the behest of their husbands, were trying to bounce people into saying things they did not wish to say and these women simply did not realise how dangerous this could be for locals. He believed their husbands were much more subtle.

He was particularly complimentary about one senior American diplomat with whom he enjoyed discussing politics. 'Hugely underrated,' he recalled, adding that the envoy was highly competent, informed and discreet, with a wicked sense of humour. 'On one occasion,' continued my father, 'at a function at one of the clubs, the American diplomat was seated next to your mother, I was next to his wife. My heart sank. Firstly because she always abbreviated my first name to "Larry", which I disliked. Secondly, because she always wanted to discuss politics with me.

'Soon she said something particularly silly and dangerous. To shut her up, I regret I was not very polite, I responded, "I only like my women in two places. In the kitchen or in the bedroom."

'The entire table went silent. I thought she was going to explode. Without batting an eyelid, her husband rose. Turning to your mother, he said with a charming smile, "Shall we dance, Mrs de Souza, or shall we stay for the fireworks?"'

For the most part, however, my father respected 'the American girls for their get-up-and-go'. He said that whereas many Western women in Iraq did not move away from the swimming pool, the Americans felt that the Middle East was an adventure and there to be explored, often without their men. In addition, they organised wonderful parties at the racecourse – always, incidentally, being used as a dead-letter box – and invited a better cross-section than did the British, who were paralysed by their snootiness.[1]

'I always believed,' said my father, 'that my Soviet friends were more anxious about the "independence" of American wives than they were about what their husbands got up to!'

He thought that the Soviets handicapped themselves by rigidly enforcing a 'no wives' policy for their own diplomats. 'They could not all go around trying to seduce the ladies!' he laughed. 'They needed educated and sophisticated wives to access women's society which always ran in parallel with the men's.'

One of my father's best stories was when the Soviets were trounced by the redoubtable 'Archaeological Study Group of the American Women's Association of Baghdad'.

In 1963, these ladies drew up easy-to-understand maps and directions to Iraq's various sites of archaeological interest. Hitherto, these sites had been the sole preserve of academics. The resulting protestations were deafening. Furious archaeologists of all nationalities made formal complaints to the Iraqi authorities, implying everybody but themselves were vandals and would destroy the sites. The American women stuck to their guns, sometimes fighting their husbands in the process, and the result was that everybody benefited. All those visiting the sites respected the women for what they had achieved and there were never any complaints.

The maps and potted histories of the sites were brilliant – I still have them. We did not go on one desert picnic without them. They were completely practical, giving directions for sites near to Baghdad, or, for the more adventurous, quite a way out into the remote areas. 'Needless to say,' recalled my father, 'eventually rumours started circulating that these maps were for the benefit of spies.'

Such rumours, although wrong, were not entirely surprising. Many say that some archaeologists of all nationalities used to act as spies or sources. My father believed that this was certainly true in the 1930s. For example, he thought that the thriller writer Agatha Christie and her husband Sir Max Mallowan, a distinguished archaeologist of the area, were British spies, if only because they were mapping parts of the desert. They certainly had very sophisticated cameras. However, in the 1960s this was not the case, any more than it is today.

Despite the rumours, the American ladies ran off extra copies of their hand-drawn directions, not least because everybody was clamouring for them. As a result, the gossip took on a life of its own. My father thought this was originally inspired by anti-American Westerners, probably from the British archaeological community, out of jealousy and spite, rather than the Iraqis or Soviets.

Eventually, however, for reasons best known to themselves, the Soviets became particularly outspoken opponents of the maps. They were able to play upon the legitimate but over-protective anxieties of the rest of the archaeological community that wished to carry out its excavations free of 'tourists'. As a result, the Soviets over-played their hand because, spies or no spies, the Iraqi authorities wanted to boost their tourism and were more than happy with the maps. In particular, the Iraqis were thrilled that the American ladies had made the ancient site of Ctesiphon, half an hour from Baghdad, more accessible.[2] Part of the site dates from the third century AD.

The women wrote directions for 'real' people. Instead of putting in grid references, they instructed:

> Leave Baghdad via the Old American embassy circle and the road past

Rashid Camp and Al-Hikma University. Cross the Diyala River on the
narrow road one-way bridge. About two miles beyond the bridge the road
forks: left to Kut.[3] Straight ahead to Salman Pak and Ctesiphon at the end
of the road (about 15 km from the fork).

These days Salman Pak is of interest because of anxieties about sites used for
constructing weapons of mass destruction. I remember the journey because
Ctesiphon became a favourite outing for the 'First Baghdad Brownie pack'.

A blind minstrel playing a bedu-style violin – goat's skin stretched across
wood, and a bow made from goat's hair – was always seated by the great arch of
Ctesiphon's sixth-century Persian banqueting hall. In front of him was a casino
attached to a rest house built by the clueless Iraqi Tourism and Summer Resorts
Administration. As we passed, Brown Owl used to instruct her Brownies, 'Do
not look, children. Nice people do not go to casinos.'

Another favourite site, an hour and a half from Baghdad (timings were
important because of having to judge how much water to carry), was Babylon.[4]
Again, the American ladies' directions did not let us down. My father
commented approvingly, 'Because of the American girls' initiative, the
archaeological community became much less snooty.' They brought the sites of
ancient Iraq to the people, trampling over the archaeologists who wanted to keep
them as their own special preserve.

'In my view,' said my father, 'the American girls did well. However, at the
height of the spy rumours about the maps, I had a run-in with one of my Soviet
friends who, at the time, was fairly influential in the Iraqi government. He
bashfully agreed that the directions to Babylon could hardly be regarded as
espionage. He was perturbed, however, by the directions to sites much further
out, for example, to Ukhaidher, an Islamic fortress palace and one of the most
impressive sites in Iraq.'

This did not stop the Soviet from asking my father for a set of the maps. The
Russian was subsequently livid to be discovered on a visit to Ukhaidher himself.
Clutched in his hand was the American ladies' excellent work . . .

I loved the expeditions into the desert. Sometimes the British Museum
archaeological team, albeit with much reluctance, invited locals, including my
family, to join them. Everybody soon fell out, however, because the
archaeologists did not like hordes of children clutching their sandwiches and
disturbing them.

Depending on the political situation, my father drove us all over the Iraqi
desert, usually in convoy with other friends and their children, so that we could
see the country. It was all a great carnival. At no time was this for espionage
purposes. 'Of course,' said my father, 'your mother and I did a lot of trips
together, when your mother acted as decoy. But we never did this when you were
present. We showed you Iraq because we wanted you to see it.'

Once, I was taken to the mountains in the north: 'Where the Kurds live, and where your grandmother came from.' We went also to Mosul and Samarra, to the Shatt where the Tigris and Euphrates meet. On countless other occasions, we drove all over much of the Middle East and into Europe, heading for England.

My father said, 'One of the advantages of espionage, as well as being your own boss, is that you can close your office whenever you want and go off travelling – particularly in the Middle East when you shut for the summer anyway because it is so hot.

'Our trips were usually for pleasure. On occasions, however, I would have to meet up with various SIS colleagues in, say, Athens. This, inevitably, led to awkward questions if, for example, you children or your English grandmother were with us, since you wondered where I had gone. On one occasion, your brother remarked, "Daddy, you cannot have a business meeting because you have not put a tie on. You must be having a meeting with someone else." His sharp observation gave me quite a scare!

'Because of my spying activities, I had to be extra careful whenever we went away. Sometimes I got into trouble no matter how much care I took.

'Once, going for a brief holiday to Jordan, we left Iraq when the border guards were asleep. As a result, our [British] passports were not stamped. Returning the following week, it cost a fortune in bribes to get back into a country we had apparently not left.

'Another close shave was again when we were in Jordan for a few days, shortly before I had a round of important SIS meetings back in Baghdad. Because the trip was partly social, we arranged to meet some British friends, who were teachers in Iraq, in Amman. Just as we drove across the Jordanian border, it was announced cholera had broken out in Baghdad. As a result, the Jordanians shut the border. We got through but our poor friends were stuck at the border for a week living in tents and much worse. In addition, we only got back to Baghdad in the nick of time for my meeting.'

Cholera outbreaks, the threat of rabies – and the terrible, 6 in. injections you had to have if you came into contact with the disease – were almost as regular as revolutions and attempted *coups d'état* in Iraq.

On one desert picnic to Habbaniya Lake, which was hidden behind a chain of low hills to the west of the Euphrates, my parents came across an American couple whom they knew by sight from the Alwiyah Club. Food hampers were immediately pooled before we all plunged into the water. Habbaniya was a favourite spot – I was almost as impressed by the Americans' ability to water-ski as I was by the contents of their picnic basket.

We saw the pair frequently after that in Baghdad and my parents became very fond of them. 'They may or may not have been spies,' said my father, 'your mother and I never knew for sure. If they were, they were a team.'

I found them great company. Having no daughter of their own, they 'adopted' and spoilt me rotten. They were familiar with the Iraqi expression: 'A family is always lucky when there is a daughter in the house.'

'Eventually, I had to put a stop to the friendship, which was a pity because they were great fun,' said my father regretfully. 'There were a lot of spies in Iraq in the 1960s – we were bound to fall over one another. I felt that they were using you as cover – this was not unusual, women and children were often used for such purposes – and I did not want this.

'Shortly afterwards they left Iraq for another part of the Middle East. I never mentioned them to my SIS colleagues. I felt a bit silly for not realising what was going on sooner. As for the Americans, I think they understood, if only because we all looked a little sheepish.'

My recollections of the couple are rather more precise than my father's.

I was well aware of what they were up to. The wife would often take me on her shopping expeditions and I can remember the routes we took. Sometimes a driver went with us. We would start off at the Eastern Trading Company opposite the Baghdad Hotel, Saadun Street. This, according to the advertising, was 'the leading Indian Shopping Centre' where you could buy 'a bikini, sari or kimono'. Next, it was off to Rashid Street to Iraq Sports where you could find 'Sports goods, photo and cine cameras, home movie and sound projectors, transistor radios, tape recorders, watches, suitcases, travel bags, Indian Novelties and Presentation articles of perpetual value'.

On other occasions we went to the Sheaffer pen shop or the Swiss Watch Company, also in Rashid Street, where I saw my first Rolex. The shop offered 'special arrangements for diplomats'. This was followed by a visit to the biggest department store of all, Orosdi-Back, where the logo was of an elephant and the caption: 'Nothing is too big, nothing is too small. If you want it, we have it.'

A particular favourite was visiting the Dar ul Kutub bookshop where the American lady allowed me to pick one Nancy Drew and one Bobsey Twins mystery without spending my 25 fils – equivalent to 5 English shillings – pocket money. Nearly four decades later, I believe American taxpayers' money was well spent. I fell in love with America through the books.

Sometimes we did not go far. We would stroll out of the Alwiyah Club and make our way to the Baghdad Hotel, the smartest one in town. Leading up to it, on either side, were expensive small shops where many people bought their jewellery. Hand-in-hand, we would look in the windows, pointing out the gold Lions of Babylon little girls were given for their charm bracelets. Then we would stroll back.

We would stop outside the Alwiyah Club, where, almost opposite, was the Unknown Soldier Monument. Nearby was the Golden Nest Restaurant, beside it, its grander rival, the El Menna, built like a ship. Opposite the Alwiyah Post Office was the Mataam al-Mataam, 'For those who appreciate excellent wines, good cuisine, gay decor and gentle music, air-conditioning. Open for breakfast, lunch and dinner seven days a week. Cocktail Bar.'

I was taken in and out of all of them, having ice creams in every one.

The only variations would be, sometimes, my 'friend' carried a different, but identical bag. I knew this trick, since I had been through the same experience with my mother.

On other occasions, usually accompanied by a driver, we would go into the old town. I adored my American friend. Unlike so many Americans, she was not squeamish. She was not, for example, worried about flies or dirt. She used to refuse to accept the sticky sweets she was offered in the Old Town, but, so as not to give offence, would accept dates. These were the best dates in the world. They used to be sold in England with the Lion of Babylon on their packaging.[5]

In a land of plentiful fruit, she knew how to choose a water-melon or sweet lemons from a hundred paces.[6] No shopkeeper could palm off poor produce on her. Her favourite food store was 'Spinneys' because, she said, 'They do not put up their prices just because I am an American.'

Wherever she went, she had her camera with her. She photographed old men in coffee shops smoking the *narghiles*, playing backgammon or dominoes. In their hands were their worry beads.[7] Sometimes, the smell of amber floated out and then you knew there was a rich man inside. Rich enough, at any rate, to have amber worry beads.

It was amazing what she photographed – the 'evil eye' painted on all the wooden buses; men stripping down ancient vehicles, a national pastime; even the 'Flit car' which drove around residential streets in the late afternoon squirting 'Flit' to kill the mosquitoes. Nothing phased her. Some streets were privately lit. Therefore, during power cuts, not all the lighting went down. When this happened, she was out with her camera photographing the richer areas that still had electricity.

She even found the flame from the Dohra – which she thought was pronounced 'Dora' – Oil Refinery, that lit up the night sky beautiful, which it was.

Her English, which is to say, her American, always included a smattering of Arabic. For example, she referred to 'zibble' (rubbish) as in, 'He's just zibble', if the person was past redemption; or 'ooti' (laundry) as in, 'We'll have to send him to the ooti man first', if the person was capable of redemption but required some initial work.

Every outing ended where it had started – at the Alwiyah Club with an ice cream. On one of the last occasions I accompanied her, I waved to the wife of a Hungarian diplomat, who was a friend of my parents. I did not know until it was too late that this was a mistake. The atmosphere between the American and the Hungarian was icy.

A little while later, I overheard the Hungarian lady remonstrating with my father, who was believed, at the time, to be a Communist. After this, I was prevented from 'going shopping' with my American friend. This was a great disappointment, since as a result I never completed my Nancy Drew or Bobsey Twins collections, which were considered 'too American' by British mothers, including my own, who bought their children Enid Blyton mysteries instead.

I was always well-disposed towards the Americans, principally because American parents were like Iraqi ones. They adored children and loved having them around. Based on my knowledge of the archaeologists from the British Museum, the same could not be said for the Brits. While Americans made all children welcome, treating them to wonderfully baked cookies, the British were uncomfortable with them, including their own.

If Britain was for grown-ups, America was definitely for children. We knew all about the United States because Americans married to Iraqi husbands ran all-American households and invited everyone in for Thanksgiving. It seemed as if they were always having parties. Nobody thought it the slightest bit odd that their Iraqi families threw themselves into Thanksgiving with gusto.

Apart from these fierce American patriots, America also had two other secret weapons.

First, Hollywood. We used to watch Hollywood movies on mild Baghdad evenings, in the open air, in the private clubs. The smell of spiced meat kebabs, barbecued on huge fires, mixed with the scent of jasmine; the noise of crickets and frogs competed with the sounds on the screen. Although all movies played to packed houses, those starring America's John Wayne had more impact on impressionable young people than, say, those featuring Britain's James Mason, who was beloved by the British abroad.

The importance of John Wayne can never be overstated. Every child in the audience wanted to be either his sweetheart or an American cowboy like him. No boy wanted to be an English gentleman like James Mason and the girls certainly did not want to be his girlfriend.

Children pestered their parents for 'American jeans' – never 'Levi's' – because John Wayne wore them. Those wearing them were always the most important in the playground. Men were judged by children on whether they wore jeans like John Wayne themselves and Americans, who did, were considered much younger and exciting than the British, who did not. British men, even if only in their early 20s, always appeared middle-aged and boring because of how they dressed.

America's second weapon was the American Jesuits of Iraq, later thrown out of the country on fabricated suspicion of espionage. These fabulous, handsome men were the messengers of Hollywood and the American Dream, every bit as much as they were the Vatican's representatives. Magnificent in flowing robes, they would join friends in the Alwiyah Club tea-gardens.

Their only Christian religious rivals were retiring Anglicans of St George's Cathedral, or the Sisters of the French Convent. The Sisters made you pray all the time; gave you statues of the Baby Jesus, even if you were a Muslim; or emptied out all your toys for the Red Crescent, the Middle Eastern version of the Red Cross.

The American Jesuits were different. In the playground, they made every child believe all things were possible. They never talked about God. Instead, they allowed children of every faith to clamber all over them, fighting for the privilege of digging deep into their pockets where they would always find sweets or tangerines. If a pocket emptied, a second was soon discovered where the last child found nougat in rice paper, with an animal picture on the box.

Next, they sorted out playground quarrels.

For example, one day – I must have been about seven or eight years old – the younger children were told by the older ones, 'The Muslims go on to a tall building dressed in black, with slits on their backs, and beat themselves with chains until they fall off the top and die.' They knew because all the servants had gone off to watch the spectacle (they had wanted to go too). We believed them because we had seen young men in the streets of Old Baghdad for days beforehand parading in their black clothes.

Spouting a thousand prejudices, we did not realise that we were hurting a small Muslim boy, with an American mother, who valiantly tried to defend his father's faith, while squaring it with his Americanism. The boy was swiftly scooped into strong arms, the Jesuit father praising Allah, and condemning those children who mocked Islam.

On another occasion, the father took a Jewish child into his arms. It was the first time I heard the expression, 'We are all People of the Book'. I remember the humility with which he expressed himself, and the care he took in explaining what had happened in Europe to the Jewish people, just over two decades before.

Today, the Roman Catholic Church is stigmatised by evidence of paedophilia. In addition, it is only belatedly admitting other matters, for example, its treatment of the Jews in Europe during the Second World War and its alleged participation in McCarthyism in the United States during the '50s. While all this is as true as it is wicked, it must not be allowed to taint the memory of many good men and of a fine teaching order.

Their aim, from a perspective only maturity has given me, was indeed to seduce young people, but only in so far as their Church and country were concerned. In this they were remarkably successful. When they left the playground, all the gaiety left with them. We thought God was an American and believed the American Jesuits were His spirit.

By the children's swimming pool, they would treat us to bottles of 7Up or Coca-Cola.[8] Then they would wait with us patiently until our parents collected us to watch the water-polo in the grown-ups' pool. They would leave at half-time, but not before calling the waiters and ordering plates of hot potato chips with ketchup: 'And another tray of pop all round.' No plate of chips with ketchup, nor any Coca-Cola since, has ever tasted so good.

The American Jesuits of Iraq sold the Gospel and the American Dream as one. The British, offering the worthy teaching and cultural efforts of the British Council, never stood a chance.

The British Overseas Airways Corporation (BOAC) did its bit for British branding, offering children's parties, the Junior Jet Club and Log Books. Meantime, older children eyed up the BOAC airline bags, eventually followed by

VC10 ones. To annoy the Soviets, menus on all BOAC flights pictured Rudolf Nureyev dancing at Covent Garden with Margot Fonteyn. BOAC's branding, however, was no match for the rival hospitality – airline bags and gifts, particularly pen-sets – offered by Pan Am.[9]

There was one organisation, however, where no one could compete with the Brits. This was the BBC World Service. I can remember one Iraqi army officer, who was not otherwise well disposed towards Britain, praising it. He would say, admiringly, as he twiddled the knobs on his radio to tune in, 'Remember this all your life. Reporting the same story, the BBC say, "The soldiers fired on the people." The others say, "The soldiers had to fire on the people." The difference is in the grammar. It is the gulf between fact and fiction. I have always trusted the BBC's version of the news.'

Because he did so, the officer was eventually purged from the army. He was later shot as a spy, which he was not.

For children, however, the BBC meant nothing. Christmas belonged to the British – Americans do not do 'panto' – as did all times of political unrest when the grown-ups, listening to their radios, waited for the World Service to tell them what was going on in the country. The rest of the year, at least for young people, was American. If branding starts early, and it does, the Brits were beaten by American Jesuits sitting beside swimming pools offering Coca-Cola, just as they were beaten by little Coca-Cola stands that sprouted way out in the middle of the Iraqi desert.

The American Jesuits, the Vatican's charismatic messengers, had an honourable agenda. Coca-Cola played its part. Today, it may stand for commercial imperialism. In the desert, in those days, it stood for all that was young and free.

Inevitably, there was speculation that the American Jesuits were all spies. (There were similar rumours about the Anglicans at St Georges; and a few regarding the Sisters of the French Covent, particularly those in touch with the American Jesuits.) Possibly some were.[10] However, they also fed the Iraqi people's love of learning, and were responsible for the exceptionally high standards of its secondary and higher education (Baghdad College and Al-Hikma University compared favourably with the best the West could offer).

In addition, because the Jesuits were so keen on Latin, many Iraqis of my father's generation, including my father, 'spoke' the language. My father and his student contemporaries were also bi-lingual in Arabic and English and most knew French or Italian, as well as having a very good knowledge of German. Comparing his American Jesuit education to his children's, my father could not believe the 'poor quality' of education available in British public schools.

The American Jesuits loved to share all they had. For example, they had a powerful telescope from which they studied the night sky. They took endless trouble with parents and children, allowing them to use the telescope to study the Milky Way and 'wonder at the Almighty's mysteries'.

The American Jesuits were totally committed to the people of Iraq and used their considerable influence for the country's good. Their eventual expulsion from the country caused them terrible sorrow.

At least, however, they got away with their lives . . .

NOTES

[1] A dead-letter box is an agreed place for secret exchanges of letters, parcels and photographs, used by those who cannot be present at the same time. For example, a spy could sit in a particular seat in a cinema and leave something attached underneath. When the next showing came on, the recipient would sit in the same seat and recover the item.

For further information see Richard M. Bennett's *Espionage: An Encyclopaedia of Spies and Secrets*, published by Virgin Books in 2002.

[2] In 1915, Ctesiphon was the site of one of the 'most disastrous campaigns in British imperial history' (Cockburn, A. & Cockburn, P. (2000) *Out of the Ashes: The Resurrection of Saddam Hussein*. Verso: London). Winning a victory against the Turks, but suffering heavy losses, British forces fell back down river, with 23,000 dead or wounded.

[3] Kut is described by Andrew and Patrick Cockburn (*ibid.*), as 'a tumble-down and evil-smelling town in a bend in the Tigris [. . .] Today, the British cemetery, a little below the level of the Tigris in the centre of Kut, has turned into a swamp, the tops of the gravestones of British First World War soldiers just poking out of the slimy green water [. . .].'

I understand that, despite problems between the British government and Saddam Hussein's Iraq, the Iraqi authorities have always dealt respectfully with the British and Commonwealth War Graves Commission.

[4] The Lion of Babylon dominated the scene. Children were photographed sitting on top of it. Otherwise, and despite the fact it is one of the seven wonders of the ancient world, Nebuchadnezzar's procession street to the Hanging Gardens – built by Nebuchadnezzar, the king of Babylon, to please his queen – was desperately dull, little more than a pile of rubble.

[5] In December 2001, Voices in the Wilderness UK, one of the organisations working to end sanctions in Iraq imposed after the Gulf War, retailed Iraqi dates again in England. Those wishing to offer support can contact them on: voices@viwuk.freeserve.co.uk

[6] Literally, sweet lemons. A fruit found only in Iraq.

[7] Narghiles, sometimes called a hubble-bubble: water pipes where marinated tobacco burns on a small bed of charcoal.

[8] Baghdad's leading dentists, including my family's superb British-trained Indian dentist, fought a losing battle with Coca-Cola.

The dentists went around placing children's milk-teeth in saucers of the drink to prove the sugar content rotted teeth. In the end, they were forced to back down because, it was rumoured, the company had found a powerful protector in the Iraqi government.

9   Some representatives of BOAC and Pan Am were believed to be spies. A senior Pan Am official in Iraq, and his wife, were charming and close friends of my parents.

10 It was even believed the debate as to whether the Garden of Eden was in Iraq – Iraqis have always said it was – was a put-up job to allow the American Jesuits to circulate and travel around the country.

5

THE FREEMASONS OF IRAQ

If the American Jesuits got away with their lives, the same could not be said for the freemasons of Iraq.[1] As with the Jesuits, there were constant rumours about their so-called spying activities – this was to lead to a tragedy. However, while freemasonry has many critics, it is sometimes forgotten it can be a force for good.

My father joined his Lodge before he was recruited by the Crown. He said, 'In those days, the men who were freemasons were of the highest moral calibre. We were aware our conduct could bring the whole Lodge into disrepute, so we policed ourselves. In addition, we encouraged young men to join. I have always said that the disciplines of freemasonry are far better for these youngsters than, for example, them becoming layabouts.'

His Lodge was consecrated on 23 May 1931, coinciding with the end of the British Mandate the following year. It is conceivable this was not entirely unconnected. It was in abeyance 1949–51 during a period of martial law, when, for example, the Communist Party went underground. However, with the exception of its start-up years, and a couple of others, the Masonic Lodge was always in Iraqi hands, albeit pro-British ones.[2]

It offered many advantages. These included the fact that it was open to all 'believers' irrespective of religious faith. Therefore, Christian and Jewish freemasons, who were otherwise excluded from Iraqi politics, were able to meet Muslim ones, some of whom were participants in Iraqi politics, as equals. As a result, there was considerably more equality in Iraqi society than the country was given credit. In addition, of course, some of the men were in business with each other. The Lodge, and freemasons in general, were cosmopolitan, years before such cosmopolitanism was universally fashionable. This suited the aspirations of many.

The Baghdad Lodge offered the United Kingdom unique commercial advantage. My father said, 'Because of freemasonry, Britain required no marketing policy and did not need to waste money advertising its products. If there was a deal or contract, or we needed a supplier, the Masonic network worldwide provided the contacts. This worked to London's advantage. However, it was also to Iraq's advantage because we could arrange the best price for quality goods. In those days anything stamped "Made in England" was indeed good quality.'

None of my father's SIS colleagues were freemasons.

My father was initiated into Dar es Salaam Lodge No 5277, Baghdad, in December 1952, long before he joined SIS. He said, 'I never, at any stage, brought politics into the Lodge, far less espionage. Firstly, this would not have been allowed. Both were expressly forbidden. Secondly, I wouldn't have done anyway.'

Freemasonry was particularly strong during the monarchy. All prominent Iraqis were members. My father said, 'It was an expensive commitment, not least because of all the charitable donations we had to give. However, because of the Lodge, I was able to rise commercially. The "pay-off", if you want to put it this way, was that as a brother prospered, he was meant to contribute more to charity. It was a way of reminding him of his good fortune. It was, I think, a good system. To the best of my knowledge, every time a brother did a big deal, he made a huge donation to various local charities.

'Through the Lodge, I met all the important people in Baghdad. When I was first initiated, I was only a poor man. However, because of the way we conduct ourselves in freemasonry, I was treated as an equal. I cannot recommend the Masonic brethren more highly. I would always advise a decent, moral young man to become a freemason.'

An example of the Iraqi Lodge's activities, dated 1955, includes the donation of £40 each to four Royal Masonic Institutions in London – two schools, a hospital and a 'Benevolent Institution'. (Overseas Lodges contributed to Masonic charities in London because they were able to send needy people from their own countries, free of all charges save travel costs, to them.) In addition the Lodge agreed 'To pass the Broken Column; the proceeds to be allocated to the Children's Welfare Society of Iraq.'

Lodge meetings, which were held monthly, except between June and September when it was too hot, were followed by a banquet. If the brother secretary was notified, members could bring guests. Dress was formal, either dinner jacket or uniform. The Lodge of instruction met each month.

In 1955, there were 84 freemasons on its Roll of Honour.

An invitation, also dated 1955, reads 'The Lodge will be tyled at 7.00 p.m.', and that the Masonic Brothers met in Baghdad at the 'Masonic Temple, Fraternity Society'. Their stated objective was 'Not so much to get more men into Masonry as to get more masonry into Men.'

Three years after my father's initiation, his boss at ICI was also initiated. My father was then assistant secretary in the Lodge. The Masonic papers read, 'To ballot for the following gentleman, proposed in open Lodge at the 188th regular meeting, as a fit and proper person to be made a mason: Mr Theodore Dodsworth Adams, Local Director, Imperial Chemical Industries Co., born on 12 March 1909.'

My father recalled, 'Adams was furious that I, as his subordinate in ICI, was his superior in the Lodge. He made his objections plain before he was taken aside by the Worshipful Master who politely told him to shut up! This was one of the beauties of freemasonry. No matter how senior a man was outside the Lodge, within it he agreed to a different and usually more meritocratic hierarchy.'

I remember my father's friends from the Lodge, and their wives and families; just as I remember my father getting ready for his Lodge meetings in his fine clothes.

During the early 1960s rumours began to spread that the Lodge had been infiltrated by the CIA and Mossad and that the Iraqi freemasons were spies and traitors. My father said, 'This was complete and utter rubbish. The Lodge was useful to some of us because we were businessmen. The majority of men, however, did not go to the Lodge for commercial reasons, far less for purposes of espionage, but because we enjoyed the company. It was like a club. Those who met at the 'club' did not use it as a cover for anything else. For one thing, there was not the time, freemasons have a lot of ceremonies in their meetings; for another, we banqueted as a group. Therefore, there was no privacy. Spies, above all, require privacy.

'We hoped we were doing good for the country in many, many different ways, as well as for ourselves. Not just our charitable donations, but other, unquantifiable things. For example, if a Brother deserted his wife and family, he was thrown out of the Lodge. Similarly, if he cheated in business. Therefore, it never happened. In addition, the age group was mixed. As a result, we tried to set an example to younger men.

'We wanted to instil in them respect for women and children; and a respect for those of age – their parents, grandparents, aunts and uncles. Iraqis are very family-minded. We recognised young men, particularly those who were unmarried, required strong moral example and we tried to give it to them.

'Things were changing because some of these young men were travelling to America and Britain and coming under the influence of Western societies. When they came back, they were not so respectful as they ought to have been. The Lodge disciplined them.

'At no time was the Lodge used for political purposes. I should know, I was both a spy and highly political. We never, once, discussed politics. It was just not allowed.'

Jewish members of the Lodge were particularly vulnerable to charges of espionage. In due course, as the political situation deteriorated in the mid-1960s and Israel became an ever-increasing issue, the Jewish Masonic brothers stopped attending Lodge meetings. They were anxious that they were endangering their non-Jewish brothers. It was a typical, chivalrous gesture that, ultimately, proved futile.

My father said, 'They were scared, honourable and courageous. What more can I say? It was a total tragedy. In previous times, when the Jews were being picked on, the Jewish community rallied round. For example, as a small boy I remember the vegetable cart of an old Jew was deliberately overturned by soldiers in the market. The next day, all the Jewish merchants of Baghdad had put him back in business. But in the 1960s the rich Jews had, for the most part, left Iraq. The Jewish Masonic brothers had no protector. It was a shameful time.'

In due course, rumours began to fly around Baghdad that all the freemasons, not just the Jewish ones, were working for the CIA or Mossad. Soon, word got out that the Iraqi authorities were looking for the Masonic Scroll, which listed all their names. To protect themselves, and at their own request, they asked that the Dar es Salaam Lodge, Iraq, be erased from the Roll of Honour of the United Grand Lodge of England. In order to protect themselves further, the Masonic Scroll was hidden.

My father said, 'The Worshipful Master, my beloved friend – our families went back years – believed that the Lodge would only be in abeyance for a few years. Until the political situation was sorted out. After all, there was some precedence for this from the early '50s. He hoped once everything calmed down, the Lodge would be able to open again.'

This was not to be. Instead, the list of Masonic names was found in 1969. As a result, some of the Iraqi freemasons, including the Worshipful Master, a Christian veterinary surgeon and the Jewish brothers, were rounded up on suspicion of espionage. They were tortured for many months and eventually hanged in front of a baying mob of thousands. The Worshipful Master's wife lost her mind. Despite the prolonged torture and barbarity, no Iraqi freemason confessed to spying for the CIA or Mossad.

My parents were living in London when the news came through. My weeping father said, 'Of course they did not confess to spying for the CIA or Mossad. They had nothing to confess. They were not spies. They were fathers, sons and brothers.'

Today, Grand Lodge, London, refuses to name its members. It cites, as one of its reasons, the murder of the French freemasons in the 1930s. It could just as easily remember the Iraqi freemasons. I do not approve of the Masonic brotherhood's secrecy. However, I believe secrecy, sometimes, can and does have honourable intent.

I recognise that Grand Lodge airbrushed the Iraqi freemasons from its records in order to protect them – some of those who survived the purge are relevant to Iraqi politics today. I also accept that Grand Lodge, and all other Lodges, say prayers for all departed brethren and those in distress.

However, 30 years after the murder of many of the Iraqi freemasons, when the men and their families are beyond such protection and/or prayers, I respectfully suggest it would be a courtesy to their memory for Grand Lodge to honour them in a more specific way, such as with a memorial plaque in London's beautiful Masonic Hall.

If Grand Lodge cannot remember its Masonic brothers from a tiny, troubled country, their generosity to Iraqi and United Kingdom charities, and their persecution and terrible suffering, who will?

It owes the memory of the freemasons of Iraq that at least.

NOTES

1   Historically, the Roman Catholic Church was opposed to the worldwide Masonic movement (as opposed to Roman Catholic Lodges). This hostility was particularly in evidence in Iraq in the 1960s. The Jesuits were especially bitter that my father, whom they had educated, was a freemason.

2   The Iraqi Masonic Lodge's founder was Brother Wing Commander H. J. Bartlett, although the founding Master appears to have been the Worshipful Brother Gordon Spencer. The Grand Secretary, 1931–42, was P. Colville Smith. The two British Grand Inspectors of Iraq were honorary members of the City of Caliphs Lodge, London. My father joined the City of Caliphs when he made his home in London in 1968.

6

SEDUCTIVE EASTERN EUROPEANS

Much to SIS's pleasure, my parents participated in, and enjoyed, the social and diplomatic whirl of Iraq in the 1960s. The horrors to come were never anticipated.

According to the Alwiyah Club Members' List, 1965, there were 49 diplomatic missions in Baghdad.[1] Of these, 38 were embassies, 3 were consulates, 4 were legations. In addition, there was an Apostolic Delegate (or Papal Nuncio – the Vatican's diplomatic representative in Iraq); the Democratic Republic of Germany had a consulate general; and the Federal Republic of Germany had an embassy. Surprisingly, the United Nations representative was not listed. He was a French Canadian, had diplomatic status, and was a friend of my parents. I remember him in Iraq, and met him again in London at my parents' house.

The Alwiyah Club Members' List of individual names reads, on the one hand, like a register of Baghdad's high society – its most prominent Christian, Jewish and Muslim families – and, on the other, like a roll call of the dead. Many of the families listed fled Iraq. Others, including some of the Masonic ones, were not so lucky and were murdered. The slim directory caused my parents such grief that my father kept it with his most private family papers.

I found it after his death.

I was thrilled. The memories that flooded back – it dated from the year I went to boarding school – were not of death, but of the vibrancy of a life made for children. Just seeing the diplomatic list re-opened a long forgotten world . . .

The restrained charm of the Finns came immediately to mind. Unlike many foreigners who fawned over other people's children if they wanted to curry favour with a child's father, the Finns were never showy or exuberant. They always held back, as if they recognised a child's privacy. I remember the charge d'affaires at the Finnish Legation in the '60s. He was a stiff, formal man. However, whenever children were present his eyes overflowed with joy.

My father was always protective about the Finns. He recognised the awkwardness of their position in relation to the Soviets. He said that SIS had very good contacts with them, although, 'Throughout the Cold War we never knew whose side they were really on.' My parents frequently attended their receptions because SIS needed help with identifying which Iraqis and Soviets were present. (My father always talked in terms of the Finnish 'Legation' but never explained the difference between that and an 'embassy'.)

I always looked forward to my parents attending a diplomatic function because the following morning I usually awoke to find a small parcel, wrapped in one of my father's handkerchiefs, beside my bed. It always contained canapés, both sweet and savoury, from the night before. As a result, I came to judge countries by their food.

I thought America was the most important country in the world because the American wives of Iraqi friends baked the best cookies. The Americans also allowed children to have as many bottles of Coca-Cola as they wanted. However, I never rated the Americans diplomatically because nobody brought me any food from the US embassy.

Of those embassies I did rate, I thought Indonesia and Pakistan were more important than Russia, because their food was so much nicer. The Russians only had 'black stuff' on awful-tasting black bread, which, in any event, was left in the refrigerator rather than by my bedside. Nonetheless, it did not go to waste, since my father always polished it off. On one occasion, he looked rather embarrassed when a messenger delivered a package of it from the Soviet embassy. It was from his friend, Colonel Michael —, the Soviet Military Attaché, who had sent him a supply.[2]

It was several years before I came to appreciate the taste of the Soviets' finest caviar. And even more years before I connected it to the fate of the sturgeon.

My father's success with the Soviets thrilled his SIS colleagues. They knew very little about them and were delighted to have a spy able to get alongside them. My mother remembers their diplomats as 'Charming. Absolutely charming. They all seemed to speak cut-glass English. They would click their heels, bow their heads and raise your gloved hand to their lips. I have always understood how women fell for them all over the world.' On one occasion, a Soviet drank champagne from a lady's dancing slipper. Her husband was furious.

This is not to say that all from the Soviet Bloc were charming. For example, my father had to attend dismal all-male drinks parties at the East German Consulate. He said, 'I always knew Communism would collapse, because the Communists did not know how to give a good party. There were no women at any of them. You cannot hope to survive indefinitely if you are against people enjoying themselves.'

All those from Eastern Europe seemed to hate each other. One group, however, could not have cared less. These were the Poles, who were constantly popping into Mass. Many of them were working for construction companies and had their families with them. Some were so poor, husbands tried to persuade wives to seduce Iraqi landlords in order to save on the rent.

One Polish couple and their daughter, Elisabeth (whom I had so rashly mentioned to the Brownie pack), lived next door to my family and were my father's tenants. Because Elisabeth and I were the same age, and although we did not speak each other's language, we spent quite a bit of time together. She and her parents were lovely people and, despite their precarious finances, were always having parties. They loved going on desert picnics – and frequently took me with them.

When they did so, it was as if the whole Polish community, including the embassy, left town (uniquely, Polish diplomats were not snooty and socialised with their non-diplomat nationals). They piled everybody into little cars that were heaving with food and alcohol. On one occasion, they forgot to take any water. The men enjoyed themselves while the women rushed around trying to find pears in syrup so they could at least give Elisabeth and myself something to drink. In the end, they gave up and were forced to give us swigs of beer.

Sheepishly, chased by women shaking fists, the men rounded everyone up, and the convoy headed home to Baghdad. On arrival, having given us water, the party continued with dancing, music and singing. Soon after, it was time for me to go home. Elisabeth's mother took my hand and walked me to my front door. Away from all the jollity, I could tell she was anxious. As we turned the corner, I looked behind. Following us was Elisabeth's father and half a dozen friends. Suddenly, life seemed full of adults anxious to share in a mutual culpability session for forgetting to take water into the desert. Leading them was the only Pole present who could speak English.

Smartly clicking his heels, a considerable feat given he was completely plastered, he explained to my parents he was from the Polish embassy. 'And on behalf of His Excellency, I would like to apologise for taking the landlord's daughter into the desert without water. I would like to assure the landlord this unfortunate incident will not happen again.'

My father was ecstatic. 'As a result, a few days later I received an invitation from the embassy to attend a function. I was very pleased because I needed to identify someone who was liaising with the Poles and the Soviets.'

My father said the Poles hated the Soviets. The Hungarians did not much care for them either . . .

Most Eastern Europeans did not include their wives on the diplomatic/social scene. The exception was a glamorous Hungarian diplomat, who looked like the film star Cary Grant, and his equally glamorous wife, a vivacious brunette. They were sophisticated bon vivants, who worked as a team, and were a very good double-act. They seemed to be everywhere, including the Alwiyah Club.

My family met them on many occasions. While the husband flirted outrageously with other women, his wife, equally outrageously, flirted with their husbands, her rather stolid young son beside her.

Supremely confident, the Hungarian couple appeared to have very little respect for the Russians and their *Babushkas*. This I found odd since my father had an enormous respect for the Russians, but very little for the Hungarians. Nonetheless, my parents liked this particular couple socially and they were a lot of fun.

The Eastern Europeans were not above a certain amount of one-upmanship. For example, various Russian friends of my parents frequently gave me presents of Russian dolls. I thanked them politely, and put them with my ever-increasing collection. In those days, Russian dolls really were 'dolls' rather than the representations of political figures they tend to be today. I became adept at reading the status of those who gave them to me, principally because the quality was different. The best set came from my father's friend, Colonel Michael —. I remember to this day my mother's pained expression when I escorted my favourite American Jesuit father to my bedroom because I wanted 'To show him all the dollies the Communists have given me.'

On one occasion, a Soviet visitor gave me yet another set of dolls. I was by this time several years older and possibly less well-mannered, or, anxious to establish I was too old for dolls, less-inclined to hide my dismay. (Particularly as I knew the son of an Iraqi Brigadier, with whom I played on the swings, had been given a model of a Soviet aircraft. The Russians were always better at accommodating boys' interests than they were girls'.[3])

The wife of the Hungarian diplomat noticed my obvious disappointment. Quick as a flash she opened her bag, out of which she produced a small and very smart little box. Handing it over, she beamed and wished me many happy returns. I opened it and was overjoyed to find a very adult-looking brooch inside. I pinned it on my dress and paraded around the garden with my new piece of jewellery. I forgot about the Russian and the dolls he gave me.

I remember, however, that the Russian looked furiously at the wife of the Hungarian diplomat. For her part, she threw back her head, her beautiful long hair twisted into three rows to rest on the nape of her neck and laughed uproariously. It was only later my father saw the brooch and realised it was a model of 'Sputnik'. My parents collapsed in laughter. They believe that what happened was that the 'Sputnik' brooch had been given by the Soviet to the Hungarian diplomat's wife. For whatever reason, this had displeased her. Therefore, in his presence, she had given it to a child.

I remember her and her dashing husband with much affection.

I was often aware, however, I was party to something I did not understand. For example, I remember being told by the Hungarian lady, who had seen me with the American Jesuits in the Alwiyah Club: 'Hungarians are Roman Catholics too, not just the Americans.' I thought she was telling me, for whatever reason, to put me at my ease and win my confidence.

Next she asked, with more directness than subtlety, 'Who do you think the American Jesuit father is having dinner with tonight? Did he tell you?'

I shook my head and said I did not know.

As it happened, I knew he was having dinner with my parents. I had become a liar, although I did not know why, nor why it was necessary. I also knew the Hungarian lady knew I was lying. Even very young children know when they are being pumped for information and it unsettles them.

On another occasion, the Hungarian saw me eating ice cream with my American friend who used to take me on shopping expeditions and bought me Nancy Drew and Bobsey Twins mysteries. The Hungarian was not her usual cheery self. For her part, the American ignored her completely which made me feel awkward. Children, as a rule, are not comfortable when adults they like are rude to each other.

The last time I saw the Hungarian lady was in 1966, also at the Alwiyah Club. By then I was at boarding school in England and had flown home with my brother on a VC10, a new aircraft and the pride of BOAC's fleet. During the flight, the captain had informed the passengers that England had won the World Cup. Neither this news, nor the new aircraft, were of much interest to me.

As always, I was thrilled to see my Hungarian friend. However, this time, now aged 11 and with the social confidence boarding schools can enrich young children, I was equal to her. The Hungarian asked what it was like to fly in a VC10. I did not know why she wanted this information but, instinctively aware of what to say, I did my bit. Although I knew nothing about aeroplanes, I knew the VC10 was important for British prestige. Therefore, like a true professional, I boasted about it, and about England winning the World Cup. The Hungarian woman listened smilingly to my enthusiastic account.

When I had finished, she put her arm around my shoulders. 'And were you given those delicious boiled sweets you used to get on BOAC to stop your ears from popping?' she asked innocently. After a few more pleasantries, she continued, 'And what about the ballet menus? Did you see the photograph of Margot Fonteyn and the Russian again?'

Finally, she asked with a winning smile, 'Were you taken to see the captain in the cockpit, darling, like you used to on the old aircraft, when you were a little girl? Did he sign your Junior Jet Club log-book? It must have been so exciting. Did you have more room to move around in the cockpit than in the other one?'

I, truthfully, shook my head. Unlike on previous occasions, I had not been inside the cockpit. The air-hostess had collected my log-book and taken it away for the captain to sign.

I saw my Hungarian friend once more, across the Alwiyah Club swimming pool. She waved but did not come over to speak. I assumed, now I was older and more canny, she had no further use for me.

The rejection hurt.

NOTES

1. The diplomatic missions listed included a bureau for Oman, and a commercial representative for Vietnam; Austria, Norway and Portugal all had consulates; and the Democratic Republic of Germany had a consulate general. Cuba, Finland, Korea and Yemen all had a legation. The Vatican was represented by an Apostolic Delegate. The following had embassies: Afghanistan, Algeria, Belgium, Bulgaria, Ceylon, China, Czechoslovakia, Denmark, France, Federal Republic of Germany, Great Britain, Hungary, India, Indonesia, Iran, Italy, Japan, Jordan, Kuwait, Lebanon, Libya, Morocco, Netherlands, Pakistan, Poland, Romania, Saudi Arabia, Spain, Sudan, Sweden, Switzerland, Syrian Arab Republic, Tunisia, Turkey, United Arab Republic, United States of America, USSR and Yugoslavia.

2. Colonel Michael —, the Soviet's Military Attaché in Iraq, was a good friend of my father's. In due course, he invited my father to defect. The colonel was subsequently posted to the Soviet embassy in London.

3. Toys were always important in espionage. SIS took them particularly seriously as a way of marketing the view it wished to project of Britain. One year, in time for my birthday, SIS sent me a handmade dolls' house – 'With electricity' – via the embassy's diplomatic bag. It was a perfect replica of an English country house.

7

THE ALWIYAH CLUB AND
THE DEATH OF PRESIDENT QASSEM, 1963

One day, the foundations of my comfortable and reassuring life were shaken. It was the week before the Alwiyah Club's Valentine Dance. President Qassem, who had killed the king, was still president.

His presidency had been marked by considerable brutality. However, there were many who admired him, not least for, in his early days, his lack of corruption. My parents met him a few days before his death. My mother recalls a 'staggeringly good-looking and charming man'.

A few months short of my eighth birthday, I remember how President Qassem died. First of all, the Valentine Dance was cancelled. Then, one moment I was watching an American cowboy movie on television, the next, the screen went blank. A few seconds later, a children's puppet show came on. About five minutes after this, live coverage of the revolution followed.

This was 'courtesy' of an Iraqi camera crew as it rushed through narrow streets behind an open truck in which were standing men being taken to detention. The truck stopped at house after house dragging more men out. Sometimes, screaming women tried to hang on to their loved ones by clinging to their legs for as long as they could hold on.

Then the screen went blank again. Many hours later, when I was supposed to be in bed, I crept under the desk in my father's study. He came in and closed the Venetian blinds. The television had started broadcasting once more. He was too tense to notice me as he started burning papers in a metal wastepaper basket.

I watched, mesmerised, as President Qassem was brutalised, and then murdered, on screen. Today, historians from all sides deny that the president's death was screened. However, I recognised the figure who was killed from his postage stamps.

My family stayed home for what seemed like months but was possibly only days. When normal life resumed, the movie I had been watching on television before the revolution was re-screened. The Iraqi broadcasting authority started it in exactly the same place as it had left off. I believe it was called *The Unforgiven*, starring Burt Lancaster.

Returning to the Alwiyah Club for the first time, I was aware some of the children I used to play with were no longer around. Soon after, there were whispers in the playground that various fathers were in prison. In addition, we noticed that the 'English girl' who lived at the club, and whose father worked for a British company, had disappeared. All sorts of rumours started flying around. Eventually, however, we found out that she had gone to boarding school in England.

In due course, some of my former playmates, brought by defiant mothers, reappeared. They were objects of curiosity, or ostracised, although we used to call their fathers 'Amu' (uncle). Other changes were also noticeable. All the portraits of the old president were replaced with the new one. In addition, at the end of the year, the club did not hold its children's pantomime. Nor did BOAC host its children's Christmas party.

There were constant curfews. In the middle of one, I heard my father go out one night. My mother let him back in a few hours later. Earlier in the evening he had sent the watchman home so that he could enter and leave the house unobserved. I did not tell my parents what I had seen. However, I knew where my father had gone and to whom.

Due to the political situation, school was cancelled but no child could profit from the extra holiday or go out to play with friends. Each day rolled into the next. The hours between the curfew were fraught as everybody rushed out to buy food. My family were lucky because of the loyalty of our cook who knew the baker and brought us *khobz* (bread) each day. The baker never raised his prices. Profiteering was unheard of. There was panic if, for whatever reason, a family had not reached home by the time the curfew started. I remember it happening to us. We drove through eerily deserted streets and I could feel my father's tension.

A long time later, life yet again got back to normal. We could go to the Alwiyah Club once more. But it was different. For example, in the car park, I saw my favourite – not least because he was so good-looking – 'Amu' getting out of his car.

He was a senior Iraqi army officer. His English wife worked for an overseas government organisation and the couple had met in Britain at a party organised by the Communist Party of Great Britain. They were both Communists. Before the revolution, in order to please him, I had referred to a trip my father made to inspect some new Soviet aircraft, saying over lunch, 'Daddy went to the airport with the Russians.' The result had been adult laughter all round, even though I knew that I had shaken my parents – it was fortunate I made the comment to someone who was sympathetic to the Soviets as I would have seriously embarrassed my father if the man had not been.

Those days seemed long gone when I saw my Amu now. I knew him, his wife and children well, and ran to kiss him. When I drew near, I found he was much thinner than I remembered. For a moment, he hovered and seemed uncertain what to do. However, his uncertainty lasted only seconds. Soon he bent to cuddle me, as he always had. But things were different. As my father approached, I realised they were both embarrassed.

They stood awkwardly, yet emotional, saying nothing. Eventually my Amu said to my father, with quiet dignity, 'You are a naughty boy, you know. You did not visit my wife and family when I was in prison.'[1]

When I saw my Amu again a short while later, he smiled briefly, but looked away. After this, I was not allowed to play on the swings with his younger son. However, in solidarity, his son and I would hover around each other without talking.

Working out adult protocol was difficult. For example, one day I was watching my parents play tennis while my Amu was with his wife on the next court. Soon, when the ballboy was off fetching a stray ball, another ball, from my Amu's court, landed at my feet. I did not know whether to ignore it, wait for the ballboy to return, or hand it back to my Amu.

Seeing my hesitation, he made the decision for me. Coming forward, he stroked the top of my head and collected the ball. Then he changed courts.

On another occasion, watched over by my father, I was playing on the swings. A few moments later there was a terrific bang followed by crying. My Amu's younger son had fallen off the roundabout at speed, crashing into a badly placed chair. Without a second's hesitation, my father went to comfort the boy. Meanwhile, as I clambered off the swing, my Amu took my hand. It was as if the only service my father and Amu could do for each other was to continue to love each other's children.

Many years later, one of my Amu's sons visited London with his bride. He had made a dynastic marriage. He was not involved in Iraqi politics and my father refused to allow SIS to contact him, saying, 'A man's child, even one grown to manhood, is still a child. And that child is sacred. I forbid SIS to make any approach that could endanger him or his family. He is the son of my friend.'

SIS, to its credit, respected my father's wishes.

Back in the playground, and without the words to explain the undercurrents, I remember the grief of two men who had once loved each other and were now separated by powerful and different visions of Iraq's future. Each man, I have no doubt, was sincere and wanted the best for the country.

A short while later, my brother arrived for the school holidays. He was a good friend of our Amu's older child. There were endless rows as my brother clashed with our father, not knowing why he was not allowed to play tennis with his friend any more.

Throughout the row, my mother looked on sad and unsmiling. Her 13-year-old son, through no fault of his own, was growing up far from home without an understanding of prevailing tensions. My brother, sensitive, loyal, artistic and talented, retreated into his shell whenever our father was present. I, as his more robust younger sister, who had been living with the atmosphere and was more adept at reading it, did not have the words to explain what had been going on.

For example, one year, shortly after my brother arrived from England, I was asked to read out a pilot's manual onto the Iraqi pilots' training-school tape. (I had to do the recording twice because, on the first occasion, I pronounced the word 'reconnaissance' the French way, never having heard it in a military sense.) I was chosen to do the reading instead of my brother because he was of an age when his voice was breaking. Not surprisingly, my brother wanted to read the manual. This sent my father off into a rage. I, on the other hand, knowing how quickly my father could react to such requests, never made them and therefore always avoided the full force of his fury. It seemed as if, through no fault of his own, my brother was constantly in trouble.

For this reason, I never told him that I had been copying letters drafted by our father and addressing envelopes to 'aunts' and 'uncles' in England I knew I did not have. I knew that my brother would ask my father about them if I did so, and that this would have ended in another row. As a result, family secrets were withheld from him. This also meant that I had no one with whom I could consult – I wanted to know what the letters meant.

I knew that the letters were important because my father had wanted me to write 'Clearly, darling, and in big writing so that the Iraqi Post Office know the letters are from a little girl.' I believe the comments were always domestic, such as, 'I hope you had a nice birthday and got lots of presents.'

I do not know whether what I copied contained coded messages, or whether my father had already written these in invisible ink. (In London, many years later, he commented, 'You can make invisible ink from onion juice if you haven't anything else.' My mother responded, 'What happens if you haven't any onions?'[2])

Eventually, my brother went back to boarding school and I forgot about the 1963 revolution. I started going to the Brownies again, but we no longer met in the British ambassador's garden. Nor did the ambassador's daughter, or her friend, rejoin. Also, Brown Owl changed. It was not just the Brownies that were different, though. Lots of things seemed not to be the same. I no longer saw my father dress up for Lodge meetings. People in general were more wary. It was as if, overnight, old certainties had been swept away.

The only people who did not seem to change were the Alwiyah Club waiters. All the goings-on in the club took place in front of them.

In the days of empire, they had all been Christians. In the '60s, the old-timers were joined by Muslims. Each and every one had a command of two languages, many knew more; all were educated.

They made the club what it was. I can still see the tall, slim, fair one, who the girls secretly fancied; the two tubby, smiley, short Assyrian twin brothers with bald heads, and curly black hair around their ears, who used to swap roles and tease the children at table. In the summer, when the weather was really hot, the waiters took turns to go into the meat freezers to cool down.

Despite the waiters' best efforts, however, even the Alwiyah Club seemed tense. In the playground, a boy who had once wanted to be an American cowboy like John Wayne beat up another boy because he had an American mother. Another boy told a little girl, also with an American mother, she must choose between 'Iraq or America'. Meantime, a little Jewish brother and sister became too frightened to mingle with the other children. Although they came to the club, they stopped going into the playground, remaining with their parents in the tea-gardens or by the swimming pools.

In addition, adults who had once socialised or played bridge together in the cardroom, no longer did so. Instead, they made apologetic, furtive smiles across the gardens when they thought no one was looking. Usually, however, they pretended to ignore each other. The communities no longer mixed, when, previously, they had celebrated each other's religious festivals and respected Baghdad's diversity.

One day, I wandered into the Alwiyah Club library. This stocked row upon row of dreary-looking books. It also had *Time* magazine and British newspapers bound in yellow volumes. I think they were the *Daily Mirror*. The library, so I thought, was empty until I discovered one of the club waiters was in there. He was reading one of the *Time* magazines and crying. Waiters were not allowed in the library unless a patron had sent for them. They were certainly not allowed to read in there. A few seconds later someone else came in. He was the Englishman in charge of the Baghdad Railways who sometimes stayed at the club. Instinctively, I held out my hand to the waiter, so it looked as if he had followed me in and was tidying up magazines I had untidied. We left hand-in-hand, after I had been mildly admonished by the railway man for 'causing the servants trouble'.

If a child can see into a man's soul and remember it, I saw the waiter's soul that day. His gratitude to me for covering up for him still fills me with shame. The following week, he had gone. I heard afterwards he had been sacked. In the playground, children whispered he had been spying on our parents. This was confusing. The waiter was a nice man. I did not believe he would want to hurt other people's parents. I did not tell anyone about finding him in the library. However, I knew *Time* magazine was American. Not having the vocabulary did not mean I was not able to guess how much this man had wanted to go to America. I wondered whether, if you spied, you could go there.

Soon after, other waiters started to be sacked. One by one, all the old favourites began to disappear. There were more whispers in the playground. So-and-so waiter was spying on club patrons, listening to what they were saying. Eventually, all the Christian waiters were sacked. The new ones were government 'plants' and all the children knew their parents had to be careful what they said in front of them.

With the old waiters, the adults did not stop talking when they brought them their drinks. With the new waiters, they always went silent or changed the subject and said something silly. In the playground, the children wondered why some waiters were sacked for spying, but were being replaced by those who were also spying. In the end, we decided maybe the waiters whom we liked were not very good government spies, and so had to be replaced by ones who were, but whom we did not like.

I do not know whether some of the original waiters were spying or not. I know, however, the waiter I found crying in the library was desperate. Desperate people do desperate things.

It seems that there is never any forgiveness.

NOTES

[1] Many years later, my mother told me that my father had wanted to visit his imprisoned friend's family. However, SIS had refused to allow him to do so. The family concerned were loyal Iraqis and were not aware my father was working for SIS. All these years later, I wonder whether SIS trains its spies to cope with their betrayal of close friends. I believe it is this, rather than the stress of espionage, that can cause mental health problems in later years.

[2] I believe lemon juice was also used. My father also said that 'Secret Writing' was referred to as 'SW' in 'the Craft'.

8

SIS AND THE PUBLIC SCHOOLGIRL, 1965

In the summer of 1965, there was another attempted revolution but, it seemed to me, nothing much happened. When it was all over, we drove from Iraq to England again. On the journey I found out that I was going to boarding school in the south of England.

This was selected with the help of Gabittas Thring, a company that specialised in finding schools for British children whose families were overseas. My parents were given additional assistance because it was crucial that a spy's child be kept apart from the children of a parent's possible SIS colleagues, or similar contacts.[1]

Despite the care taken, a problem soon arose when one of my classmates, who was the daughter of the British ambassador to a Soviet country, invited me to spend part of the holidays in that country. Very little could have embarrassed my father's so-called 'anti-British' reputation more than if his daughter was holidaying with this particular British ambassador's family.

At boarding school, my memories of disappearing waiters at the Alwiyah Club gave way to weekly baths and *Dr Who* on television. I kept quiet about the things that cut me off from normality. I did not explain to my new schoolfriends why my father signed his otherwise typed letters from 'Daddy Lawrence and Mummy Julia'. Nor did I tell them that I had had to practice recognising his handwriting or why.

'Check for Daddy's signature, darling,' my father had instructed before leaving with my mother for Iraq. 'If you ever receive a letter from Daddy that does not have his signature, it is not from him. Do not do anything the letter tells you to do. Give it immediately to your headmaster. Say, "This letter is not from my daddy. Please inform my 'daddy's London office'."'

I learned later that 'daddy's London office' was a euphemism for SIS.

My father's instructions were not without their drawbacks. On one occasion, I was met off the school train by a 'Mr Parker' from my 'daddy's London office' who had to take me to Heathrow to catch the flight to Baghdad. The arrangements had been made direct with my headmaster but I had not been informed of them.

Therefore, at Waterloo, when matron handed me into the care of SIS's 'Mr Parker', I refused to go. I believe the scene I made, a little girl in her school uniform looking like a pudding in a boater, prompted the arrival of a British bobby.

Finally persuaded, I got into a taxi with 'Mr Parker'. He was a tall, stringy man, with an Adam's apple. As I sat back in my seat, I noticed that beads of sweat were pouring down his face. He was old, harassed, in a state of considerable distress and clearly unused to children.

Sensing my advantage, I asked politely, 'Will you be meeting me when I fly back to London? I am returning a day early.'

'Very possibly. If your grandmother has not recovered her health,' he replied.

Speaking loudly so that the driver could hear, I added informatively, 'Matron said I had to come back early because I have to be measured for my first brassieres . . .'

Subsequently, SIS asked my father to make alternative arrangements. My parents were to hear later that it was several days before 'Mr Parker' recovered from the ordeal of being in a taxi with their daughter.

Before I returned to London, my father took me aside again. This time it was to stress how important it was to be careful about what I said in letters. 'Otherwise, darling,' he said quietly, 'it could be dangerous for Daddy. You know how silly the people in the Iraqi Post Office can be. Always opening other people's letters.'

I took him literally and therefore was careful about what I said in my letters. However, I did not realise I had to be careful about parcels. He had made no mention of these and, besides, by the end of the Christmas term I had forgotten the seriousness of his warning anyway.

Thinking it would be a nice surprise if I sent my parents all the Christmas cards I had received from my classmates, I bundled them into a bulky parcel. In addition, supposing they would want to show the cards to all their friends, I addressed the parcel to the Alwiyah Club, instead of my father's office address. Finally, in a further spirit of helpfulness, and assuming my mother would want to hang up the cards, I strung them together in what I considered a methodical pattern.

They all contained the childish scrawls and comments of schoolchildren. I put pictures of Christmas trees, animals and stars together. Regrettably, some of the stars had six points. I did not know this could represent Israel's Star of David, nor that it was a banned symbol in Iraq.

My parents were in Jordan when my parcel arrived. When they returned to Baghdad, my father was called into the Alwiyah Club. Iraqi Post Office representatives and the Alwiyah Club management were waiting for him. While they accepted that the cards were from children, and the parcel had been sent by a child, they did not immediately accept that there was no sinister intent. Children's handwriting, as I knew myself, could often be a ruse.

Two, typically childish greetings had caused particular concern. These, by chance, were written into cards picturing the Star of David. In one was the comment, 'To Podge, Tunzaluv, Beaky.' ('Tunzaluv' = tons of love.) In the other were the words, 'To Coca-Cola, love, Pepsi. PS Have a 7Up on me in the holidays.'

The Iraqi authorities believed that these were coded messages. In addition, they thought that the word 'Tunzaluv' was an Americanised Hebrew word they had not come across. Eventually they accepted my father's explanation that the Christmas cards were wholly innocent. However, many years later, he told me that the incident had placed him in considerable jeopardy.

In addition to being vigilant about what I did in writing, I had to be careful of what I said in speech. This was pretty much a hit-and-miss affair. Nevertheless, at the end of every school holiday, my father would patiently remind me, 'Remember, darling, when you are back in England, try to avoid discussing Mummy and Daddy with anyone. If, however, you cannot get out of it and, for example, your friend's daddy asks what your daddy does for a living, tell him, "Daddy is a British Commission Agent." Can you remember that, darling?'

I remembered only part of it. Spending one half-term with a schoolfriend whose father was the head of a shipping company, the conversation went as follows:

'Where do you live, my dear?' asked my friend's father.

'In Iraq,' I replied.

The man beamed. 'How wonderful! Is your pa with the embassy?'

'No,' I replied, trying to remember exactly what I had been told, '. . . he is a British Agent.'

Following this brief exchange, and mindful of my father's instructions to avoid further discussion of him, I asked politely, 'What are you reading in your newspaper?'

'The cricket results, my dear,' came the response. 'Tell your pa these, no doubt, are read by British agents everywhere.'

After this, I was taught to say, 'Daddy is a merchant.'

The most marked difference between myself and my schoolfriends was that I read the newspapers – they never read them – scouring for news of Baghdad. These, during term time, were placed in the school library, after they had been skimmed by the history mistress to ensure that there was nothing upsetting in them, or any reference to a girl's family.

So far as I could tell, there was never any news of Baghdad in them. However, I learned three things. Firstly, only three newspapers told stories which were not about England: *The Times*, the *Daily Telegraph* and the *Daily Express*, then a broadsheet. And only one of these, the *Daily Express*, was written in big writing and had pictures. Finally, the *Daily Mirror*, which I had read in bound yellow volumes in the Alwiyah Club library, and, more importantly, had understood and enjoyed, was not considered an 'acceptable' newspaper by my teachers and therefore was not available. Slowly, I was absorbing the class structure of England. My parents had told me something about this. They had omitted to mention it extended to newspapers.

There were also differences in the way my friends and I behaved. For example, children brought up in Iraq were never rude about the Iraqi president. In England, I found my schoolfriends were always rude about Mr Wilson, the prime minister.

In history, I also heard about the 'wicked Communists who are trying to destroy us'. Grateful for my days in the Brownie pack, I concealed the fact that I knew Communists, liked them, and that my father went to parties at Soviet Bloc embassies. I slipped once, calling the Russians 'Europeans'. (The Iraqis regarded – and taught their children – the Russians 'Europeans', lumping them with the French, Italians, British and so forth.) I had to sit in the gym with a book on my head because I refused to be corrected.

I also struggled in general knowledge. For example, I was marked down because I did not know the anniversary of the French Revolution (14 July), although I did know the anniversary of the Iraqi Revolution (14 July) but was never asked the appropriate question. One of the strangest things I had to get used to was the idea that although in Baghdad Britain was central to our lives, the reverse was not true.

In addition, I knew nothing about the death of President Kennedy. Instead, I knew about the death of President Qassem. When it was explained to me that President Kennedy had been assassinated, I understood his death in Iraqi terms and assumed that the new American president had killed Kennedy, in the same way as the new Iraqi president had killed Qassem. As a result, I was back in the gym with a book on my head. It was roughly about this time that I realised some countries were more important than others. And that America was definitely more important than Iraq.

Returning to Baghdad in the school holidays, I was welcomed back by old friends. However, things were different. The American Jesuits never went to the Alwiyah Club anymore. Nor did anyone joke about spying, when spying, and joking about it, had been a national pastime. Worse, Iraqi television no longer showed American movies or series such as *My Friend Flicka*.

There were good things too. For example, our cook's eldest son qualified as a fighter pilot. We were all proud of him.

At home there were tensions I no longer understood, such as an 'atmosphere' around a table. My parents always seemed too jolly when they went near it. I later found out that it had been provided by SIS and had a secret compartment for papers – one of the legs was hollow and could be unscrewed.

I was relieved when the end of the school holidays arrived, and I was able to return to what I now considered my normal life in Britain. It was autumn 1966. I did not know I would never see Iraq again.

For subsequent school holidays, my parents flew to London. When they arrived for Christmas a few months later, they seemed different and tired. My father had a lot of meetings at 'Daddy's London office' and we seldom saw him. They celebrated New Year at a London nightclub with 'friends of Daddy's from Baghdad' who he 'put on expenses' but neither my brother nor I were allowed to meet them, which was unusual. In addition, my father spent a lot of time with 'my Arab visitors' at the Pigalle nightclub.

What was also a surprise was that my mother and father returned to Baghdad before the end of the school holidays. The whole vacation had been fraught and my brother and I were relieved to see them go.

NOTES

[1] I understand that the private school chosen for me 'catered for those whose parents' background is understood'. This meant that if anything happened to my parents, my fees would be covered. I also understand SIS had a contact at the school 'in case the child has any difficulties'.

I believe this could have meant that it was not unheard of for a child to be indiscreet, either deliberately or inadvertently, about her parents and, if a problem arose, a member of staff would know how to handle things. I think that the SIS contact in my school was either my elderly headmaster, who taught divinity, or my English teacher who had been a missionary in Africa.

9

AN SIS SPY IN DANGER, 1967–68

In 1967 the Six Day War with Israel broke out and the American and British embassies in Iraq shut. After the war, my parents came to England again for the summer holidays. So did various Iraqi friends. As usual, the latter all went shopping in Oxford Street. However, they were not allowed to buy anything from Marks & Spencers – hitherto a favourite London store – because it was 'Zionist'. Those who did make surreptitious purchases cut off the shop's 'St Michael' labels to avoid being found out. I thought this a dangerous strategy – so many Marks & Spencers tags were being snipped off, particularly at London Airport before everyone flew out again, that their goods were instantly recognisable.

In London, my father told SIS that he wanted to leave Iraq for good. SIS's response was that it wanted him to defect to Moscow. (Colonel Michael — of the Soviet embassy, Iraq, who was not aware of my father's allegiance to the Crown, had invited him to make his home there.) SIS was very keen that my father accept.

Much to its disappointment, my father declined – 'I could have named my price,' he said – because my mother refused to accompany him. He went on to say, 'Your mother would have come with me had it not been for you children. Instead, she suggested she move to London, so she could be close to you and I travel to London to see her. I turned this down immediately. How can a man "visit" his wife? I could not face such an arrangement. Your mother was my life, I was not "whole" without her. Therefore, I told SIS I would not go to Moscow.'

Next, SIS asked my parents to consider moving to South Africa, a significant posting.[1] This suggestion they similarly turned down because of the colour bar then in operation. Eventually, it was agreed that they remain in Iraq for one more year. This was particularly important for SIS since the British embassy was still shut.

My parents found returning to Baghdad hard.

My father said, 'One Englishman, a businessman, remained in Iraq after the Six Day War. He was not involved in espionage. However, SIS had many local contacts in Iraq who were. Of these, I was the only one who was British. Therefore, I was HMG's sole representative in Iraq during this time. SIS was very, very grateful.'

It was a nerve-wracking time. My father was particularly worried about my mother because, on several occasions, he had to leave her on her own. If something had gone wrong – he was very active during this period – SIS would not have been able to get her out. If this was not enough, my father had terrible financial problems.[2] These circumstances, coupled with the closure of the British embassy, meant my parents felt 'naked'. They particularly missed my father's SIS case officer 'Frank Tay'. 'Tay' had run my father since 1964 and the two men, with their wives, were close friends.

My father said, 'When the embassy was functioning and "Frank" was around, it never seemed as if we were on our own. I felt that whatever happened to me, your mother could go straight to the embassy if things went wrong. With it shut, I no longer had this reassurance.'

He held the fort for SIS for a year and a half.[3]

He explained, 'It was a terrible time. Just terrible. The pressure under which your mother and I were living was indescribable. Every time we went to bed at night, we were frightened. We did not, for one moment, doubt what we were doing. We wanted Iraq to be Britain's friend. This way, the three major communities of Iraq – the Christians, Jews and Muslims – could thrive. We all got on so well. However, the pressure took an awful lot out of us.

'Every time I sent information back to London, I did not know whether I was going to get caught.'

My father, as I discovered when *The Mitrokhin Archive*[4] was published in London in 2000, was not exaggerating the danger he was in. If anything, he was understating it. For example, the *Archive* declares that in 1967, 'Of the greatest interest [to the Soviets] is the identification of an SIS agent group [in Iraq] consisting of a courier and two agents in the highest government circles . . .' Although my father was not in the government, I believe this refers to him. I can identify two of the three mentioned. For this reason I think my mother saved my father's life. Even though the Soviets had not yet discovered actual identities, they had certainly identified a specific agent group.

It was not known then that the Soviets were aware of a specific SIS group operating in Iraq. Therefore, had my father gone to the Soviet Union, as the Soviets had invited him, and as SIS had wanted, it would have been only a matter of time and a process of elimination before he would have been identified. My mother's refusal to defect to Moscow spared him.

Further evidence of my father's role in Iraq is inadvertently confirmed by Sir Dick White, the former head of SIS and MI5. In Tom Bower's biography of

White,[5] Sir Dick is quoted as saying with pride, 'Baghdad was one of the few locations where SIS could insert a locally born British national into the government.' This refers to my father. Although, as I have said, he was not in the government, he was particularly close to it, and to the best of my knowledge there were no other 'locally born British nationals' fitting this description. I think the discrepancy arises because Sir Dick was unfamiliar with the details. He was never personally interested in the Middle East. The reference is one of the few SIS success stories in Tom Bower's biography.

When, finally, the British embassy reopened and 'Frank Tay' was able to return, my father said that he almost wept with relief. 'In fact, I think I did weep. "Frank", like Sandy Goschen before him, was the best type of SIS diplomat. I literally believe he would have done anything for me.'

The 'Tays' lived in the next street to my family.[6] In the middle of the night, they or my parents would slip into each other's houses. It was easy for them to do so without being seen, because nobody went anywhere on foot in Baghdad. The streets were always deserted. As often as not, because of his young children, 'Tay' would slide along the road to my parents.

'If I went to him,' said my father, 'your mother always came with me. Once, when your mother was away, I got home in the small hours of the morning to find the telephone ringing. It turned out to be a friend wondering where I was and if I was all right. I had to pretend I had been with a woman. This upset me.'

Although the Western embassies reopened, everyday life in Baghdad for foreign nationals and locals remained difficult. It was even worse for our Jewish friends. They were all trying to get visas so that they could leave with their families for the West.

They were particularly hurt by Israel's attitude. My father said, 'The Israelis did not want the Iraqi Jews. They were racists. It was as simple as that. We used to joke, if "joke" is the right word, that the Israelis did not want the Iraqi Jews because they could not stand the competition. The Iraqi Jews are the cleverest in the world.'

Their plight became much worse after the Six Day War when the Israelis boasted, 'We even made soldiers out of the Iraqi Jews.' This, naturally, got reported in Baghdad, placing those Jewish families left in Iraq in even more danger. My father said, 'Some of the Baghdadi Jews escaped via Iran, but this route was dangerous. It was all so sad. The Jews, like the Christians, were Iraqis. They did not wish to leave their homes or their friends, including their Muslim ones, any more than the Iraqi Christians did. We were linked by local and regional ties and loved our shared values, way of life and country.'

By early 1968, my parents set about discreetly winding up their affairs. Other than SIS colleagues, the only person who knew of their plans to leave the country, at this early stage, was our cook, who had been our loyal friend for many years. My father asked him to come with us, but he refused. He said he was too old. Also he had a large family in Baghdad and many children. One of his sons now flew aeroplanes – when his father was illiterate – taking his family into prosperity and the middle classes.

My father said, 'When we finally left, the old man broke up. So did I. We felt as if we were deserting him. We left him as much money as we could, so that he would never have to work again, or be dependent on his sons. But how can you put a price on loyalty, love and years of service?

'Our cook had only ever worked for British families. He did not want them to leave. I have always believed many Iraqis felt the same way.'

The decision to leave Iraq was determined by the deteriorating commercial and political situation, as well as domestic problems. Many years later, my father told me, 'Your brother was nearly 18. Despite his British passport, he was born in Baghdad, so he would have had to do his military service. I was frightened my teenaged, fair-skinned son would become a target for every rapist in the Iraqi Army. Also, you were almost a teenager too, a time when good families try to choose husbands for their daughters, after they have completed their education. I did not want to snub any of my Muslim friends if they wished to encourage a match.

'For these reasons, I knew we had to leave. When a man becomes a father he must not see the babe. He must see the adult and plant the child where it can thrive. I was haunted, literally haunted, by my children's future.

'In addition, I was 47 and my nerves were shot. If I left it any longer, I did not know whether I would be able to earn a living in London. Your mother and I only knew London for holidays. We did not know what London was like to live in. Your mother had left after the [Second World] War, and there had been so many changes since then. As importantly, our children were virtual strangers because we were distanced from the culture that was influencing their young lives.'

The decision to leave was made a little easier because of the loyalty of a senior British oil executive and his company in London. My father knew that if it were at all possible, the oilman would do all he could to help my father establish himself commercially in England. 'He was a perfect gentleman,' said my father.

My father was equally loyal, postponing his return to England by one month in order to secure a valuable contract for the oil company concerned. The deal was eventually successfully concluded. I believe that my father knew the revolution was on its way, and was aware of the date on which it was scheduled. This allowed him to delay his departure to win the oil tender, with enough time left over to leave safely with my mother in June 1968.

He told me, 'We packed up our house, sold what we could and shipped the rest of our things back to Britain. With SIS approval, we gave the dolls' house its craftsmen had made for you to the French Covent which ran the orphanage. We were pleased about this although we would have liked to bring it back to Britain.

'SIS kindly sent my books, and a private collection which I treasured, via the "diplomatic bag" because otherwise I would not have been able to get them through Iraqi customs. My SIS colleagues collected everything when they picked up the "table" with the false leg. Regrettably, SIS did not accept for the "diplomatic bag" my framed, old maps of Iraq, or your mother's dinner service. It was her pride and joy.'

On their return to London, my parents learned SIS had paid their shipping costs. While 'delighted with this gift', my father said, 'I was very hurt "Frank Tay" had not told me this would happen before we left. Had he done so, your mother would have been able to keep so many small things of immense sentimental value. It was particularly heartbreaking for her to leave so much behind. SIS, while being generous, also has a mean streak which can sour its generosity.'

My father continued, 'At long last came our day of departure. I had said goodbye to "Frank Tay" a short time before. We had worked together so closely it was like saying goodbye to a brother. He had a very different character to Sandy Goschen but I liked them equally. In those days, all we did was shake hands. Our word was our bond. We never ever let each other down. I liked working like this.

'Your mother and I were given a wonderful party and send-off at the airport by all our Iraqi friends. We were very, very sad to go. I cannot begin to tell you what it is like to leave behind all you know and love. Everybody had such respect for people. For example, a dear Muslim friend had always said, "If you ever have any problems with the British embassy shut, take your wife immediately to my mother. She will be safe there." How could I ever replace such love and loyalty?

'However, we were also drained. Even at the last moment, we thought something could go wrong and the Iraqi authorities would catch us.'

One month after my parents left Iraq came the first of the July 1968 revolutions.

The minute their aeroplane left Iraqi air-space, my parents were approached by a beaming air-stewardess with champagne from 'your London office'. Throughout the long flight they only had to blink to find champagne at their elbow. On their arrival at Heathrow, they were taken off the aircraft and whisked through customs. Waiting for them was an SIS diplomat formerly based in Iran, now back in Whitehall. His name was Norman Darbyshire. He was carrying a huge bunch of flowers for my mother.

'Welcome to London,' he said with a dazzling smile.

'In a daze,' said my father, 'your mother and I got into a staff car and were taken to be debriefed. We stared silently out of the window as the streets of London passed by in a blur.

'It was the end of a long, long nightmare.'

NOTES

1   SIS's interest in South Africa in the '60s was summarised in *Lobster* 43, published summer 2002: 'South Africa was an important player in the imperial game. It was a recipient of considerable British overseas investment and a magnet for exports. By

1967 it surpassed even Australia as a market. But South Africa's value to Britain was not only economic . . . Arms exports were good for the balance of payments and domestic employment; it guaranteed the defence of the South Atlantic and Indian Oceans; and security of sea lanes around the Cape . . .'

[2] Following the Six Day War, trading conditions for businessmen like my father were particularly harsh because the Arabs boycotted any country that traded with Israel. As a result, the only money he had coming in was from SIS. In a letter to his nephew in America in 1972, he wrote, 'I traded with the US, UK and West Germany. After the Six Day War, all these countries were caught up by the Arab boycott. It was a very difficult time . . .'

[3] As HMG's sole representative in Iraq, my father bitterly resented the fact that, unlike SIS diplomats, his children's school fees and travel were not paid by the Crown. He believed this was unfair, and that what was good for one crown servant, should have been good for another. He remarked, 'Although we were all taking terrible risks, those I was taking, particularly after the embassy shut, were by far the greater. There was a two-tier system operating that, presumably, existed throughout the empire.'

[4] *The Mitrokhin Archive: The KGB in Europe and the West.* p. 443.

[5] Bower, T. (1995) *The Perfect English Spy: Sir Dick White and the Secret War 1935–90.* Heinemann: London: p. 236.

No doubt unwittingly, the emphasis Sir Dick gives is to praise SIS. I believe such praise could have been reserved for the spy, whether or not he was my father, since it was not SIS that 'inserted a locally born British national into the [Iraq] Government', but the heroism and courage of the man concerned.

[6] Watching a documentary on Iraq in February 2002, I was surprised to learn that the street in which my family lived is now the 'Fifth Avenue' of Baghdad.

TWO

An SIS Family in London
1968–78

10

ESTABLISHING AN SIS SPY

All those who move country will recognise adjusting to another can take a considerable time. The change is particularly traumatic if dramatic events unfold in the previous country of residence and those lucky enough to be outside it can do nothing but watch from the safety of their new homes. This was the position in which my parents found themselves in July 1968, when, shortly after their departure from Iraq, two revolutions followed in quick succession.

Throughout this time, they had the support and kindness of Norman Darbyshire, the SIS diplomat who had met them at London Airport.[1] He was one of the country's most dashing and courageous intelligence officers who joined the Foreign Office from the Special Operations Executive after the Second World War. His career, especially his involvement in the downfall of Iran's Prime Minister Mossadeq in 1953, may be considered controversial today.[2] My comments are on the man I knew, who, with his then young wife, were my parents' first friends – and in Darbyshire's case, SIS mentor – in London after they left Iraq. Those who might judge his overseas career by today's standards could miss the flavour of the man, his heroism and, from an exceptionally young age, his years of loyal service to the Crown.

Good-looking and charismatic, albeit not the easiest of men to get on with, Darbyshire took his role as mentor seriously and he was always remembered with affection and gratitude. Darbyshire's job encompassed everything from having to write 'Beirut' rather than 'Beyrouth' in his report because, 'Otherwise the clots at "The Office" will think you are talking about a town in Germany' – to what London clubs to join; to finding my parents a private family dentist and doctor who were acceptable to SIS. Those chosen were Darbyshire's personal friends.

He recommended London clubs – 'So Lawrence can have an idea of the social life here before he becomes active and starts circulating again' – and membership of these was quickly achieved, i.e. we were able to jump the various waiting lists.

He painstakingly explained language traps – 'Our sort tend not to say "settee", we say "sofa"' – because he didn't want 'Lawrence getting tripped up socially'. In addition, he cleared up cultural misunderstandings. For example, my father had trouble accepting that the well-known American actress Ali McGraw was not being 'disrespectful to Islam' by calling herself 'Ali', the name of the Prophet Mohammed's son-in-law. 'Ali' is, of course, the abbreviation of the name Alison.

Darbyshire had strong views about the Middle East, many of which my father profoundly disapproved. A dozen years after the Suez fiasco, the diplomat could not accept Egypt had had a 'right' to its canal, any more than he could accept President Nasser had had a 'right' to be a nationalist.[3] Darbyshire's real passion, however, was for Persia. His heart belonged to its people and he knew the country, literature and language well.

Although often argumentative, Darbyshire could be charming and entertaining. He was adept at using humour to raise spirits in otherwise desperate days. One of his funniest stories was when he reported the battle the London police were having because 'every Egyptian accredited to the Court of St James appears to be stealing the pigeons in Trafalgar Square. They want them, apparently, for pigeon-pie [a delicacy in Cairo].'

He would continue, 'When they have run out of pigeons, they are nicking the ducks in St James's Park.

'. . . We discovered it when a friend from "The Office" found out that his favourite duck, which he fed every lunch-time, had disappeared. He's so upset his feathered chum has been swiped for "Duck a l'orange", rumour has it he's going to get Special Branch on to it to bring the miscreants to justice.'

I first met Norman Darbyshire in the school holidays of summer 1968. I was 13. So far as I was concerned, he had one great virtue: he was straightforward with children, even when the news was distressing. For example, he explained matter-of-factly, 'Go easy on your father. Do not fuss him. He is upset. There has been another revolution in Iraq.'

I continued to rely on his straightforwardness, even after he had been posted overseas again and had ceased to be my father's case officer. Once, when he was home on leave, I turned to him when events in Iraq had further deteriorated. A so-called Zionist spy-ring had been discovered in Baghdad which resulted in 17 'spies' being rounded up and eventually executed. Spotting him when I was walking past his house, en route to the golf-club opposite, I asked, 'Would Daddy have been rounded up as well?'

Darbyshire shook his head, saying, 'Unlikely. But if not this time, then probably on another occasion. Your father is well out of there.'

Next, I asked, 'Does this mean that we will never go back to Baghdad?' It was the first time, despite all that had been said, and all that had happened, I fully realised that I would not be going 'home'. He shook his head.

On another occasion, I asked about the head of Coca-Cola in Iraq who, shamefully, had been tortured and killed. I already knew what had happened, but wanted it confirmed. Again, Darbyshire responded straightforwardly, adding quietly, 'How did you hear about the poor chap? Were you listening to your father's phone calls?'

I nodded. Although I did not speak Arabic, I had understood the gist of what I had overheard. With his arm around my shoulders, Darbyshire said quietly, 'You must never listen to your father's phone calls. You would not like him to listen to yours, therefore it is wrong to listen to his. Your father will always tell you what you need to know. If he does not, there will be a reason for it and you must trust his decision. In addition, never trust anybody who gives you information – including me – your father does not want you to know.'

I accept that throughout the ten-year period my family knew him, he could be a difficult and overbearing man. My memory of him, however, is of his sweetness.

Not even an SIS mentor could help those not used to London adapt to the city. My parents also found it difficult connecting with their children, particularly with my brother, who, now aged 18, was a young adult with his own way of life. For obvious reasons, his preferred *modus vivendi* was automatically in conflict with our newly arrived parents, particularly our father. This was the '60s after all – the era of long hair for young men, mini-skirts and the pill for young women.

My parents had other problems too, not least London's lack of cosmopolitanism. In many respects, my mother suffered the most. She had left Britain just after the war, aged 25. She returned, aged 44, to a very different nation from the one she had left. This reinforced her impression of isolation, especially as my father had his SIS career where, unlike herself, he had the benefit of colleagues. She had no close female friend to ease her back into life in the United Kingdom, let alone one who understood the nature of her husband's work or their joint sense of dislocation.

My father also had financial worries. Six months short of his 48th birthday, he did not know how he was going to support his family in the long-term. SIS, while being exceptionally kind, had not yet given an indication of my father's future role. In addition, he was virtually penniless as, ever since the Arab boycott, his business had suffered and he had, for the most part, been keeping his family on savings.[4]

Using his SIS salary, he set about doing what he knew best – commerce – establishing his import–export business from scratch. Given the acknowledged frustrations with red tape, this was no easy task, particularly in a country he had only previously visited on business or for extended holidays. SIS were naive about commercial matters and did not understand why, for example, it took him so long to establish a telegraphic address.

He said, 'They kept pressing me to get on with this, as if the delay was my fault. They did not know how slow departments of their own government could be. In the end, SIS had to speed things up for me. This came as a shock since up until then I had believed anything to do with British bureaucracy was well organised and all British civil servants were gods.'

SIS, quite rightly, let him get on with things, keeping strictly in the background. He rejected their one suggestion.

Through high-ranking SIS freemasons, he was introduced to two British businessmen, on various Chambers of Commerce circuits, one of whom had been an MP. Both had knighthoods. SIS suggested that it would be beneficial to my father's new business if, because of their knighthoods, he put their names on his letterheads. A fee would be charged. My father refused to employ the two men because he saw no reason 'to fund their retirement'. He explained: 'I worked for my money. I could not understand why I was being expected to carry anyone else.' SIS did not mention the subject again.

Many years later he remarked that his decision not to employ the two businessmen 'was a mistake for my espionage career. I know now that SIS was more comfortable, particularly when it came to the placing of contracts, if someone familiar to them was on the board of a spy's company. It was also a mistake commercially. I did not know then, this was how British business worked. Most of my other friends from the Middle East who also set up companies always included those with knighthoods, even though the conduct of some of these knights was bad for the country's reputation.

'My friends had no respect for them, and HMG did not realise to what extent they and, in consequence, the country, was despised for tolerating such parasites, but my friends believed them to be essential for the prosperity of their businesses, which, as it turns out, they were. There is very little difference between the practice in this country and in, for example, Saudi Arabia, where it is mandatory to have a Saudi Arabian partner. In fact, there is an argument which suggests that at least the Saudis are not hypocrites by being straightforward about the arrangement.'

At a later stage, my father gave a more graphic description of politicians and former public servants throwing themselves, and being thrown, in his direction. He said, 'I could not believe what was going on. They were absolutely shameless in their demands and convinced of their own superiority. It was shocking. It was as if I was expected to fund their retirement by providing them with so-called employment, in exchange for which I would receive certain benefits . . .'

Nor, for the most part, was my father impressed with what today would be called 'networking' events (in those days referred to as 'cocktail parties') which were often hosted in Parliament. These occasions were organised by the various Chambers of Commerce and country-specific or area-trade associations. He was impressed, however, by the Masonic parties and concluded several business deals as a result of those he met through them.

Masonic functions always contained a sprinkling of Arab guests – 'The Arabs have long been comfortable with freemasonry,' he said. My father told how on one occasion the chairman of Rolls Royce 'hilariously mistook me for the ambassador of an important Arab country. I only figured it out when he called me 'Your Excellency' not once, but three times. When he found out his mistake, he was profoundly embarrassed. I said, "Not to worry", and arranged a meeting for him anyway since the ambassador was my friend.'

However, it should also be noted that my father was bitterly upset that the United Grand Lodge of the United Kingdom had expunged all records of the Iraqi Lodge, which, at its own request, had closed down three years earlier in 1965. He also had his criticisms of freemasonry in England, which he said was too snooty – 'The Iraqis are snooty people too but at the Lodge in Baghdad, all men were equal. I did not find this in the UK. I went to the smart English Lodges, obviously, because this is where all the contacts were. I could not have been more warmly received. My Masonic brothers were all cosmopolitan people and thrived on meetings with those from foreign lands.

'However, this deep affection was not offered to one of my friends from the North of England. He was a fabulously wealthy self-made and lovely man. I was hurt for him. He was philosophical and angry he was looked down upon. I think he became a Rotarian instead. Some years later he bought the company of one of the Masonic brothers who had been particularly rude to him. I was very, very pleased for him. I always tried to warn my Masonic brothers that freemasonry in England would die if they did not put an end to such revolting and arrogant behaviour.'

Six months after his arrival in the UK, my father secured his first commercial contract. It was a nerve-wracking business with many of his letters having to be smuggled into, and out of, the Middle East. The contract was worth £18,675, of which my father's commission, after he had paid disbursements, was £2,241. This represented a lot to him but was a minuscule piece of business for the British oil company concerned. However, it proved to SIS he could deliver contracts.

Now established in business, SIS provided him with a first-class sophisticated administrative infrastructure. This was organised by its lawyers and accountants. My father's SIS solicitor was the late Derek Sinclair, who had distinguished SIS family connections – Sinclair's father was Rear Admiral Sir Hugh Sinclair, who succeeded Sir Mansfield Cumming as SIS Chief in 1923.

Derek Sinclair's office, which I knew well because I was always delivering letters to it, was just off Portman Square.

My father's SIS accountant, whom I shall call 'Mr Smith' and to whom I also delivered letters, had offices in Mount Street.[5]

My father had nothing but praise for his SIS accountant and lawyer. They were always happy to act as buffer if he had problems with SIS, or as conduit if he wished to raise issues which he felt would be more appropriate coming from them. For example, citing SIS commercial naiveté, my father provided Mr Sinclair with a report on the problems he was experiencing setting up a business, mentioning a specific issue which he presumed would be encountered by all SIS businessmen-spies.

Mr Sinclair had the 'fault' corrected immediately, and it was in due course passed into legislation.

Mr Sinclair was particularly kind when one of my father's relatives – a businessman and professional gambler – went through a troubled period. In order to protect my father from publicity, inevitable in the fall-out, Sinclair ensured that there was a blanket ban in the media. (This also served to protect my father's SIS career, since his employers hated publicity.) Mr Sinclair subsequently speeded passport applications for the relative and one of his children.

Sinclair was absolutely scrupulous in upholding the law, and, without a doubt, one of the most powerful men in the country at this time. (An example of how little the public knew, in those days, about who was really powerful in Britain.) He made it clear that my father was 'a crown servant, answerable only to the Sovereign'. As a result, there was never any confusion in my father's mind as to who his employer was. Sinclair was the first to hint that my father was likely to become operational again, discreetly suggesting that his career could 'become dangerous. For this reason, my dear, I must strongly advise you to make a will.'

He made it clear what arrangements had been made in the event of anything happening to my father. 'SIS will be very generous to your widow and children. Moreover, there will be no tax on your estate. It is the least the Crown can do. I would most likely be a trustee. I advise you to leave your money in trust for your children. . .'[6]

My father interrupted, 'My children? What about my wife? She is the one who would need help if I died.'

Mr Sinclair responded, 'Naturally SIS would look after your widow. However, in my experience it is unwise to leave money directly to a widow since she is likely to marry again, or spend the money, to the detriment of the children of the marriage. For this reason, SIS tends to separate the widow's interests from that of the children.'

Much to Mr Sinclair's dismay, my father replied, 'This is a recipe for a widow to have to approach her own children with a begging bowl. Tell SIS my wife is my heir. She has shared all the dangers of my life. She is entitled to anything and everything it is worth.'[7]

Mr Sinclair's colleague in Mount Street, 'Mr Smith', settled all accountancy matters.

When my father first arrived in the UK, he was what was known as, in banking terms, an 'external account'. These were for overseas residents (SIS loved them because, since they were tax-free, the Inland Revenue did not need to become involved). My father also had several numbered Swiss bank accounts. The former eventually subsided as he became a UK resident; the latter he wound up because he was 'uncomfortable' with them.

All my father's commercial commissions were paid into his London account. He had separate accounts, agreed with the Inland Revenue, for commissions he held for third parties who were resident overseas. (SIS, through its accountants and lawyers, was absolutely scrupulous in ensuring its businessmen-spies conformed to all aspects of the law.)

My father found the assistance of his SIS accountant 'Mr Smith' vital, because he was looking after the savings of many old friends from the Middle East whose governments did not permit them to have money or assets outside their own country. As a result, my father had to explain specific circumstances to the Inland Revenue. 'Mr Smith' did this on his behalf.

Sometimes all my father needed to do was set up British bank accounts for his friends before, as they requested, transferring the bulk of their money to the United States or elsewhere. However, others required more sophisticated investment advice and assistance. Others again, wanted to purchase property. 'Mr Smith', British banks and the Inland Revenue were kind and adept at handling the savings of those from, or still living in, troubled countries. All recognised that, sometimes, citizens from these countries had more money outside of them than they did inside.[8]

My father could not praise 'Mr Smith', the Inland Revenue or Coutts Bank more highly for the 'sensitive and humane way they handled things'. He continued, 'Some people had a considerable amount of money. Other people had only pennies. "Mr Smith" and Coutts provided them with an identical service, as if they had all been millionaires and made no charges. In my opinion, the way "Mr Smith", the Inland Revenue and the banks handled such sad cases did more for the good reputation of this country than anything else.'

Despite SIS's superb relationship with the Inland Revenue, there were communication problems. For example, some years after my father had settled in the UK, the Revenue queried his accounts. He attracted its attention because of all his SIS travelling. Unfortunately, its letter arrived when 'Mr Smith' was on holiday. The matter was therefore handled by a subordinate, who was not aware of my father's SIS connection.

As a result, my father had to justify his visits to Abu Dhabi, Lebanon, Copenhagen, Stockholm, the Gulf, Athens and Egypt. He was able to cover himself by truthfully explaining that he had gone to Abu Dhabi to follow up 'a large business for the supply of kitchen equipment to the Royal Palace at Al-Ain'. (Lockhard Equipment Ltd, a company in the Trust Houses Group, whom my father represented at the time, had submitted a quotation to Messrs. J. L. G. Poulson.)

However, my father found explaining his visits to Copenhagen and Stockholm not quite so easy. In the end, he told the Revenue, 'I tripped over to Copenhagen and Stockholm several times in the hope of concluding arrangements for the supply of about 1,500 tons of Frozen Chickens to Egypt. I enclose cards relating to such contacts.'

Fudging a visit to Greece was even more difficult – 'I went to Athens to meet one of my Egyptian clients' – because of his many trips to Cairo. The

Revenue, rightly, queried why my father did not see his Egyptian client in Egypt.

My father gave a huge sigh of relief when 'Mr Smith' returned from holiday and personally handled the matter. Soon after, SIS agreed that my father withdraw his accounts (with the exception of his non-SIS commercial income) from tax-authority scrutiny. Instructed by 'Mr Smith', my father wrote to inform them that '. . . until conditions change in the Middle East, which is the field of my specialty, I have decided to cut down my losses and continue to operate on a minute scale with the least possible expense. Therefore, I shall not be submitting to the Inland Revenue an Import–Export Account in future.'[9]

In addition to his SIS work, my father's non-SIS commercial career slowly prospered. As always, my mother wanted him to concentrate on this, preferring he make his way in the world as a *bona fide* businessman, rather than as a spy. She was particularly anxious he leave espionage behind because, she said, 'Our children were growing up. I did not think it was fair on them. Espionage is too intrusive for children.'

My father refused, saying, 'I was hooked by this time, absolutely hooked. I loved working for the Crown and would neglect everything to do so. I thought it was vital work and more important than anything else. You cannot imagine the excitement of working for Whitehall during the Cold War.'[10]

Even my mother admitted, 'I felt we had to show our gratitude to HMG for all it had done for us. The country had not let us down, and we could not let it down.' Therefore, and as always, she supported my father in his work.

Politically, two events dominated the British agenda and television screens in 1968. One, the start of the (modern) Troubles in Northern Ireland, meant nothing to my father. He did not believe these to be serious and thought they would soon 'blow over'. The other, the Soviet invasion of Czechoslovakia, was a different matter.

I sat with him as he slumped in front of our black-and-white television, watching events unfold. Any number of his friends from the Middle East were living in Prague. A short while later, he had a telephone call. This was the start of countless whispered conversations. At the end of one, he told me, 'Always remember what you see on television today. It is the only way you will realise the Communist system, despite many temptations, is an evil one. Whatever you do in the future, never go anywhere near it.' The crushing of the Prague Spring re-confirmed why he served HMG.

One of the main delays, however, for the re-starting of his SIS career was because he could not pass his British driving test. My mother passed first time. As he bashfully admitted many years later, 'No self-respecting spy does not have a British driving licence.'

While he was thrilled to be operational again, my mother, still harbouring doubts as to whether this was the best thing for him and their family, was cross to discover that, because of his work, he, and therefore she, was excused from jury service. All SIS diplomats, civil servants, spies and their families are excused this. Outraged at being deprived of her right to perform a minor civic duty, she was even more incensed when given the reason: 'Your husband's work for the country is civic duty enough. If the wife of a spy is on jury service, it is likely to be a distraction or inconvenience to the man.'

This message was conveyed to her, rather sheepishly it has to be admitted, by 'Geoffrey Kingsmill', my father's second London case officer.

NOTES

[1] Norman Darbyshire MBE OBE served with the Special Operations Executive 1943–45. He joined the Foreign Office in 1945, becoming third secretary in Teheran in 1945, moving to Cairo in 1948. Two years later, still aged only 26, he became vice consul in Meshed. The following year he was back in Teheran, moving to the British Middle East Office, Cyprus, in 1952. He returned to London two years later, before becoming consul in Geneva in 1956. He was first secretary in Bahrain in 1958, returning to London in 1960. In 1964 he was back in Teheran again, this time as SIS Head of Station. He returned to London three years later, before being posted to Beirut as first secretary in 1969. He returned to Whitehall in 1973, and retired from SIS in 1978.
   Source: 'A Who's Who of the British Secret State', *Lobster* special (1989).

2 See Dorril, S. (2000) *MI6: Fifty Years of Special Operations.* Fourth Estate: London.

[3] As a result of Suez, President Nasser of Egypt had made SIS look particularly silly in Whitehall and a desire for revenge dictated the British agenda for years. I believe, but could have misunderstood what I overheard, particularly in view of accepted interpretation of the Suez crisis, SIS bitterness had been exacerbated by the fact that Israel had secretly wanted the Suez Canal kept shut and had backed the Americans. This had played on some SIS anti-Semitism and, for a while, I understand, SIS had hoped to overthrow the Egyptian president by offering information on Israel in exchange for his murder.
   This is not a view, however, that has been reflected in the history books, and I accept I could have misunderstood the discussion.

[4] On my father's arrival in London, SIS paid his salary as a tax-free lump-sum of £3,000. This was for the half-year July/December 1968. Subsequently, his salary was taxed although arrangements were made with the Inland Revenue for this to be declared on a separate tax form to his non-SIS commercial accounts. So that the reader has the benefit of comparison, Michael Foot MP said in the House of Commons in 1968, 'No one needs an income of more than £6,000 per year.'

[5] I have not named my father's SIS accountant because, I understand, he is in poor health and of great age. Nor have I named the legal and accountancy practices. This is because, although neither exist today – having amalgamated with other partnerships and changed address – I have no knowledge of their present status.

[6] I cannot help but contrast the integrity of my father's SIS lawyer Mr Sinclair, as

prospective trustee, with that of a modern counterpart. At the time of writing, an SIS lawyer is currently in prison for fraud. His crimes include embezzling the trust fund of two orphans whose father I knew and admired.

7   I believe that in the late '60s, following the death of a spy, SIS pastoral care could have been principally about the financial well-being of children. I do not think, but could be doing SIS an injustice, such care, despite all the promises, would have been particularly fair to widows.

8   This was why my father always argued, particularly with an SIS insurance broker interested in the Middle Eastern market for financial products, personal insurance products would never sell in the area.

Another reason was because Islam's Sharia Law forbids Muslims from receiving interest payments, although dividends on shares are permissible, so long as they are not derived from alcohol production, gambling or pornography – possibly the earliest example we have of an 'ethical' investment policy. At the time of writing, the financial products industry is seeking to provide Sharia-compliant products.

9   One reason why SIS was so determined to remove my father's import–export accounts from the Inland Revenue was because, in order to substantiate his cover, British embassy representatives in Stockholm and Copenhagen had had to run around obtaining the visiting cards of local suppliers of frozen chickens.

Hilariously, some years later, my father really was offered a contract to supply frozen chickens to Egypt. However, the Egyptians only ate 'corn fed' poultry, which made the carcasses yellow, whereas the UK, in those days, only had 'white' poultry. Complaining to his old SIS friend 'Frank Tay', then awaiting another overseas posting, he had had to use a Spanish rather than a British supplier, 'Tay' responded, 'Actually, Lawrence, SIS do not know a great deal about frozen chickens.'

10   With the benefit of hindsight, I believe that my mother's wishes should have prevailed. I think 'foreign' spies like my father are wholly unsuited to Whitehall/Foreign Office culture when they are based in London. This culture is especially difficult for the spy to absorb if he is closer to 50 than 40.

11

OPERATIONAL AGAIN

My father served in London with 'Geoffrey Kingsmill CMG' (not his real name) from 1969–73. They continued to operate together after 'Kingsmill' had been posted in 1973.

Events in the Middle East during this period included the arrival of Colonel Gaddafi of Libya in 1969 and the death of President Nasser of Egypt in 1970. The same year, Ba'athi President Assad came to power in Syria, to twin with the Ba'athis running Iraq who purged their rivals. In Jordan, the Palestinian Liberation Organisation (PLO) virtually set up an independent state.

'This time also saw an increase in fighting between the Lebanese Army and the Palestinian fedayin fighters who were making cross-border raids into Israel and provoking retaliatory attacks by the Israeli Defence Force.'[1] The expulsion by the Royal Jordanian armed forces of members of the PLO the following year led to conflict between the Palestinians and Lebanon's Phalangist Christians, in what was becoming the beginnings of the civil war that was to rip Lebanon apart.[2]

SIS diplomat Sir David Spedding, who was to become SIS Chief in 1994, was the second secretary at the SIS Beirut Station at the time, 'Where he cut his teeth collecting intelligence on the various Palestinian factions which were to become his main area of expertise . . .'[3] He was subsequently 'outed' as a member of SIS by Kim Philby – a British agent who defected to the Soviets in 1963 – in Moscow.[4]

In Iraq, came the end of the Kurdish rebellion in the north without resolution of the legal status of Kurdistan. As a result, the early '70s were dominated by Kurdish alliances with the Soviets and various Western powers. 1972 saw the nationalisation of the Iraq Petroleum Company, and subsequently Kirkuk's Kurdish oil being changed into Arab oil. At this time, the Kurds were not aware that the Western powers were not in favour of an independent Kurdistan because this would threaten the integrity of Iraq and complicate relations with Iran and

Turkey. Meanwhile, the Iraqis signed a 15-year Friendship Treaty with the Soviet Union, a follow-up to its 1969 treaty with the Soviets to produce oil. In 1973, there was an abortive coup in Iraq led by the Iraqi security chief and the Yom Kippur War in Israel.

My father was an expert in all these political developments. This complimented his acknowledged authority on issues pertaining to Iraq and his superb understanding of the Arabic language, cultures and faiths.

I met 'Kingsmill' when I was 14. Compared to the wildly attractive and immaculately dressed Norman Darbyshire, he was a bit crumpled, and therefore something of a disappointment. It was to be several years before I appreciated the subtlety of his character, humour and understated appeal. Of the men with whom my father served in London, 'Kingsmill' was to become the most senior.

Today, the British intelligence services advertise for new recruits in the appointment pages of major newspapers and magazines. Had this been the habit in the 1970s, 'Geoffrey Kingsmill' would have taken out a small advertisement in *Loot* (or its equivalent in those days) and, under 'Car Boot Sales', would have inserted the caption, 'Spooks Wanted: GSOH. Must like curry'.

I was introduced when the situation in Iraq had deteriorated again. Fourteen men, most of whom were Jewish, were executed in Baghdad, their bodies placed on public display.[5] As news of various atrocities drip-fed into London, 'Geoffrey Kingsmill' was a constant source of solace to my parents. However, he did not have Norman Darbyshire's detached skill in comforting 14 year olds. For this reason, when further distressing news arrived from Baghdad, I turned to his more 'child-aware' colleague.

The run-up to the escalating troubles saw the Iraqi community living in Europe and America chasing around for news of relatives and friends. As one family heard something, they passed it to the next. In a letter dated 2 July 1969, one of my uncles who had also left Iraq wrote to my father to let him know that various friends and acquaintances had been imprisoned. His letter concluded: 'Things are so bad there that everybody is afraid of everybody else.' He wrote again a few days later naming other friends who had been arrested, adding, '[. . .] the list of names was in an Arabic newspaper. What is going on in Iraq?'

In September, a letter dated 17 August 1969 arrived. It was from a family friend still inside Iraq and had been smuggled overland before being posted from Europe. After detailing various inhumanities too distressing to repeat, the writer went on to say: '[. . .]You may also be interested to know, in case you do not hear about this in the Western newspapers, that the situation between Iraq and Lebanon has now blown up to hell and that Iraq has recalled all the Iraqis from there, stopped all shipment through Beirut and all imports from Lebanon and they are referring the matter to the Revolutionary Council to take whatever other measures they deem necessary to take. This is official and broadcast on Baghdad Radio [. . .] Why is all this happening?'

I do not know why it all happened. Nor do I know whether SIS had more to do with it than any of the other national intelligence agencies that have contributed to the type of country Iraq is today. I do know, however, the Iraqi society I knew as a child worked, albeit imperfectly, and had the promise of working better. More than 30 years later, three generations of gifted and wonderful people have been sacrificed on the altar of greed of all.

I remember constant discussions in hushed voices between my father and his SIS colleagues. These were sometimes in English, more usually in Arabic – so I could not understand.[6] ('Geoffrey Kingsmill' was always sad I had not been brought up to speak Arabic, believing this to be 'a golden opportunity lost'. My father explained to 'Kingsmill' that he did not want his children, particularly his daughter, becoming involved in espionage because, he said, 'I want a nice life for her, with a husband and children. What decent husband would want a wife who is a spy?')

I do not remember any of the contents of what I understood of the discussions I overheard. However, I believe the Treaty of Mosul was mentioned by 'Kingsmill'. Similarly, I recall my father saying, 'When we are contented with Iraq, Kuwait is not important to us.'

Like all children, I ran on instinct, tip-toeing around the adults. If there were things on my father's desk I ought not to see, I automatically averted my eyes. My family existed in a sealed environment of espionage and sorrow. This gave a young person many false ideas about being adult. I could not, even in passing, mention anything about my home life to my contemporaries. Nor could I give any indication as to my parents' friends and visitors. Many of these turned up in what seemed to be the middle of the night, when I was assumed to be asleep.

This, of course, was a silly assumption because, as I was packed off to bed early, I usually knew when a visitor was expected. Anxious not to miss anything, I would sit in the dark peering out of my bedroom window for what seemed like hours. It was always annoying if the visitor slipped in through the back door, because my bedroom was at the front. When the visitor did come through the front I was equally disappointed because he came in so quickly, I usually missed him. It was almost as if our house had one identity during the day and another at night.

My father, in the early hours of the morning, would sit in darkness, chain-smoking. Wearing tatty old pyjamas, he would hunch over my mother's radiogram, twiddling the knobs of the carefully selected Grundig, to pick up Arab radio stations. On his head would be powerful headphones, supplied by SIS, which I still have. As often, there would be countless strange telephone calls shattering the stillness, followed by brief conversations. The following day, he would wait for his BBC *Bulletins* (Middle East) – translated verbatim reports of those same radio stations – to arrive. These he would study from cover to cover, breaking off only to listen to the news on the radio once more.

An example of the information in the BBC *Bulletins* is one dated 19

September 1971, from the Cairo Home Service, naming President Anwar-as-Sadat's cabinet. In January the following year the *Bulletins* detail the president's new cabinet, and give the full text of the Egyptian Statement on US–Israeli Arms Production Understanding. Today, this sort of information is compiled by, among others, public affairs specialists and lobbyists. In those days, such information was accessed solely by intelligence services' eavesdroppers and passed to SIS for analysis.

Another example of the wealth of information in the *Bulletins* is dated 7 February 1976. This reported that the Baghdad Home Service had announced: 'Two decrees have been issued establishing two new provinces. They are Salah ad-Din and Najaf provinces. The decrees have also changed the name of Kirkuk province to Ta'mim (Nationalization) Province.'

In the margin of one *Bulletin*, my father had written: '7 April 1947 was the birth of the Ba'ath Party by M. Aflaq.'

He kept all his *Bulletins*, plus his detailed notes, neatly filed and cross-referred 1969–79, in special steel boxes in the basement. He destroyed most of these, as well as his comments, shortly before his death. In addition, as per all SIS safety rules, he kept no copies of his reports.[7]

Drafts of his SIS reports, which he wrote in longhand before typing up on the SIS-supplied typewriter, were torn into little pieces and flushed down the lavatory. On one occasion this created a blockage and SIS had to send out their own plumber to sort things out. All meetings and comments noted in his diary had to be in pencil. As a result, he had a stock of good-quality ones, as well as an excellent pencil sharpener (things had to be in pencil so that, if necessary, they could be erased).

He used a portable SIS-supplied Olivetti typewriter, for which a receipt was taken. This was exchanged at regular intervals. SIS was particularly security conscious about the typewriter ribbon. He also had a similar, non-SIS one, for personal use. On one occasion, he was so exhausted, he typed his SIS report on the wrong typewriter (it was always important not to confuse them) and had to re-do it on the correct machine before submitting it. However, my father never told SIS of his mistake and so the ribbon of the incorrect typewriter was not submitted.

Sometimes, if he had a meeting at home, all the radios and taps had to be turned on. Sometimes too, I was able to glean partial information about what was happening. For example, once I heard a torture victim had arrived from the Middle East for treatment in one of the big London hospitals. The man had been so brutalised, the only movement he had left was the ability to lift one of his little fingers. If it is possible to talk in terms of 'reputation', Britain had a 'good' one because of the expertise our doctors and nurses had in caring for such victims.

At a particularly grim time, when my father feared for his own safety and knew, if caught, he would be similarly tortured, he asked if I remembered our

Baghdad telephone number. When I recited it, he replied, 'Good. This is our family code. If the worse happens, look up the whole telephone number in the relevant page references in my Bible. You will find a message from Daddy because he loves you all very much.' The telephone code was used in one operational matter with my father's third London SIS case officer.

The only British newspaper my father took – somewhat to my embarrassment since all my friends' fathers read *The Times* – was the *Daily Express*. This disappointed 'Geoffrey Kingsmill', who believed that my father ought to read *The Times* and the *Daily Telegraph* because, he explained, 'You can get the line from them.'

My father disregarded the advice on the basis, 'I get better information from my BBC *Bulletins*. This is of more value to the Crown than me being influenced by HMG's line in *The Times*.'

To this day, I believe my father is the only person 'Geoffrey Kingsmill' ever knew who read the popular press. Despite his SIS colleague's snootiness, my father highly rated the *Daily Express's* political and foreign news.

Soon after, as the 1970 General Election approached, came a discussion on voting. 'Geoffrey Kingsmill' was very shocked that my parents had decided not to vote because they believed there was a consensus on foreign affairs. 'And we have not been in the country long enough to know anything about domestic politics and the differences between the parties. It would not be fair to the country if we voted.'

SIS colleagues placed my parents under so much pressure to vote Conservative, eventually my father asked me, 'Do you know who all your schoolfriends' daddies vote for? Do they really all vote Conservative, as "Geoffrey" says? I thought everybody voted for different parties here. I cannot believe certain people vote the same way. "Geoffrey" is very cross Mummy and Daddy are not voting Conservative.'

My response further confused him. This was because the distinguished businessman father of my closest schoolfriend voted Labour because 'The Labour Party are not as anti-Semitic as the Conservatives'; while the parents of another schoolfriend were holding election parties for Edward Heath.

It was not until the 1974 General Election that my parents voted (Conservative) for the first time.

'Geoffrey Kingsmill' was never happier than when he was holding business meetings in curry houses and kebab shops (his colleagues preferred Overtons restaurant). The hotter the curry, the better 'Kingsmill' liked it. On one occasion, my father said the curries they had eaten had been so hot, 'I thought "Geoffrey" was going to keel over. However, I was in a worse state than he was . . .'

(Several years later, their liking for curry had an impact on me when I became an undergraduate at London University. Much to my fury, I was prevented from eating in kebab shops for fear I might bump into 'Kingsmill' or my father entertaining their contacts. This placed me in some difficulty since it was not always easy to steer a student group away from one reasonably priced restaurant to another. To 'Kingsmill's' credit, he took the problem commendably seriously. Anxious to come up with a compromise, he suggested I eat in Greek restaurants with my friends, although he conceded, 'Greek kebabs are not nearly as good.' To which my father replied, 'This is because the flies are better in Arab restaurants.')

The son of a distinguished military civil servant, 'Kingsmill' was raised in India. As a result, he loved Indian and Middle Eastern food. His visits to my parents' home noticeably increased whenever they received gifts of food from friends arriving from the Middle East. This gave 'Kingsmill' the opportunity to eat his beloved *Kubba* and *Basturmah* which, in those days, were not available in London.[8]

If 'Kingsmill's' palate was exotic, his character was wholly British. For example, having been invited for lunch, my father would sometimes return home and report to my mother, 'I'm starving. "Geoffrey" produced an apple, a tomato and a bench in the underground to sit on.'[9]

The civil servant was very careful with the nation's funds, which he always referred to as 'the taxpayers' money'. In marked contrast to some of his SIS colleagues, he was scrupulous in avoiding, unless operationally necessary, eating in expensive restaurants.

My father would complain: '"Geoffrey" will never spend any money. He is mean with himself and mean with the nation's money too. I feel like a spendthrift if, overseas, I have even a finger of kebab and charge it up. He will ask where I ate it and invariably comment that I could have got it cheaper around the corner. He was usually right too. He knew all the restaurants in every town.

'The only time he was not mean, and would spend anything, was on security. This gave me, and my sources, enormous confidence. I always knew "Geoffrey" would move heaven and earth to protect us. He always recognised I was firstly a businessman, not a spy; and the men I was running were similar. "Geoffrey" made safety his personal responsibility.

'I only came to appreciate the extent of his concern when I worked with Alexis Forte [see next chapter], when I realised safety was a matter for the individual case officer. If the case officer, for whatever reason, was not safety conscious, his spies and their sources were always in jeopardy. "Geoffrey" was the best in this respect. He valued life, fretted constantly about all of us, was always taking risks he would never let me take, and would not sleep until everyone was accounted for. I trusted him implicitly and in this regard he never failed me.'

Occasionally, the men had disagreements. When this happened, arguments were always made up over food. Once, when they were particularly annoyed with each other, I took a call for my father who instructed, 'If it's "Geoffrey" tell him I am not here.'

Hearing the message, an ecstatic 'Kingsmill' responded, 'Tell your father when he comes in, I have tracked down some Qammerldine.'[10]

If food was a major bond between the two men, the friendship between their wives was an even greater one. 'Mrs Geoffrey Kingsmill' was much loved by my parents and retained their affection to the end.

NOTES

1. *Guardian*, 14 July 2001.
2. *Ibid.*
3. *Ibid.*
4. My father never mentioned David Spedding by name. I had no idea they knew each other until I was told by the Foreign Office in 1994, by which time Spedding was SIS Chief. At the time of Spedding's 'outing' my father said, 'Sometimes I wonder whether Philby is not working for us after all. The chap he has named in the Lebanon is a pip-squeak. Not significant at all. If Philby had wanted to, he could have done far greater damage.'
5. I grew up with the knowledge of the atrocities of Iraq. In December 2000, the British press carried a story – video-taping of a daughter's rape and other details – that was identical to stories my family were hearing from the late '60s onwards. As many have pointed out, methods of torture tend to repeat themselves.
6. Former SIS officer Richard Tomlinson, in his book *The Big Breach: Inside the Secret World of MI6*, published by Cutting Edge Press in 2001, says, 'Even if an agent speaks good English, it is preferable to speak to him in his mother tongue – that way his real character is more exposed.'

     I believe in my family's case, my father and 'Kingsmill' spoke in Arabic so that I would not understand what was said.
7. I think this was a mistake. I believe all SIS spies, except when they are overseas or face other dangers, could keep copies of their reports in case their relationship with SIS, especially when their case officer changes, goes wrong.
8. This could, of course, have been a sort of SIS bonding exercise my father would not have known was contrived. If it was, 'Kingsmill' deserved his CMG. However, I do not believe anyone, even for the sake of the Realm, could eat that much *Kubba* or *Basturmah* unless they really liked it.
9. Hugh L'Etang, in *Fit to Lead?* published by William Heinemann Medical Books in 1980, says: 'Gastronomy has a part to play in diplomacy and international relations. In the days when Britain was a world power, her negotiators ate a solid breakfast and thus would deliberately prolong the morning sessions to discomfort their continental opposite numbers whose levels of blood sugar were not being adequately sustained by their scanty continental breakfast.' It is possible this could have been 'Geoffrey Kingsmill's' intention.
10. Dried apricots flattened into sheaths of apricot papers, much loved in Iraq. At the time, not widely available in London.

12

WORKING WITH 'GEOFFREY KINGSMILL CMG'

In his memoirs, Albert Speer, Hitler's architect, wrote: 'Espionage is so dirty, only a gentleman can do it. This is why the British are so good at it.' This phrase could have been written for 'Geoffrey Kingsmill'.

He was deeply committed to intelligence gathering and equally committed to those he was running, who had a wonderful sense of belonging to something that was powerful and right. A natural optimist who did not have a gloomy bone in his body, 'Kingsmill' gave his spies and their sources maximum autonomy but ensured they had a sense of purpose and were not working in a vacuum.

Unlike his colleagues, 'Kingsmill' did not call himself a 'diplomat' but a 'civil servant'. The distinction was important. My father, however, perhaps because he was not born in this country, never understood the difference. He raised his children believing his SIS associates were all diplomats.

'Kingsmill' never presumed himself to be more important than non-SIS Foreign Office personnel. He thought espionage was the appetiser to the main meal – diplomacy – and, sometimes, the pudding as well, but did not make the mistake of thinking the main meal could not be satisfactorily enjoyed by itself.

He had a profound respect for the law and people's liberty. I remember one of my father's biggest operational complaints was 'Kingsmill's' refusal to bug people's telephones. In so far as other rules were concerned, 'Kingsmill' made it clear: 'SIS can bend the law. It cannot break it.'

He refused to discuss, let alone provide, 'a certain type of woman' when my father, believing it to be operationally necessary, requested it, on the basis that 'We do not do that sort of thing, Lawrence.'

As a result, my father said, 'I will never understand the British. "Geoffrey" expects a hot-blooded Middle Easterner whom we have been cultivating to get off his aeroplane and go straight to the conference table. He simply does not realise no Middle Easterner does this. They are lusty people, red-hot males chasing blondes, and cannot think straight unless they have had sex. In these circumstances, I see no reason why we should not provide such a man with professional women.

'"Geoffrey", bless him, simply does not understand this. He does not realise if you make a man happy, he is much more disposed to sign a commercial contract with one country than another.'

My father continued: 'So I tell "Geoffrey" to make arrangements for the man to arrive in time to enjoy a weekend in London at the Bunny Club, so that come the Monday morning he is refreshed and ready for business. Instead, "Geoffrey" makes him arrive on the Monday, and expects him to be immediately ready for business. It is hardly surprising the man stops off in Paris first and, by the time he gets to London, is exhausted, having had not only a million women, but signed several contracts as well.

'The Americans are much better about this sort of thing. They understand sex. I have told "Geoffrey" that unless the British are prepared to loosen up, we will lose all our commercial contracts to the French and the Americans. If a man likes pretty redheads, the British will carefully note it, their records are second to none, but will do nothing about it. The Americans, on the other hand, like the French, will not take a note of anything. They are lousy record keepers. Instead, they will go off and find ten redheads.

'In addition, the Americans use straightforward language. To them a tart is a tart is a tart. To the British, she is a "Lady of the Night" and this is how she is described in the records. I think the British pour all their sense of romance into their reports. I bet in a thousand years, SIS records will still be written in faultless grammar and matchless romantic prose. Meantime, the Americans, along with the French, will be running all our former markets.'

Whenever 'Geoffrey Kingsmill' was in the company of my father, they spoke in Arabic. 'Kingsmill' never wasted an opportunity to practise it. My father said that he spoke the language beautifully, adding, 'Grammatically, he is better than I am. His accent, however, is terrible and this upsets him since he is a perfectionist. For me, however, as a Middle Easterner, he is a joy to listen to and I hope he is never able to correct it. It is part of his charm.'

Both men believed deeply in the supremacy of British Intelligence over the Americans, and my father thought, as did his sources, they were all working for the Foreign Office. They were not aware, as we are today, the Foreign Office could be dismissive of SIS.

When my father was with his sources, he would refer to 'British Intelligence' since, in those days, this expression was more commonly used than the abbreviations SIS or MI6. The abbreviation CIA, on the other hand, was in common usage. With 'Kingsmill', my father referred to SIS or MI6; and, in appropriate context, HMG or 'The FO' (Foreign Office). In due course, the expressions 'Six' or, alternatively, 'Five' were used when referring to MI6 or MI5, or, more likely, 'The Office', 'The Firm' or 'Head Office'.[1]

At one stage, my father came home and said, 'Now they want to be known as "DI6".' ('Defence' rather than 'Military' Intelligence.) However, he never used the initials on the basis that 'It is silly. Who on earth are we trying to kid? Besides, we all keep forgetting and therefore still call it MI6.'

My father did not believe that the UK shared much information with the Americans, despite the official line, 'Because "Geoffrey" trusts no one. Good SIS diplomats do not even tell their superiors what is going on. They only tell people what they want them to know. This includes the hierarchy. Besides, "Geoffrey" thinks that the Americans talk too much.'

My father shared 'Kingsmill's' view. However, my father had an enormous admiration for certain American diplomats whom he said loved and understood the Middle East. 'They have been undermined by the CIA with their own government,' he added sadly.

One of SIS's drawbacks, and one it recognised, was that its personnel had little understanding of all-important Middle Eastern family relationships. My father was valuable because, given his background, he usually knew which half-brother was married to which cousin by which mother. However, his main purpose was to gather political intelligence that could inflict as much damage as possible on the Iraqi Ba'ath Party.

SIS also knew very little about the Soviet Union's activities in the Middle East. Again, my father's knowledge was second to none. This was of particular importance as various Palestinian groups began to make their presence felt by direct action; and the Soviets, for a time, colonised Baghdad after they had been booted out of Cairo.

My father believed SIS's job, and his role within it, was to promote British political/commercial interests in the Middle East; resist Soviet penetration; and protect Britain's oil investment, or, when this was no longer possible, ensure the safety and supply of cheap oil. He believed this could mean, if necessary, SIS could actively seek to influence the internal affairs of sovereign states, in whichever way it saw fit.[2]

To do so, SIS required a detailed understanding of Middle Eastern politics, personalities and commercial alliances. My father excelled in all of these issues, was always comfortable with his work and 'Geoffrey Kingsmill's' direction and handling.[2] At no time did my father anticipate problems with the Foreign Office or elected government. He believed these did SIS's bidding. It came as a profound surprise when he found out this was not always the case.

On one occasion in 1971, my father was incensed by the Conservative government's attitude towards the Middle East. 'They are complete imbeciles,' he said, continuing, 'Our motives are pure. We are doing what is best for this country and Iraq. The government try to clip our wings, and hand our work on a plate to American oil giants, because they distrust so-called SIS "romanticism" for the Arabs. What they actually mean is that SIS refuses to over-sentimentalise the State of Israel. So who are the real patriots? SIS or government?'

My father aged 27, at the time of his marriage, London, 1949.

My mother aged 25, at the time of her marriage, London, 1949.

ABOVE: My parents (*centre*) at the Alwiyah Club, Baghdad, New Years Eve, 1951.

BELOW: My mother (*left*) and father (*fourth from left*)
at the British embassy, Baghdad, on Coronation Day, 1953.

ABOVE: HRH the Crown Prince (fifth from right), Lady Wright, wife of the British ambassador (fourth from right) and others. Second Row: my father (behind Lady Wright); my mother (almost behind the Crown Prince). British council School Sports Day, Baghdad, 1957. A year after the photograph was taken, the Crown Prince was murdered with the Boy King and the British embassy sacked and looted.

BELOW: My parents at the Afghan emabassy with the wife of the Afghan ambassador and the wife of the Afghan charge d'affairs, Baghdad, 1961.

ABOVE: My parents at the Finnish Legation, Baghdad, 1961.

BELOW: My parents with military attaché and wife, Baghdad, 1961.

ABOVE: The blind minstrel of Ctesiphon and a
member of the First Baghdad Brownie Pack, 1962.

BELOW: The belly-dancer 'Princess Amira',
who came from Yorkshire. Baghdad, 1963.

ABOVE: My English grandmother in Babylon, 1965.

BELOW: Me, aged 25, in 1980 — the year I was approached by the intelligence services —
in the company brochure advertising its specialist parliamentary consultancy.

Me, aged 18, with my father, in 1973.

Eventually my father felt that nobody could say anything about the Zionists without being regarded as anti-Semitic. (Much to my disgust, he was a Zionist himself.) He complained bitterly that young British diplomats knew they would not be promoted unless they were pro-Israel. 'This is not right,' he said, 'Israelis talk against Israelis – all Semites, including Arabs, talk against each other. We enjoy it. It is part of our personality. So why, suddenly, does the British government make it a crime for someone to criticise Israel? It is not only demeaning but wrong. It will cost the country our Arab markets.'

Exasperated, he would continue, 'You do not think the Americans are so sentimental about Israel they are prepared to give up their markets in the Middle East for it, do you? Of course not. However, they artfully play upon British sentiment, which dates from the treatment of the Jews under Hitler, while they move in on our markets. SIS are disgusted with our politicians.'

While my father was in full flood, 'Geoffrey Kingsmill' never interrupted. Nor in my presence did he ever make a political comment about Israel. However, he rated Mossad highly and commented admiringly, 'They recruit from the prostitute to the bishop. When it comes to recruitment, the Israelis are the best.'

All my father's SIS colleagues admired Mossad's courageous priest who lost his life working for the Israelis in Beirut (later depicted, in a cameo plot, in a Hollywood movie). However, despite the admiration for Mossad, I believe the SIS personnel whom my family knew were privately pro-Palestine. For this reason, the growth of Palestinian terrorism embarrassed them. All recognised that the future of the Middle East could not be settled until there was a solution to the Palestinian problem, not least because the Palestinian diaspora was unsettling Arab countries and causing these substantial internal problems.

One of my father's SIS colleagues believed: 'The Israelis will try and prolong the Palestinian problem for as long as they are able. Without the Palestinians as a problem, Israel is of no consequence to the West.'

My father, not least because of his Kurdish mother, was more interested in the plight of the Kurds. He believed SIS were 'wedded to their belief in Palestine, whereas they had no similar feelings for an independent Kurdistan'.

He was pragmatic enough to recognise that 'giving the Kurdish people their homeland would mean disrupting relations with Iraq, Syria, Turkey and Iran. For this reason, I cannot see us ever doing so. After all, there is nothing in it for us. More importantly, the plight of the Kurds has nothing to do with Israel so the Kurds are denied the publicity that keeps the Israelis and Palestinians in the news.

'Nevertheless, looking at things realistically, it is difficult to see how, once the Palestinian problem is resolved, there can be any excuse not to make arrangements for Kurdistan. One day, the map of the Middle East will have to be redrawn. This is not only right and as it should be, but, unless the Kurds are given their own nation, Kurdish terrorism will replace Palestinian terrorism.'

I believe my father and SIS were straightforward in their dealings with their Kurdish sources, who were always politically sophisticated. However, at one time, the Kurds were given to believe that HMG favoured their sovereignty financed by the Kurdish (northern) oil-fields of Iraq. At a later stage, it was left to my father to inform his sources, that HMG had changed its mind.

This distanced HMG from betrayal, but devastated my father because his sources trusted him, not least because his mother had been a Christian Kurd from a well-known tribe. However, well used to superpower treachery, they were pragmatic and philosophical.

My father said, 'My Kurdish friends were gentlemen. Complete gentlemen. They did not hold anything against me. They knew it was not my fault. We parted as brothers. HMG reneged. It is as simple as that.'

NOTES

[1]   Writing in the *Mail on Sunday*, on 26 May 2002, and commenting on the BBC's six-part series *Spooks*, former MI5 officer David Shayler queried, 'Why do the characters insist on calling MI5 "Five", which it is never called in real life?' This could be a generational thing. Certainly, in my father's day, the expression 'Five' was in fairly common usage.

[2]   One of the issues brought to public notice by David Shayler is what has become known as the 'Gaddafi Plot', i.e. whether SIS had the right to participate in the overthrow of a government it did not like. My father believed SIS did have this right. So, I understood from him, did many of the SIS diplomats and civil servants with whom he served. This was to ensure a leadership in other countries, irrespective of its internal sins, favourable to the Crown's interests.

However, what a spy of one service might have thought appropriate, a young staff officer like Shayler, in another service, many years later, rightly did not.

Declaration of interest: I am a friend of David Shayler and his partner Annie Machon who, like Shayler, is also a former fast-stream MI5 officer.

13

SOURCES AND SCHOOLGIRLS

My father was responsible for talent-spotting, recruiting, developing and running some of SIS's most senior Arab and Kurdish sources, 1968–78. Those unable to deliver intelligence to a required standard were passed by SIS to the CIA.

His sources were not naive, and, with one exception, were not young men. They were sophisticated in the ways of dealing with the foreign intelligence services, and, if they refused to assist, did so with great dignity on the following basis: 'You, my brother, are working for your country. Let me work for my mine, and you for yours, separately. Otherwise, we can no longer be brothers and this would be a loss to both our hearts.' For the most part, they were commercial, politicised and educated.

My father always met his sources outside their own countries, or other Arab countries, where there was less chance of their meetings being noticed. Some of them were persona non grata in their own countries and were 'temporarily' living in places like Prague[1] – never in Yugoslavia since Tito was too independent and the Roman Catholic and Orthodox Churches too powerful for the Soviets to trust them.[2]

My father met those living in Eastern Europe, in northern or Western European countries since at no time would SIS permit him to travel to a Soviet Bloc country. Nor were his children allowed to travel there. As a result, I was unable to participate in a school trip to Moscow.[3] This, to my shame, I played for all it was worth, since it coincided with discussions on an increase in my pocket money. (My father was ruthless in business. However, and despite the fact he was crisply advised by my mother that 'She is playing you like a violin', he was wholly unable to be equally ruthless with his daughter.)

There were even worries about some non-Soviet Bloc countries such as Austria. Nonetheless, my father travelled frequently to Vienna because it was an ideal SIS location for precisely those reasons. Whenever necessary, SIS arranged entry visas for his sources in whichever Western country they wished to meet.

He had complete control over those he chose to recruit or not. Sometimes, SIS made suggestions. On one occasion, the daughter of one of my father's former contacts, who had married into an Arab family of particular relevance, was brought to his attention. He turned SIS down, on the basis that 'I held her in my arms when she was a tiny tot. Now she is a mother herself, you ask me to befriend her husband in order to nurture her father-in-law? No. This is not correct.'

SIS behaved impeccably and withdrew the suggestion immediately.

My father particularly respected four of his sources, one of whom he loved like a son. I met three of them, and inadvertently identified a fourth – always a danger when there are children in the house. Two had SIS code names; one an SIS alias; a fourth used his own name. The SIS diplomats and/or Whitehall civil servants they met through my father usually used an alias, i.e. some sources never knew the names of SIS staff although they always knew the identity of my father. An alias usually incorporated 'The correct first name with a false family name. There is less chance of making a mistake that way.'

Only one of my father's sources told his wife what he was doing. Another was so paranoid that his chatterbox spouse would put her foot in it, he did not even tell her the 'rented apartment' they stayed in every time they visited London was in fact their own, purchased from monies paid by SIS.

Of the sources for whom my father had no respect, one, under separate SIS patronage, was to become fabulously wealthy. His company was 'littered' with former British public servants. My father recruited his, at the time, more senior colleague when they were all living in Iraq.

Some sources, for different reasons, were less than satisfactory, not least because of laziness. Others had no political objectives and would be of assistance so long as the price was right. My father paid them in cash, although on every occasion he took receipts which he filed with SIS.

He said that under 'Geoffrey Kingsmill' and those who served with him, SIS was corruption-free. 'Kingsmill' kept very careful accounts, particularly when my father was paying sources. As a result, my father said that when he submitted his personal accounts to SIS, they read like a complete confessional – a method he employed with his commercial accounts too. He was always aware that if he did anything wrong and, for example, the Inland Revenue had occasion to query his non-SIS commercial accounts, SIS would have sacked him immediately.

'"Geoffrey" was absolutely adamant on this one,' said my father. 'Because of him, I do not think that any of SIS's businessmen-spies would ever have done anything wrong. Our good name was far too important and precious to sacrifice.'

My father was hard-nosed when it came to getting the best price out of his potential sources. At times, 'Geoffrey Kingsmill' (himself thrifty with public money) thought my father too mean, instructing him to raise the amount on offer.

The correspondence below, translated by my father from Arabic into English, illustrates how a prospective SIS source tried – and succeeded – in raising his price.

The correspondent wrote:

> I hardly saw any place except the hotel, your house, the embassy and the airport [. . .] I came on the strength of the open invitation [. . .] I was taken by complete surprise when I was faced with subjects which had never occurred to my mind, while at the same time you neither allowed me the opportunity to think nor gave me sufficient time for re-assessment in addition to all your persistence on the subject, all of which led me to withdraw in the manner already known to you after I had incurred the expense of not less than 300 pounds [. . .]

Using commercial language as cover, my father sent the following soothing reply:

> [. . .] in respect of the consignment of air conditioners for the Gulf, the Company has scolded me severely for not being receptive to our brother in a manner which should have pleased him.
>
> After due consideration and a keen desire for continued cooperation with our brother, the Company has decided to compensate him with £500 on the damages of the first consignment and is further prepared to pay him a commission of £1000 for the outstanding new consignment as soon as he confirms the order and opens the Letter of Credit in the full amount.
>
> All these payments will be made in cash on meeting me in London or any nearby town like — on the Continent.
>
> The Company will, of course, defray all travelling expenses and arrange for entry visa to the UK or anywhere he desires. To avoid the occurrence of any misunderstanding, he will be introduced to the Director responsible for exports to enable him to discuss the Agency Agreement in general and the percentage of commission for all other consignments in future [. . .]

If my father loved his SIS work, there were also huge frustrations. He was always angry at the coverage of the Middle East in the British press and failed to recruit a valuable source because of bias in the reporting of a particular issue. 'Geoffrey Kingsmill' was sympathetic but adamantly denied that anything could be done because 'We have a free press here. We do not interfere, although "Five" are sometimes able to do so if there is a serious industrial dispute.'

This dismayed my father. He said, 'The coverage, especially the ridiculing of Islam, is costing us contracts. Huge commercial contracts. If the press has no sense of fairness, do they not at least have a sense of duty towards the United Kingdom? Everything, including all the employment that goes with it, will shift to America, Germany and France unless we do something about it. How can the ambassador of an Arab country justify giving us a contract if, back home, his people know the British newspapers have been insulting their faith? I simply do not understand the point of having a free press if it is biased.'

He always complained that the press did not know how diasporas worked. 'If the British press are rude about one Middle Easterner in London,' my father would say, 'he will tell his cousin in France. His cousin in France will tell his wife's nephew in Detroit. His wife's nephew in Detroit will tell his second cousin in Bombay . . . and so it goes on.'

My father thought that the attitude of the British press was a shame because 'Fundamentally there is huge goodwill for Britain . . . And our press are squandering it, and mutual prosperity in the process. The Arabs, like the Indians, want to do business with the British. However, they can take their business anywhere in the world. We will not realise what we have lost until it is too late.'

When my father eventually drew breath, 'Kingsmill' would take the opportunity to ask for another cup of tea.

The only time I ever heard 'Kingsmill' react strongly to something my father said was when the latter made an appalling comment about the Pakistanis. 'Kingsmill' hit back very quickly, admonishing my father soundly. ('Kingsmill's' father, who served in India for many years, similarly ticked off my father for making an equally poor comment about the calibre of Indian troops during the Second World War.)

Where 'Geoffrey Kingsmill' and my father were agreed, however, was the tragedy of Britain's denial of the Commonwealth, and its Muslims in particular. 'This,' my father said, 'is hugely important to our national prosperity. And yet, all we hear about the Commonwealth is what a millstone around our neck it is because we are having to pay lots of money to poor countries. What we do not seem to realise is that many of the Commonwealth countries will one day be rich countries. If Britain, out of self-interest, cannot accept the immorality of racism, it should realise at least a brown man's money has no colour.'

NOTES

[1] Sir Richard Dearlove, SIS's present director general, served in Prague from 1973–76. It is possible, therefore, there could have been some overlap between him and my father.

[2] The Soviets encouraged many Middle Easterners who had fallen out with their governments to make their homes in, for example, Prague, which offered a comparatively free and easy-going lifestyle. Others chose Prague because it was a cheap place to live, prostitution was inexpensive and their pensions went further. However, some Middle Easterners had African blood and this posed a problem for the Soviets

because of the racism in some parts of the Soviet empire. As a result, these people were often offered residence in Moscow.

[3] I was given no guidance as to what explanation I could offer my classmates as to why I could not go to Moscow. Being left to my own devices meant, as always, lying. A spy's child is forced to embrace lying as a way of life from a young age.

14

CHILDREN AND SECURITY

I have no knowledge of SIS security precautions made for my father when he was on an overseas visit. However, I remember how angry and 'rattled' he was when 'Geoffrey Kingsmill' informed him of the maid who had been discovered in 1971 bugging the British embassy and SIS station in Beirut.[1] At the time, my father was frequently in Beirut on SIS business.

I have a detailed recollection of SIS safety measures taken to protect my father in London. Hedges at the front of our house had to be cut back so that nobody could hide in them. Every junction of the residential street in which we lived had a sign with the street name, not common in those days, so that in the case of a security alert all the police cars converging on our house would have no problem finding it.

Next to my father's bed was the 'buzzer' that connected him directly with Special Branch in Scotland Yard, while simultaneously alerting local police stations. In the event of a terrorist attack, all my father had to do was 'hit' it and there would be a major armed police presence within minutes outside our front door. In his study was the connected 'red' telephone with a private telephone number. My father was one of three in the area who had similar VIP status and level of protection. One of the others was Lord Hailsham, the former Conservative Lord Chancellor.

Our telephones did not have our ex-directory telephone number across the dial and we were given a special number that could be dialled which would result in the telephone ringing the minute the receiver was replaced. 'This way, you can pretend to have a conversation with someone if you want the person in the room to be convinced you are passing on a message,' All 'unusual' telephone calls, including wrong numbers, had to be noted.

In addition to the alarm system, decorative grills, courtesy of the taxpayer, went up on all our windows; the doors into our house had to be reinforced, the front and back door being bullet-proofed. Meantime, with all the creativity and ingenuity of SIS's superb master craftsmen, two safes were put in. One was pencil thin and used for storing documents; the other was a discreet wall safe. (The latter, many years after my father's death, took the relevant company 12 hours to dismantle.)

Everybody in the house had to lock all outside doors, even if they were merely walking to the garage at the bottom of the garden for a few minutes, if, no matter how briefly, the door used was out of eyeshot. We had to be vigilant when walking past parked cars and had to be especially careful about waiters in restaurants and bars because 'out of uniform they always look different'. We were warned we must never leave our drinks unattended and always had to drive with our car doors locked.

Sometimes, it was difficult not to become paranoid. Things that had rational explanations appeared sinister. For example, one morning my father found our milk, which was delivered to the front door, had been opened. It was only when he discovered that the sparrows, with a liking for the cream on top of the milk, were the culprits that he accepted there was nothing 'suspicious' going on. (The family's milk bottles had suddenly become of interest because we had changed from 'silver' top to full-cream 'gold' top! My father, always alert to the possibility he could be poisoned – something all Middle Eastern spies have to keep in mind – had a sense-of-humour failure when I drew him a picture of a robin wearing Arab headgear with a bubble proclaiming 'The sparrows are innocent').

My father's anxiety about security was a complete embarrassment because I could not explain to my friends why certain precautions were being taken. In addition, being brought up to believe I could be a kidnap target – always a possibility in order to put pressure on an espionage parent – meant I had to take everything my father said seriously. To prove this, I could not make jokes about another increase in pocket money.

In addition, I always had to be careful what I said. On one occasion, I mistakenly mentioned to 'Geoffrey Kingsmill' that I remembered going for a picnic in the Iraqi desert with his colleague 'Frank Tay' and his wife. Later, my father took me aside and said, 'Darling, first of all, we never went picnicking in the desert with the "Tays"; secondly, you must remember not to refer to any connection between us. It could be very dangerous if you did this in front of the wrong people.'

The worse nuisance was finding out something by accident, because this usually meant, through no fault of my own, I was penalised. For example, I identified one of my father's more sensitive sources when I took a call – as always from a coin-box – when, again as always, the source gave his alias. A few moments later I took another call from a person with an identical voice. As a result, I knew who my father's source's brother was, since, having no involvement in espionage, he gave his correct family name. This meant that I was not only able to identify the source, but explain contradictions I knew were not understood by the source's wider family, some members of which I knew well. Therefore, I was never allowed to meet my contemporaries from the family again. Nor was I able to explain why I was being kept apart.

As a result, I lost out on friendships. In addition, existing arrangements I had agreed with friends were obliterated. For example, one of my girlfriends from the Middle East had left her Marks & Spencer jumpers with me because she had disobeyed her parents' orders to cut out their 'St Michael' labels (see page 65). The compromise we had reached was that she would wear them when she was in London. In the meantime, I was allowed to wear them.

Or at least I was until our two families had to cease contact because of my father's work.

In the end, in case of 'slippage' – making an innocent comment to the 'wrong' person – and to protect the adults at risk, I was not allowed to mix with any Iraqi or Arab friends. Similar precautions were taken when I met members of my father's family. This was because they were in touch with the Middle Eastern community in Europe and America. I was told, 'A wrong word, darling, could endanger Daddy, or his friends, and, more importantly, contaminate the rest of the family, or his friends' families. You must be very careful what you do or do not say.'

I also had to be careful about who I gave our telephone number to or invited home. However, I was given no guidance as to how I might invite one child but not another. For example, I was not allowed to become friends with the daughter of an overseas businessman, because of her father's connections with the Middle East, although we had many schoolfriends in common. I think, while understandable, such measures are far too heavy a burden for a child to carry. I hope today much greater thought is given by parents involved in espionage, and their employers, so children can maintain contact with friends and members of their wider family.

Older children and young adults throw up different problems not least because the connections they make can be unpredictable. For example, my then teenage brother remarked over the bridge-table one night, 'How is it every time you come back from a business trip, Daddy, two weeks later there is a revolution somewhere?' My father was rattled but laughed the comment off as best he could. It was obvious it had unnerved him.[2]

By the time I did my 'A' levels at a London day school, my brother had left home. I was therefore on my own with two parents pretending our lives were normal, when I knew they were anything but. In 1972, two months before I took my exams, came the proof. We were hit by a massive security alert.

The problem was heralded by a series of 'odd' telephone calls at home and, finally, by the singing of an Iraqi lullaby, in the middle of the night, outside our front door. In those days, to increase terror, Iraqi execution squads moving in on London would 'warn' their target a few days before the intended attack by singing in classical Arabic outside the victim's house.

My father immediately asked for a gun. 'Geoffrey Kingsmill' refused.

Instead, before the police presence under SIS instruction swung fully into operation, 'Kingsmill' stayed with us. I was moved out of my bedroom and into my mother's. My father slept at the front of the house, and 'Geoffrey Kingsmill' at the back. To the best of my knowledge, neither had guns.

When I awoke the following morning, I found we were living with Special Branch officers inside the house and an armed, uniformed police unit outside. It was incredibly exciting, not least because the men from Special Branch were so good-looking. This added to my parents' burdens, as their hitherto demure daughter launched herself at the men. (The men behaved impeccably and, much to my chagrin, were too professional to flirt. It is always possible that the thought of my Arab father – breathing fire if any male aged 11 and over even looked at his teenaged daughter – could have been off-putting.)

My mother found the security alert particularly upsetting. She disliked the fact that she and my father had to be escorted everywhere, especially to evening engagements. (Special Branch had arrangements with all the major London theatres and other places of entertainment. Tickets were upgraded in order to accommodate the two-man Special Branch team accompanying patrons.)

The police, their guns clearly visible, were stationed for several days at the front and back doors of our house, as well as at the bottom of our garden. All of this was an unlikely sight in the London suburb in which we lived. Over 30 years later, a much-loved local friend said to me at a drinks party, 'I have always wanted to ask you this. I remember when the police were outside your door. What on earth was that all about? I have waited all these years to ask because I did not think it right to do so before. We thought perhaps your father was a drugs dealer and had been arrested. Then we saw all the guns and realised it was political.'[3]

In due course, the visibly armed police gave way to uniformed police with concealed weapons. These stood, around the clock, outside our front door.

Apart from the first night that heralded all the problems, and the eerie singing in the dark, I never felt physically under threat. I believed my father and the police were in control of the situation. However, it was a frightening reminder about what my father did for a living. It reinforced my increasing anxiety that anything I said carelessly could impact, with dangerous consequences, on him.

This, I believe, is espionage's real legacy, not least because, through fear of my father being assassinated, I lost all sense of balance. I hope far greater assistance is given to young people today when facing similar events. What made things worse was that I was given little instruction as to what to say to explain the commotion when I arrived for lessons. ('If anybody asks about the police guarding the front door, darling, just explain it is "friendly" not "sinister".') This, not least because two of my schoolfriends walked past our house on the way to school, was embarrassing.

Moreover, neither SIS nor my parents had any idea that leaving me to explain a police presence as 'friendly' rather than 'sinister' led to a host of other awkward questions. The best was posed by one of my schoolfriends, who said, 'We had the same thing when my father invented parking meters. Has your father invented another type of one?'

NOTES

[1] See *The Mitrokhin Archive*: p. 443.
[2] I have no knowledge of my father's operational life. However, because of his response to my brother's question, I believe, while not involved in 'Special Operations', my father could have been a paymaster.
[3] The local press quickly heard about what was happening. It was not allowed to report matters.

15

SIS CAREER PROSPECTS AND TRAVEL

If 'Geoffrey Kingsmill' looked after my father's safety, he also knew how to raise my father's value and give him confidence. In March 1971, he called in my father to discuss his career. He explained that, at the time, my father had the rank equivalent to first secretary (diplomatic). This is to say, in Whitehall terms, my father was a Grade 5 civil servant and therefore paid the commensurate salary (£3,292 p.a.). A plate in his 1971 diary lists the diplomatic grades that 'Kingsmill' gave him – from Grades 5 to 1 (Head of Diplomatic Department) – and the corresponding salaries, '*w.e.f.* 1 April 1971'.

'Geoffrey Kingsmill' also explained to my father that, if my father agreed, he could work for another 8 years, when he would reach the automatic retirement age of 58. My father was 'delighted' to be able to do so. He said, '"Geoffrey" was thrilled to advance my career in terms of status and salary. He never begrudged me a single penny of my pay. He was always appreciative of my work.'

Regrettably, this was to change under 'Kingsmill's' successors. Those who came after him were extremely jealous that my father was being paid by SIS, in addition to having a commercial income. This jealousy hurt my father bitterly, not least because, he said, 'Unlike "Geoffrey", my new colleagues were so lazy and knew so little. I was doing all their work, and yet they were not only being paid substantially more, but also refused to pay me properly. I have absolutely no doubt that had "Geoffrey" been made aware of what was going on, or had still been around, he would have put a stop to it.'

My father spent much of his time travelling. An indication of his expenses, paid by SIS and dated 21 January 1970, included: 'Airfare to London–Cairo return –£112 and fifteen shillings'. His UAR (United Arab Republic) visa cost £1 18 s. Subsistence at the Shepherds Hotel in Cairo came to £205. My father believed, as did his colleagues, that SIS gave the taxpayer good value for money.

An idea of my father's SIS and commercial activities is given in a letter to my mother from the Shepherds Hotel in Cairo, dated 26 January 1970:

> Today I had a meeting at the supplies department of the Ministry of Defence and business prospects could be promising. Yesterday I called at the Libyan embassy as a last effort to obtain a visa but was politely turned down by even the Consul himself. Therefore it is now absolutely definite that I shall not be visiting Tripoli and shall be flying direct from Cairo to London [. . .]

Some of the businessmen he met on his overseas trips were his sources, sometimes unwittingly so. His correspondence with those who were aware he was working for SIS was usually genuine commercial exchanges, with, additionally, other paragraphs slipped in. For example, a letter to a contact in the Middle East, dated 22 June 1971, concludes:

> You might recall our meeting in the Tivoli Gardens with a businessman called —. We have discussed this matter with The Chairman and it was considered as a most favourable prospect. Therefore, please proceed with preparatory discussions. The terms can be discussed at a later date.

In the period leading up to an overseas visit, my father was usually tense. A chain-smoker and an insomniac, he scarcely seemed to go to bed. However, on departure day, he was always calm and focused, his mind uncluttered. He only ran into difficulties once, he explained, 'And this was my own fault.'

He said, 'I was in Cairo and, returning to my hotel late at night, I felt like a stroll to unwind. It was unbearably hot, the day had been busy, and I was leaving the next morning. My brain was too active for rest and I knew I would not sleep if I went back to my room. I hated the loneliness of hotel rooms anyway, no matter how luxurious, and always missed your mother. So I ambled along, not thinking where I was going. Eventually, I came to an underpass. Absent-mindedly, I assumed it was for pedestrians to cross from one side of the road to another. I entered it.

'The minute I did so, all hell seemed to break loose, with Egyptian soldiers running around in all directions. I had foolishly walked into a proscribed area. They treated me with absolute courtesy – the Egyptians are the politest people in the world – but arrested me and took me to their superior officer. He was equally polite, he called me *Bey* [a term of deference, meaning, roughly, 'my lord'] throughout, but was a thorough, perceptive and sophisticated examiner. I was with him for hours even though I told him I had a plane to catch in only a few hours' time.

'Eventually, the mess was sorted out, the error understood, and profuse apologies accepted. In addition, I was driven back to my hotel in a staff car, where they checked my passport (some of the difficulty had been in accepting I was a British citizen. I do not look like an Englishman. I look like an Arab and, with the scar on my face from the "Baghdad boil" [a distinctive facial disfigurement, previously common in Iraq], an Iraqi one at that). It helped that I was able to say I had had meetings at their Ministry most of the week and had the appropriate visiting cards on me.

'Afterwards, back in the safety of my hotel room, I kicked myself. Literally kicked myself. And thanked the Good Lord for protecting me. Sometimes things go wrong because of bad luck. You cannot complain about bad luck because this is what it is. A bad break. However, I had not had a bad break. I had been very, very careless.

'I never made this mistake again. I also knew how lucky I had been for it to have happened in Egypt. Anywhere else in the Middle East and they would have asked questions last, and tortured me, even for a simple, genuine error, first. Then, look what a treasure trove they would have stumbled upon!'

At a later date, my father said, 'The very idea of torture always frightened me. I am not a brave man and always knew that I would not be able to resist torture. SIS were very kind about this and offered me a cyanide pill (which could be fitted into a back tooth) for whenever I travelled ("in case you get into difficulty"). I declined. I thought that it was bad luck. I pretend I am not superstitious but I am. Also, I was worried in case I crunched my tooth by accident.'

Back in the Shepherds Hotel in Cairo, my father was so shaken he could not even pack his suitcase properly. (My mother always packed this for him, and hid little treats she would never let him eat in London because he was getting so tubby. If he was going to cold countries she would pack a big bar of chocolate; if he was going to hot countries she would pack wine gums, sherbets and hum-bugs which didn't melt.)

'So I just threw everything in my suitcase,' explained my father, 'sat on it, which was the only way to close it – I do not pack as well as your mother – and ate all my sweets. Sweat poured down my face. I left for the airport a few hours later. Except when we flew out of Iraq for the last time, I do not think I have ever been so grateful to get on an aeroplane to London in my life.'

He visited Abu Dhabi, Athens, Beirut, Brussels, Cairo, Copenhagen, Helsinki, Madrid, Oslo, Paris, Rome, Stockholm, Tripoli and Vienna, sometimes regularly, on behalf of SIS. Wherever he went, he sent me a postcard.

(This simple act came back to haunt him because, as a young adult, I tracked them. As a result, some years after his retirement, many of the postcards he sent me as a schoolgirl were confiscated, as SIS were concerned about the locations and dates they revealed. My father was particularly upset and made clear he 'would not have sent them to her if I had been told I could not'. At SIS's request, the cards were later destroyed. However, because of my untidiness, I was unable to find all of them. As a result, I still have many of them. Also destroyed were the notebooks I kept as a teenager. These included character sketches of my father's then colleagues and their wives. Although amused by their contents, my father agreed with SIS that I could not be allowed to keep them and they were all destroyed.)

Wherever my father travelled, SIS put him up at the best hotels. In Beirut, he held his meetings at the beautiful St George's Hotel before these were switched to an SIS-owned property in Lebanon.[1] In Vienna he would stay at either the Ana Grand or the Hotel Bristol. In Holland, the Hotel Amstel (often, however, he went to Holland on no more than day-trips). In Sweden he would stay at the Anglais. In Paris, he checked into the obviously grand hotels, or the equally grand but more discreet, such as the Hotel de la Tremoille.

His visits, at his own request, never lasted longer than a week. The one exception was a tour of three weeks. 'When I came back from that long trip, I was dead, absolutely dead,' he said, continuing, 'After that I said to "Geoffrey" I could never go on such a long visit again. It was not the work and danger – I thrived on that – but the loneliness. I admire men who can stand it. I cannot. Loneliness is exhausting. I do not mind meeting after meeting; risk after risk; danger after danger. I just could not bear spending another three weeks in hotel rooms without your mother.

'I could not take her with me, although she would have accompanied me like a shot if I had allowed her. I had endangered her life when we were in Baghdad, I could never let this happen again. Nevertheless, I hated being separated from her. I suppose I was not a very manly spy.

'I apologised to "Geoffrey". He was sweet about it. After this he ensured that I never went on long overseas trips again. Only short ones. Those I loved. Danger, in bursts, does not eat at you, not least because you have no time to be lonely.

'Working with "Geoffrey" was a treat, a privilege. He did everything he said he would do and ran a very well-managed office. I never found working with anyone else the same. Regrettably, I did not know then, he was the exception, not the rule.

'He was even responsive about little things which were big things to me. I liked his temperament. He was the complete opposite to me. Where I was volatile, he, like your mother, had a calm personality. I have always admired the English temperament.'

The appreciation was obviously mutual. One of my father's overseas trips to an Arab country was so successful, a thrilled 'Kingsmill', bubbling over with enthusiasm, left a dated hand-written note beginning 'Welcome back and well done!' To the best of my knowledge, it was the only time 'Kingsmill' left any trace of himself, a mark of how important had been the success.

My father said 'Kingsmill' always supported him, even against his own staff colleagues. 'On one occasion it was necessary for me to snub a young man at the embassy in Beirut because he would not heed what I was saying. I dealt with him severely.' On his return to London, 'Kingsmill' backed my father to the hilt.

The 'young man' later became SIS Chief Sir David Spedding.[2]

NOTES

1   So far as I am aware, SIS's UK and overseas property portfolio has never been consolidated. For example, my father was involved in the purchase of an SIS London property in November 1975. This was in the Sloane Square area and cost £19,250 (address withheld). Under a later case officer, he queried the sale of a 'safe flat' because he did not think the transaction sum quoted was appropriate. It had been turned around within a six-month period. He was disappointed by SIS's response and refused to withdraw his report. He felt there was a possibility for corruption if the sale of London properties was not handled 'more professionally'.

2   Sir David was Chief from 1994 to 1999.

16

AN SIS SPY IN LONDON

My father was a regular visitor at various Arab embassies, consulates, military missions and airline offices in London. Many of the Arab embassies were located in Queensgate, South Kensington. In those days, it was the custom for all Arabs visiting London to pop into their embassies to pay their respects to their ambassadors. As a result, the atmosphere all along the road, let alone in the various embassies where there was little, if no, security, since it was not necessary, was more like an Arab coffee shop.

As an Arab himself, my father was able to mix freely and pick off those he was interested in. These people, in all innocence, thought they had bumped into him by accident. He was always alerted to their intended visits to London because of their visa applications; and by their actual presence in London by 'friends' at Heathrow airport when they landed.

He joined the Directors, Hurlingham, Playboy, Saddle Room, RAC and Roehampton clubs, as well as CAABU (Committee for Anglo–Arab Understanding). Part of the annual subscriptions for these were paid by SIS, in proportion to the amount they were used for SIS rather than bona fide commercial and/or personal use. In the case of the Playboy Club, the whole amount, including all expenses within it, were paid by SIS, since, my father said, 'I have no interest in the Playboy Club. I entertain, or spend many evenings circulating there, solely because of SIS.'

The venues were carefully selected because, as my father explained to 'Geoffrey Kingsmill', 'Most Iraqis, when they are not at the Bunny Club, are at the Hilton next door which is why they like staying there. Quieter Iraqis stay at the Dorchester or Claridges All of them, at some stage or other, go gambling. The Clermont, White Elephant or the 21 Club are favourites for many; Crockfords for the serious gamblers who want no other distractions.'

SIS encouraged my father to frequent some of the London casinos and paid for all his food and alcohol, as well as the hospitality he offered his guests. However, it did not pay gambling money. My father, who was not a gambler, resented this because he had no option but to use his own.

'As a result, I did not go to casinos as often as SIS would have liked. My colleagues accepted why I did not, as much as I understood their reasons for wanting me to. It was a disappointment on both sides. SIS knew the majority of important Middle Easterners, including the women, gambled. Many years later, SIS lifted financial controls. I could have had access to all the gambling money I needed, even though, by then, the casinos in London had closed. However, I never availed myself of this because I did not like the new SIS breed that took over. This was long after "Geoffrey Kingsmill" had been posted overseas again.'

Operating at the peak of his powers, with enormous social confidence, my father had access to a substantial SIS expense account and entertained frequently at the following restaurants: Cunningham Oyster Bar, Overtons, Poissonerie (affectionately nicknamed 'The Poison-rie'), Simpsons on The Strand, Directors' Club Dining Room, the White House and the Playboy Club. He also offered hospitality at the following hotels: Browns, Goring, Grosvenor House, Hilton, St Ermins, Regents Palace, the Ritz and the Royal Lancaster. Meetings took place in railway hotels such as the Charing Cross or the Great Western in Paddington.

In the evening, if my father and his source were accompanied by their wives, the White Elephant Club on the river (sister to the White Elephant gambling club) was a preferred private nightclub. If their wives were not with them, the men went to Les Ambassadeurs. During the day, said my father, 'We arranged to meet up with our wives at the Lansdowne Club. This was one of the most useful places in central London because there was no possibility of bumping into other Arabs. If my contact had children with him, English SIS friends would invite them to Queens, so the young people could play tennis. I did not go with them because in those days there were very few Arabs at Queens and therefore we would have been too obvious.'

He took less sophisticated sources, sometimes with their wives, to cocktail bars and nightclubs. These included The Beach-Comber, Talk of the Town and Raymond's Revue Bar. Some sources, particularly those with well-educated wives, declined nightclubbing in favour of more traditional entertainment. Therefore, they went to the Royal Opera House or Royal Albert Hall instead. Beforehand, they were invited to dinner in one of the private clubs. The Travellers was always a favourite.

Modest venues were chosen for daytime meetings. Dino's, in South Kensington, was popular because it was conveniently sited . . . until I started going there with my student friends. 'Geoffrey Kingsmill' favoured Mohi Mahal in Glendower Place. 'Kingsmill' usually entertained, however, at the RAF Club, where he always stayed if he had to remain in Whitehall during the week.

One of my father's sources always craved salt beef. As a result my father took him to the Jewish restaurant Blooms, where they were received 'with tip-top kindness and discretion. If it had become known my source had eaten there, it would have been immediate proof we were working for Mossad. My source, who was very bold, could not give a damn. He liked his salt beef, and Blooms' salt beef was, he said, "The best salt beef in the world, including the Middle East." He would continue, "In addition, I am served by —, who speaks my language better than I do. If the whole lot of them are working for Mossad, good luck to them. I have no quarrel with Israel. My quarrel is with my own country.'"

My father had to be very careful where he entertained prospective sources because anything could, inadvertently, make them suspicious. On one occasion, he and 'Kingsmill' were having a sensitive discussion with a valuable contact in a modest restaurant. The waiter seemed cheeky and full of himself. This made them all nervous. As the waiter removed the floral decoration in the centre of the table, he said, 'Sorry to bother you, gentlemen. Don't mind me as I remove the bug.'

My father said, 'I presume he, and doubtless other waiters, have made the joke many times before and since. However, he could not have said it at a worse time. The contact was already jumpy. The joke made him more so. As did the fact the waiter constantly made eyes at him. I paid the bill and we left as soon as we could. Regrettably, the contact refused to meet us again. Afterwards, I insisted we eat in places where the waiters did their job correctly – this is one of the advantages of the private clubs or traditional, albeit expensive, restaurants in some London hotels. "Geoffrey" accepted without demur. He was as cross as I was.'

Some London restaurants were 'off limits'. For example, the Baghdad House was rumoured to be a hotbed of Iraqi spies. It was eventually closed down. The Omar Khayyam nightclub also had problems. In an undated letter to his brother-in-law in the Gulf, my father wrote:

> You may remember — from Baghdad who came to England about 15 years ago. He owned the 'Omar Khayyam' nightclub in London. He was fabulously rich, driving in a Rolls Royce. Unfortunately, he died mysteriously some three weeks ago when he was returning home in the early hours of the morning from his nightclub.

The event sent a frisson of terror throughout the growing Iraqi community in London.

Most of my father's sources, particularly if they stayed in London for longer than a month, moved into serviced apartments. These were in, for example, Chelsea Cloisters or Nell Gwynn House. (One of my father's case officers also lived in the latter. The apartment was owned by his wife, an SIS secretary.) Those coming for medical treatment rented similar apartments in blocks close to Harley Street.

Some medical doctors, and some hospital consultants, were participants in some SIS activities. The prestige of British medicine was an essential SIS component, maintaining London as a key destination. Many countries got wise to this, and those with the resources soon established superior hospitals locally, inviting Western surgeons to travel to them.

It is impossible to overestimate the importance of some of London's centres of medical excellence, such as the Great Ormond Street Hospital for Sick Children. This did more for Britain's prestige, as well as spreading goodwill for the country throughout the world, than can be imagined. SIS piggy-backed on this prestige.

If they preferred, my father's sources stayed in hotels rather than serviced apartments. The Goring, located in Victoria, was a favourite. Others were more comfortable at Claridges. Sources whose hospitality was organised and paid for, by SIS, were put up at the Green Park Hotel, Half Moon Street. Dinner was usually at the Grange. If it was too dangerous to run the risk of being seen in Central London, and there was insufficient time to drive out of town, sources were entertained in the suburbs. Fisherman's Wharf in Wimbledon was a favourite; as was The Mitre near Hampton Court.

Outside of London, my parents entertained certain sources and their wives at the Bridge House Motel in Reigate or, depending on their seniority, the Compleat Angler in Marlow, and the Randolph in Oxford. They would all stay the night and, sometimes, the weekend. This would assist bonding and/or impress the source by the amount of money my father apparently had at his disposal.

They met at venues where, in those days, there was less chance of bumping into the source's fellow countrymen. 'On one occasion,' my father said, 'your mother and I, with our guest, came face to face with someone we knew from Baghdad. Luckily, the woman was not with her husband, but somebody else's. For this reason, we knew we were safe. This is to say, she would never mention bumping into us, let alone our guest, since this would invite inquiry as to why she had been there herself and with whom.'

There were entire areas and towns where my parents could not be seen with their sources. Brighton, for example, because of the large community from the Middle East that visited or lived there, always had to be avoided. This was forcefully brought home when, one weekend, I strolled along its seafront with my parents. Slightly ahead, I was stopped by a young person who asked me to take a photograph of him and his family. Thinking nothing of it, I was happy to do so. When I turned around, my parents had disappeared. In all innocence and by complete coincidence, I had been requested by the relative of one of my father's sources, to photograph the source's family. My father was later to remark, 'In espionage you can plan for everything except chance. "Chance" is the biggest killer of all.'

Meantime, a member of the family noticed I was wearing a particular type of gold bracelet, peculiar to Iraq. This invited immediate and friendly comment, which I warded off as politely but non-committally as possible. That is to say, I lied, by implication denying any connection with Iraq. I told them that I had been given the bracelet by my (English) schoolfriend's father who worked as a contractor in the Middle East, thus switching the conversation to my fictitious birthday. I always found this upsetting. No matter how many times I did it, I never got used to hiding my background and identity. Over time, I became more adept at handling myself. Nevertheless, I lived in constant terror that, however much I tried to avoid problems, I would still end up being 'ambushed' by my father's separate worlds.

I was.

One night, aged 17, I had dinner at a private club with someone who represented my 'English' life. Coincidentally, it turned out we knew some of the people at the next table. The group, however, also comprised a teenager with a Western mother and an Arab father, whose friendship I was obliged to snub because of the connection between those our fathers knew. The young person concerned was not aware of the sensitivity of our relationship.

Nothing prepares you for your sense of shame at being cold to someone who is nice and innocent of motive, nor for the awkwardness when this is noticed by others. You cannot explain yourself. There is also a sense of loss – only four years earlier, I had had as many mixed-race Western-Arab friends as English ones, although the two worlds were still kept separate. I missed one half of my life desperately because it had been severed.

My father met his SIS colleagues in cars, tube and railway platforms. On other occasions, dental appointments were co-ordinated so my mother could pass papers to 'Geoffrey Kingsmill' as he came out of his appointment and she went into hers. (This, presumably, was the reason we had been introduced to our dentist by my father's first London case officer, Norman Darbyshire. I have always assumed that the dentist, long retired, and one of the nicest men one could hope to meet, was 'active'.)

He met other SIS colleagues in offices and private apartments in London, mostly in Victoria, in particular Whitehall Court, Barclay Mews and Artillery Mansions; as well as at addresses at Claridges and Prince of Wales Mansions in Battersea.

In due course, permission was given for the purchase of a 'safe' apartment for my father's use. Comments in my father's diary read as follows: '"Geoffrey" phoned urging me to find a flat.' The following week he notes: 'Discussed finances of purchase of No — Sloane Street with "Geoffrey".' Finally, he confides: 'Flat now in operation.'

My father was in regular contact with the Army & Navy store. (SIS used it to build/develop things, including, for example, a cabinet and a camera.) Scribbled reminders in his diary include: '"Geoffrey" rang 11.30 a.m. Army & Navy store delivering cabinet'; and '"Geoffrey" phoned Army & Navy store about the key.' In addition, my father frequently collected 'Kingsmill' from outside the shop, 'So we can have a chat on the way home from the office.'

My father attended debates at Westminster when these were considered to be 'useful and informative'; and, for a ten-week period, had a portable telephone at home (long before the communications revolution) because 'it was considered necessary'.

Over ten years, his SIS colleagues were noted in his diaries only by their first names. Regulars included, 'Alan', 'Clem', 'Geoffrey', 'Peter'. Personal dates were recorded, for example, when they were on holiday. Less regular SIS colleagues figuring in the diaries included 'Jack' – e.g. 'See "Geoffrey" at the Grosvenor Hotel, followed by meeting with "Jack" at the Ritz'; 'Terry and Margarita', a married couple; 'Michael', 'Tim', 'Oliver' and 'Stephen'. Uniquely, in the case of 'Stephen' my father noted his surname.

The SIS secretaries included 'Susan', 'Yvonne', 'Jill', 'Liz', 'Penny' (who lived near my parents), 'Heather', 'Sheena' and 'Sheila'. 'Sheila', at a later stage, was to act out the role of my father's 'mistress' at an SIS 'love-nest'.

My father was uncomfortable with this. 'I am not an actor,' he said, 'I am a happily married, middle-aged man, with a daughter not much younger than this girl. It is not nice for her, nor for me.' (This is one reason why the 'James Bond' image of SIS has always struck a false note. While, no doubt, many middle-aged men would have jumped at the opportunity of kissing young girls while being paid for it, as many again were appalled by it.)

My father strongly believed that SIS should not 'encourage these acting games. To be an effective spy, the best thing to do is to be yourself as much as possible.'

The SIS secretaries were trusted implicitly by their bosses. Many of them were very pretty. My father's diary shows he met them frequently, including such entries as: 'Grosvenor Hotel: Penny'. This was in order to pass on letters and reports; or, more usually, to collect travel money and the appropriate details. He always organised his own airline tickets and charged them up later.

I could always tell if sources were ringing in because they only used call-boxes. I could hear the 'pips' as they put their money in. No matter how small the amount, SIS always refunded it. The sources never spoke for more than a few seconds because of the danger of crossed lines. Their calls were to confirm and arrange times of next meetings and little else.

Some sources were too frightened to even use call-boxes, but would press the doorbell late at night. This was one reason why spies like my father never moved house. For some, the spy's home address was their only constant. (This, as my father later discovered, can be a problem for retired spies, as well as after their deaths, for their widows and family. Some sources, unable to communicate or leave their countries for several years, head immediately for the spy who ran them when they eventually reach London. I can still remember a man's desolation when he was informed that my father was dead. SIS's handling of the matter remains one of my most serious operational complaints.)

Cock-ups, of course, are inevitable and often humorous. On one occasion, my father put his briefcase, containing important SIS papers and sensitive documents, in the boot of his car. Prior to his meeting, he had arranged to take it into his garage to check out a rattle in the engine. Thinking nothing of it, he allowed it to be hoisted, so the mechanics could check underneath.

However, before it could be lowered to the ground again, there was a power-cut. He was stuck without a car and, more importantly, without his papers. In addition, because of their sensitivity, he could not leave his car unattended to go to his meeting. (SIS are anxious about garages at the best of times, in case a bug is placed in a car when it is being serviced. It is even more concerned during national crises.) My father could not insult the garage owner – 'He was a fellow mason and as honourable as the day is long' – nor could he arrive at his meeting late, as '"Geoffrey Kingsmill" was always severe about time-keeping. He was always punctual. All good spies are.'

Luckily, just as he was beginning to give up, the power came back on.

Other mistakes were just as infuriating. My father said, 'On one occasion I had an important diplomatic contact. SIS were very pleased at the way things had developed, not least because we had been angling for a particular contract for Britain for quite some time. At long last, it was in the bag. The contact was all ready to sign on behalf of his government. All the arrangements were made and the British manufacturer was absolutely cock-a-hoop. With such an order, many jobs go to our workforces.

'Unfortunately, what SIS did not know was that MI5 had been watching our man on suspicion of espionage. On the very day that I, accompanied by a senior official from our Ministry of Defence, was to take the man down to sign on the dotted line, he was exposed in the newspapers and given 24 hours to leave the country. It was maddening. Absolutely maddening. Needless to say, Britain lost the contract. I had to telephone the manufacturer to apologise for the fact the man had been busted by "the other lot", who had also managed to get his face plastered all over the press.

'The manufacturer was very good about it, but it was a disappointment. I learned later that because we did not get the contract, many men had to be laid off. It was so sad. And unnecessary. It was plain incompetence one side did not know what the other was doing.'

Sometimes the incompetence almost drove him mad. For example, he instructed SIS to warn Heathrow Immigration not to constantly send Arabs back to their country of origin if their documentation did not always check out, especially if the birth dates they gave did not conform to those they had given on previous visits to Britain. My father said, 'There are three reasons why dates of birth seldom check out. Firstly, many Arabs do not know what year they were born, and do not care either. Therefore, when they get their passports renewed, they just make up a date.

'Secondly, and more importantly, many Arab men bring their age down if they have older unmarried sisters because this makes their sisters younger so they can remain in the matrimonial market. It seldom works, but, because in the Middle

East it is so important for a woman to have a husband, you cannot blame them for trying. There is a certain amount of self-interest in this too. This is to say, a brother always remains unmarried himself if he has an unmarried sister, so she always has a man to protect her – i.e. his own personal life is blocked until he has settled his sister's future.

'Finally, I have to accept, many Middle Easterners bring their ages down for reasons of vanity. Including, incidentally, various members of my own family.'

My father found all this amusing until one day he went to Heathrow to meet an Arab contact. SIS had gone to quite considerable trouble to bring the man out of his country, using some imaginative paperwork to convince the man's own authorities why he had to fly to Britain.

My father said, 'I waited and I waited. I could see on the board the plane had arrived hours ago and my visitor should have cleared customs. Eventually, I started to panic. I telephoned "The Office" and they started to panic too. They said they would contact a "friend" at Heathrow to find out what, if anything, had gone wrong. The visitor could, for example, have run into difficulties at his own end and not been on the aeroplane. This is to say, the ruse had failed.

'Eventually, we found my contact just as immigration were about to put him on the first aeroplane back to where he had come from. The visitor was steaming. Absolutely steaming. And all because of those ruddy birth dates not checking out. Immigration were a law unto themselves. Despite all the instructions they were given, despite the fact they knew he was our man and we were expecting him, they *still* decided to send him back. It was only by luck we managed to nab him before they succeeded.'

17

SIS COMMERCIAL AND GOVERNMENT CONTRACTS

My father thought it was the duty of all loyal businessmen to do their best for British exports. He also believed, 'Not all businessmen are as fortunate as I am to be offered the privilege of serving my country in the way I do. I have never met a businessman yet, particularly if he is a freemason, whatever the colour of his skin or Commonwealth country he comes from, who would not jump at the opportunity of serving the Crown in any way he could.'

However, as a businessman, my father thought that the country's export drive was being frustrated by civil servants in the relevant departments of state. Used to working with SIS, who were on duty around the clock, my father was unprepared for what he considered the laziness of other British civil servants.

He said that this was not a problem for big companies, the giants of British industry, but it was a huge problem for small businessmen like himself. He complained that it was as if only one section of the business community, the giants, were important or allowed to prosper, despite the fact that sometimes small companies managed to hook enormous contracts which should have gone to Britain but in the end did not, 'because we could not be put through to the right civil servant in the right department to find the right supplier.'

My father continued, 'The only suppliers our civil servants were aware of were the giants who usually had a waiting-list of months on end. However, because they did not want the tender to go to one of their local competitors, and had no knowledge anyway of smaller suppliers, they deliberately frustrated the deal instead of behaving like patriots and passing the enquiry on to another British company.

'Meantime, our civil servants had no sense of commercial urgency. They simply did not seem to know or care that when I contacted similar departments of state on the Continent, I was put through immediately to the correct person, who knew all the correct suppliers, and who, moreover, was so keen to promote his nation, he also suggested other lines of exports which his country could also supply. And all this in good English too!'

The exception to the rule was the Ministry of Defence (MOD). My father found it a relief to deal with it since it was staffed by senior military civil servants, with the rank of full colonel – 'which, by this time, was my own rank' – who were used to getting things done. In addition, they were an asset socially, which was vital for exports.

'These boys are used to dealing with foreigners,' said my father approvingly. 'They know how to circulate in any environment – they are more flexible in this regard than British diplomats. Defence personnel are like businessmen. Even if they know nobody in the room to begin with, by the end of the evening they will know everybody, even the most insignificant. They know how to flit from one group to another. They are also socially confident with women. For example, a diplomat will not be respectful of a man's mistress. A soldier will. He is not judgemental, and does not care whom she is sleeping with.

'British officers are snooty but not racist. Which is to say, they are completely at ease with a brown-skinned nabob, but uncomfortable with a white-skinned Communist. Again, they differ from diplomats in this regard.'

My father also praised MOD personnel for their awareness of cultural nuance. (For example, not serving ham sandwiches to Muslim visitors, as happened at one of the departments of state he took important Muslim guests to.) They also understood entertainment and that, 'Sometimes a man likes to have fun. They like fun too, and, unlike representatives from the Foreign Office, join in.'

My father made clear that military civil servants were always careful not to embarrass his guests. For example, they were quick movers and were never photographed with them in case it compromised anybody. They were invariably wary of waiters and photographers. (Unless, as one of my father's visitors good-humouredly pointed out, the photographers were working for HMG anyway, in which case the MOD staff went out of their way to get in the photographs so that they could compromise people!)

My father praised the MOD because its representatives were commercial, knew how to read tender documents and, as importantly, could work out logistics and costs immediately. He was so impressed by one of the MOD colonels SIS introduced him to that he suggested that the colonel send out 'field officers' to all the other departments of state. The colonel jokingly threw his hands in the air and said, 'No, no! There would be a mutiny. All my good men would resign. They would far rather a march through the jungle than into the Board of Trade.'

My father recalled, 'He was a very funny man, a real soldier, and I loved him.'

Another MOD colonel for whom my father had an enormous respect, 'although he had a much more severe character, was Colonel ——. He had a Jewish surname, but I do not know whether he was Jewish or not. My Muslim visitors thought he was and trusted him implicitly because of this.'

My father continued, 'The colonel was a personal friend of —. The latter trusted the colonel so much that on a private visit to the UK to attend to his wife's medical condition, he stayed with the colonel. He did not trust his life or personal safety anywhere else.

'My own contacts liked doing business with men like this colonel because they used to say, "The Jews have not got where they have in business by cheating people. They have got where they are by giving people a fair deal." The colonel was very understated. He had the best manners in the whole of Whitehall. Manners matter to Muslim visitors.'

My father also praised the military academies Mons and Sandhurst, on the basis that 'these train officers from all over the world. This is a wonderful investment for Britain's future because genuine friendships are made.' He thought it 'a very bad move' when Mons,[1] which offered a six-month training course for officers, was closed down: 'men from overseas do not always have the time to study at Sandhurst for a couple of years'.

He added, 'The best thing about dealing with military civil servants is they use straight English. If my contact is buying, they are selling. They know exactly where to go for the correct suppliers. These they rotate so that everybody gets a fair crack and takes their turn. If the contract is a large one, and for Britain to get the order, they have to get all the suppliers on side, they round them all up, get their workforces working around the clock – they have no union problems because they know how to treat men, and solve all problems on the football field – and deliver on time and within budget.'

My father was, to use a polite term, a military supplier working as an SIS intermediary or middleman between the manufacturer and the client overseas government. For example, in 1969 a British company, with my father's and SIS assistance, was trying to sell its photo reconnaissance systems to an overseas air force flying Soviet MIG21s. (Unbeknown to the Soviets, UK manufacturers were adapting equipment to fit Soviet aircraft supplied to Middle Eastern and African countries.)

In a letter dated 14 November 1969, my father wrote to the British manufacturer:

> It was finally agreed by our mutual friends and myself that the best way
> of proceeding further at this stage is to request you to kindly send HM
> Air Attaché, at the British embassy, a copy of your proposed offer [. . .]

Readers will note my father's use of the phrase, 'Our mutual friends'. This is a long-standing agreed form of words confirming SIS involvement.

The British company proceeded along the lines my father advised. Acknowledging my father's help, a senior executive responded:

> Thank you for your letter regarding your work on our behalf with the —

Air Force. I have very carefully noted the instructions contained in your letter [. . .] Naturally, I am very pleased to note that things are moving along, and I would like to say how pleased we are that you have been able to contribute considerably to this affair.

Attached to the correspondence was my father's detailed, five-point advice note, part of which can only be described as a euphemism for bribery:

If Colonel — is successful in being nominated to visit the UK to discuss the tender, it will be possible to make financial arrangements with him which should increase the chances of the tender being accepted. However, it is essential that there is no suggestion at any time of the existence of middlemen working in favour of the firm or that commissions may be payable to third parties.

The British manufacturer followed my father's advice to the letter. In due course, my father wrote:

[. . .] you would now do well to send your formal offer to the Air Colonel at his Ministry of Defence. You are requested to let me have a copy of your letter to enable me to follow up the matter further. At the same time, I would appreciate it if you would please let me have your confirmation that your price will include a margin of 10 per cent for me so that I may commit myself accordingly [. . .]

A senior executive from the company responded:

[. . .] I should like to confirm that I have included not only your commission of 10 per cent but also a small margin for bargaining since this is likely to be a contingency which we will have to face [. . .]

An idea of other commissions payable in 1969 is given in a letter to my father from a British construction company involved in a defence project in an African country. It offered approved middlemen like my father rates of 5 per cent commission on projects up to the value of one million pounds; 3 per cent between one and five million pounds; and 2 per cent on all projects above five million.

According to my father's commercial records, it appears that in some instances the MOD, by using different SIS businessmen, knowingly supplied two sides of various protagonists. For example, my father quoted for 'Complete mobile hospitals, collapsible for packing but inflatable for erection, ready to be dropped by parachute in the rear lines of battle and supplied complete with a standard box of all surgical and medical equipment' to one African country, when another SIS businessman was supplying the other side.

My father also sold the country concerned army blankets, overcoats, berets, belts, boots and socks when the same businessman, quoted above, was similarly selling identical goods to the opponents.

SIS was also keen my father quote for small amounts of used military equipment that the MOD was trying to off-load. This always infuriated him because 'My contacts want new weapons, not cast-offs in stupid numbers. The British simply do not realise if they keep treating people like donkeys, they will purchase elsewhere. Moreover, they diminish my status with my contacts who think I am off-loading junk which, regrettably, I am. Quite sensibly, they are not stupid enough to buy it.'

Nevertheless, he wrote to his contacts offering to supply:

> Ex-British Army Weapons and Spares including 303 Rifles, 303 Bren guns, 30 Brownings, 3.5 Rocket Launchers, 2" and 3" mortars, 25 pdr Guns and many other American and Continental Weapons and equipment which include optical and REME Stores plus supply of ammunition for all these weapons and other types.

My father's commercial files also detail the dealings he had with Western chemical companies, most of whom, by the late 1970s, were represented in the Middle East, especially Iraq. He was also in business for a while with his former case officer, SIS diplomat Norman Darbyshire.

Norman Darbyshire, after he retired from SIS, joined Euro-Gulf Developments, based in Buckingham Gate, London. In July 1976, he wrote to my father about military spare parts, saying:

> [. . .] From time to time, governments like Iraq, who already have equipment from the UK or Europe, find it politically difficult to obtain the spares which they need. This is where we can help.
>
> Arnold is a director of a highly reputable arms company and we can always cover the spare parts market without difficulty. Equally, if the Iraqis wish to dispose of any of their spare and unwanted armaments or ammunition in the international market, we can find buyers. I believe that your idea of re-enforced plastic water tanks for use by the Iraqi military could be a good one [. . .]

On another occasion, my father wrote to his contacts in the Middle East about machine-gun equipped vehicles:

> [. . .] I lost no time in surveying the possibilities through my Associates, Euro-Gulf Development Ltd. The actual type M113 was easily identified and is now superseded by a later model Type M113a delivery of which is almost impossible because of the demand in other markets. However, we

may be able to meet your requirements for identical or similar vehicles from Italy or even from British Leyland in England [. . .] You overlooked to mention whether these vehicles are to be equipped with or without machine-gun or a communication system etc. because these are the questions we are being asked [. . .]'

In May 1977, Darbyshire wrote to confirm

> [. . .] We have immediately available 80 Saladin Armoured Cars which have been in use by the Federal German Border Police. In fact, very little use has been made of them and they are virtually in brand new condition. For example, one of them has only 400 miles on the clock [. . .]
>
> The beauty of this proposition is that we can obtain them very cheaply, and that they carry with them two years spares according to the manufacturer's list of spares to our own Ministry of Defence.
>
> The F.O.B. price from a UK port would be £97,750 per vehicle, including the two years' spares. I also confirm that in this price there is 15% for your end [. . .]

My father also hosted overseas military delegations. Teams fielded by their governments usually included the financial controller, engineering corps commander, quartermaster general and the ammunition factory commander. If inducements were being offered, there was usually a pecking order . . .

One delegation arrived in London on the same day that there was a coup in its home country. Its members ended up asking for political asylum. This was granted immediately. Nevertheless, and ever the pragmatists, the following year MOD/SIS tried to resurrect the contracts.

On the suggestion of the MOD, one of the British construction companies involved wrote to my father:

> [. . .] you no doubt appreciate that so much has happened since the visit of the last delegation under the Brigadier, that due to their Revolution last year many of their documents were lost. I understand that the Lt. Col. was killed by —.
>
> Last week, I had the pleasure of meeting the new Quartermaster-General, who is on a private visit to London, and our discussions confirmed the prospects of reviving the project with the possibility of certain modifications.
>
> However, because of the loss of documents in the chaos of their Revolution, please can you copy the previous correspondence and drawings to him. In addition, I believe you should be hearing from his country's Ministry of Defence by the end of this month, bearing in mind that their budget for the new financial year will shortly be allocated [. . .]

Some time later, the same British construction company wrote to my father again:

> [. . .] With all the changes going on in —, and your intended visit overseas, I thought I would enclose a list of certain projects which I envisage. As you know, we specialise in the design as well as construction of these, so perhaps you would like to chase things up whilst you are there on our behalf and see if anything comes of it . . .

NOTES

[1] Mons: Some of those who worked for the Crown, particularly if they had no requirement for money were offered other inducements such as the placing of their children in Western institutions of higher learning, including military academies. I understand that Mons was one of those academies.

18

A RELATIONSHIP SOURS

Much to my father's grief, his relationship with SIS soured after the death of his beloved colleague 'Frank Tay', who had been a frequent visitor to our London home. Simultaneously came the collapse of the pleasant working relationship my father had enjoyed with 'Geoffrey Kingsmill'.

In 1971, out of the blue, 'Kingsmill' requested that my father sign a blank sheet of paper stating that 'Kingsmill' was my father's employer. To this day, we do not know why it was so important to 'Kingsmill' or SIS. No explanation was offered as to its purpose.

Without a moment's hesitation, my father refused on the basis that the contract was not on official Foreign Office stationery. 'I work for the Crown. I do not work for individuals,' he explained to 'Kingsmill'. The latter was as stunned at the refusal as my father was to have been asked in the first place.

'Working for me is working for the Crown,' replied 'Kingsmill' indignantly, continuing, 'You must sign it. It is better for you. It makes you staff. This way you will be eligible for promotion. It also protects your wife.'

'I have protected my wife all the years of our marriage,' responded my father, 'I do not need any lessons on how to continue to do so. This scrappy piece of paper does not say who you are, or who your employers are. How does this protect my wife?'

'Kingsmill' retorted furiously, 'You know who I am and who my employers are.'

'In which case say so, on this piece of paper.'

The pressure and emotional blackmail was relentless. My father told us, '"Geoffrey" is being very rough with me. He is playing dirty.' This caused enormous distress, particularly to my mother who was very fond of 'Kingsmill's' wife.

'Kingsmill' was adamant that my father sign the blank sheet. My father was equally adamant that he would not. The civil servant took it as a personal insult. My father, almost in tears, responded, 'I, insult you? After all we have been through together, and what you, your wife and children mean to me? No, my dear, this is something I would never do. However, you must understand, blank sheets are not a legal contract. If I sign, and you give me an order, which, by mistake, subsequently turns out to be illegal, what is this blank sheet of paper worth? What if I am ordered to do something with which I am in disagreement or could send me to my death? Am I in breach of my contract if I disobey?'

'Kingsmill' replied angrily, 'Neither I, nor SIS, would ever be unreasonable. You know this.'

The conversation bounced from one man to the next, my father always making it clear, 'This blank sheet of paper is not an agreement with you as SIS, a department of HMG. It is an agreement between two individuals, where one individual is signing away all his rights to another.'

Absolutely distraught, he continued, 'I do not know how this has happened. It would never have happened in "Frank Tay's" day. I do not, and have never seen myself as your personal employee. I believe us both to be employees of the Crown. If I have ever given you a different impression, the error is mine and I apologise. You wish to turn me into your employee, without putting the name of your employer. Put the name of your employer, who is also mine, write the contract on the correct government stationery, and I will sign.'

The discussions grew increasingly nasty. 'Kingsmill' had never been thwarted and my father was stunned by his arrogance. Reeling from the pressure, and shattered by what he believed to be the civil servant's betrayal, my father told him, 'If you were the owner of the tiniest little tobacconist shop and asked me to sign a contract of employment with you as proprietor, nothing would give me greater pleasure. In such a contract, the limits of the agreement, and the intentions, are clear.

'However, there is nothing on this sheet of paper that says who you are. Who is "Geoffrey Kingsmill"? Unless, underneath your name, you put your title and have the agreement typed on Government stationery, I cannot sign. It is not a legal document and I do not put my name to documents that are not legal. My signature is all I value.'

That evening, the first of what we were later to recognise as SIS nuisance telephone calls came through at home.

Eventually, after discussing things with my mother and myself, my father decided to resign from government service due to the pressure from 'Kingsmill' to sign the contract. Before leaving for his meeting, he commented bitterly, '"Geoffrey" thinks that I should be grateful he is offering me a contract. Who the hell does he think he is? He is not HMG. He thinks I cannot refuse and will break eventually. I will not do so. I am in my own country. I do not have to do anything I do not wish to do. I have never seen a man so cold and ruthless. He seems to think that he is God.'

My father came back from his meeting reeling. Without even taking off his coat, he told us, "'Geoffrey" says I can never resign from SIS.'[1] Meantime, my mother had taken a call from 'Kingsmill', one of several, asking her to pressurise my father into signing. She refused to do so.

A short while later, my parents and the 'Kingsmills' met for a long-standing lunch engagement. A few months short of my 16th birthday, I was also present. Drinks beforehand at the 'Kingsmills'' house were a tense affair. Soon after, as we walked to our respective cars to drive to the restaurant, 'Kingsmill' asked mildly, 'Anybody coming with me?' As he did so, he opened the car door behind the driver's seat at the precise moment that I was passing it. Usually he opened the passenger door for his wife. I got in, while his wife settled herself at the front.

Within minutes of me being separated from my parents, 'Kingsmill' asked quietly, 'Anything to report?' As he pitched his question, he ostentatiously adjusted his driving mirror. As a result, when I looked up, I stared straight into his crystal-blue eyes. Where these had once been warm with affection, they were now icy. (I have always called this SIS technique the 'eye-drop'. Those who see it, never forget it. The change of expression happens very quickly. It was a chilling display of power.)

I cannot say that I was shocked by 'Kingsmill's' conduct, although I was surprised. (Having witnessed my father's betrayal of a friend in Iraq, when I was a young child, adult betrayal was not new to me.) I continued to like him, but never trusted him again. Realising too late why he had placed me directly behind him, I gave a monosyllabic answer. The rest of the journey was in silence.

Thirty years later, I still wonder how 'Kingsmill' could really have believed my liking for him and his wife could have outweighed my loyalty to my father.

At the restaurant, I re-joined my parents with relief. We all managed a superficially polite lunch. After it was over, my father drove my mother and I back to London. The minute we were on our own, my father exploded with rage. Over the years, he was to comment with deep anger, "'Geoffrey" should never have invited my daughter into his car. I did not like it. It was wrong.'

My mother was even more upset. She said, 'When the "Kingsmills" were posted overseas again, they asked us to look after one of their children, who was undergoing substantial dental treatment. Although their need was genuine, it was also a blatant attempt to restore trust.

'As a result, one whole year of our family diary is taken up with the child's dental appointments. In addition, we constantly picked the child up from the school train, saw the child to the airport, to the aunt and uncle, to the child's grandparents. At no time would your father have asked that child anything about "Geoffrey". Whether the child had been five years old, fifteen or fifty. Your father was the more honourable man. It shocks me even now that "Geoffrey" tricked our daughter into his car to rattle your father.'

In due course, the two men repaired their relationship. It was the end of innocence but not of professional respect. In London and overseas, they continued to work well together, and with great affection.

As for the blank sheet, 'Kingsmill' eventually conceded defeat. My father never signed it.[2] 'You are unique, absolutely unique, to the whole of SIS,' 'Kingsmill' informed him.[3]

However, the civil servant got his revenge by, first, dropping my father's salary and, a few days later, dropping it even further; as well as cancelling a proposed pension.[4] Nevertheless, on 13 May 1971 my father signed the Official Secrets Act (OSA).

Afterwards, my father told my mother, 'Signing the Act is different to signing a private contract with "Geoffrey". I felt it was insulting to sign the OSA, and said so. After all, I had been HMG's loyal servant for many years. "Why," I asked, "did SIS suddenly think I had become untrustworthy?" But nonetheless I signed. Moreover, I had no objection to doing so. It formalised the relationship between myself and the Crown and was a check on "Geoffrey" and his games.'

Soon after, my father's SIS account with a local high-street bank was set up. This was used for remittance of his monthly salary, expenses and other disbursements.[5] Two months later, he reported, 'Now "Geoffrey" has let me see his power, he is all smiles. He is the "Geoffrey" I used to know. He seems to be as thrilled as I am that my pension has been approved after all.[6] I gave him my sincere thanks. Only "Geoffrey's" genuine kindness could have secured it for me. However, at the back of my mind is the ever-constant thought he is not the man I thought he was.'

My mother – who liked 'Kingsmill' but always had poor expectations of him – told my father to 'put things down to experience'. However, inside she seethed. 'Kingsmill's' behaviour had appalled her.

At the end of the year, the civil servant telephoned to tell my father about a 'pleasant Christmas surprise'. 'Kingsmill' had arranged for my father to receive a Christmas bonus. My father said, 'This made up my money to what it ought to have been. I do not know whether this had always been within "Geoffrey's" gift, and he had been playing games, or whether he had fought long and hard for me. I felt ashamed and sad about my cynicism. In addition, "Geoffrey" confirmed that despite the fact I had not signed the blank sheet, I would not lose status after all and would rise through the ranks accordingly. I was relieved and very pleased.'

My father continued, '"Geoffrey" tried to pretend the past had never happened. However, I knew it had. Moreover, I knew it could happen again. "Geoffrey" was a ruthless man. He could be all smiles one minute; and change the next. I was in his debt, and he knew it. I shudder when I think what could have happened if I had signed that blank sheet. It would have made me his slave. He could have ordered me to do anything, and I would have been breaking the law if I had refused.'

The whole experience had been bruising, not least because my father had loved 'no other man more than "Geoffrey" – like a brother'. What made the situation worse for my father was that he had no colleague in whom he could confide. Isolated, he relied on my mother and myself. However, we were not sufficiently sophisticated to give him the advice he needed. Moreover, the three of us believed that SIS and the Foreign Office were not only all-powerful but widely respected. This was a mindset that SIS had deliberately encouraged.

Therefore, it came as a relief when we finally learned that while the Foreign Office was indeed all-powerful, it was not remotely widely respected. Nor could its civil servants and diplomats take criticism from those with equal, or grander, professional standing.

For example, one of my father's close British friends was the chairman of a European bank. At a drinks party hosted by my parents, the banker, in passing, made a none too respectful comment about the effectiveness of British civil servants, particularly Foreign Office ones. 'Geoffrey Kingsmill's' response was instantaneous and rude. Soon after, the banker and his wife moved to the same town as the 'Kingsmills'. The civil servant snubbed him every morning on the platform at the railway station as they waited for the same train to Waterloo.

The banker thought it hilarious. However, his opinions contributed to my family's long overdue maturity. It was the first time that we had heard anyone, let alone someone of the banker's professional standing, criticise senior Foreign Office personnel.

(Some years later, at another drinks party hosted by my parents at which Norman Darbyshire was present, there was a similar run-in. This time the argument was between Darbyshire and another senior British banker who had been in Iran. My father's diary reads, 'Norman and — recognised each other from Persia. Towards the end of the evening, they exchanged sharp words, because — had a poor opinion of the British embassy when he was in Teheran. It is interesting that he shares the same views as —. Maybe British bankers do not rate the Foreign Office.')

My father served with SIS for many more years. However, as his non-SIS life developed, he became increasingly less awe-struck. Nevertheless, he was very sad when 'Geoffrey Kingsmill' was posted overseas in 1973.

'Kingsmill' arranged a meticulous handover. He even sorted out administrative details. For example, shortly before he left, and after my father had submitted a list of his business activities, my father's diary reads, 'Discussed with "Geoffrey" and Michael legal aspect of trading name.' The following day he notes: 'Explained my problems to "Geoffrey" who was to ask legal opinion.' Finally he writes, 'Had a meeting at 3.30 p.m. with "Geoffrey" and Michael and cleared all outstanding points.'

Also set in motion was a false persona for my parents. This, it was intended, would be developed by my father's new case officer.

In the meantime, my parents took 'possession' of an SIS apartment in Dolphin Square, a privately owned London housing block. They also rigged themselves out in a new wardrobe at the taxpayer's expense – everything they purchased had to have a Harrods label. Next, using their false names, they had to arrange for Harrods to courier their new clothes to 'their' Dolphin Square address. My father's diary reads that my mother spent the day shopping at Harrods. '[. . .] I joined her for lunch at the store. We stayed at the flat that night for the first time.' Today, his Harrods green silk dressing-gown hangs behind my own bathroom door.

The following afternoon, wearing their new clothes and using their fake names, my parents drove to Marlow, where they had dinner at the Compleat Angler. They hoped they would not be spotted by the restaurant staff who knew them under their real identities. The next day, my father met his new case officer and an SIS secretary 'for a rehearsal at the flat'. She was to pretend to be his mistress. From September 1973 onwards, my parents were sleeping as often at their SIS apartment as they were at their own house. I was delighted. By then an undergraduate, I was very pleased to have their house to myself.

In addition, my father prepared for an SIS trip to Miami, and one to Detroit. This, disappointingly, was cancelled. However, soon after, prior to visiting Beirut, he flew off to meet 'Geoffrey Kingsmill' in his new posting. The two men rendezvoused at an SIS-owned apartment, where they embraced like brothers. 'I forgot he was not an Arab,' said my father, adding, 'I have never known "Geoffrey" so affectionate.'

During the meeting, 'Kingsmill' specifically confirmed my father's rank. This, had the country been at war and required him to go into uniform, would have been at the level of full colonel. Looking through the report my father had written, 'Kingsmill' commented, 'I have had some of this intelligence before, but it is not nearly as good as this.' My father was very pleased.

As importantly, returning from a follow-up visit, he told my mother and I about a 'sincere warning' that 'Kingsmill' had given him before my father again flew on to Beirut. His old friend had told my father, 'Never, irrespective of the pressure SIS might put you under, ever travel overseas on false documentation or carry a false passport. If things go wrong, you will be shot as a spy immediately.'

My family were to remember 'Geoffrey Kingsmill' for several reasons, including his many kindnesses. However, we were particularly grateful for the sincerity of that warning. In later years, my father was to say, 'Whatever happened between "Geoffrey" and myself, I owe him this at the very least.'[7]

It was in this frame of mind he got to know his third, and penultimate, case officer, SIS diplomat Alexis Forte.

NOTES

[1] A letter dated August 1994 from the Foreign Office stated those who work for SIS do so 'voluntarily'. I believe this is true at the point of joining. However, what is not made clear is that, having worked for SIS, resignation is not an option. Therefore, it is not as 'voluntary' as the Foreign Office seek to imply.

2   My mother and I believe that although my father's refusal to sign the blank sheet impacted negatively on his career, it ultimately saved his life. He concurred, saying, 'After "Geoffrey" was posted, Alexis Forte became my case officer. Had I signed the blank sheet, I would definitely have been dead. Alexis did not have the same respect for a spy's life that so distinguished "Geoffrey's" career. Because I had not signed it, I was able to refuse Alexis Forte's shameless orders.'

3   In 1994, the Foreign Office tried to imply that the use of the word 'unique' meant that my father's contract was 'unique to him'. This is not what 'Geoffrey Kingsmill' meant at the time he said it, unless he deliberately gave a false impression, which is always possible.

4   My mother and I believe that this was when my father should have been allowed to cease SIS employment. This way, our family and SIS could have avoided the catastrophic breakdown in the relationship some years later. In addition, it would have enabled my father to develop his personal and professional life in what was still a strange country, free of SIS input. It would similarly have allowed my family to escape the long shadows of espionage.

5   I took full responsibility for my father's paperwork when he became terminally ill. On his death (1986), I was so anxious about SIS's conduct, which included interference in his private safety-deposit box, I turned his SIS bank account into my widowed mother's personal account. I advise all those who take responsibility for former SIS employees, or their dependants, to do the same, to prevent any attempt to deny the widow's rights, or use the account against the widow with the Inland Revenue.

6   SIS did not backdate my father's pension to his first year of service. Therefore, his work in Iraq was not taken into account. Nor was he allowed to backdate his national insurance.

7   My father felt so strongly about the Crown's attempts to make spies travel on false passports (see page 153 and Note 3 on page 154), that he said, 'If I could offer only one piece of advice to a new generation of SIS spies, it would be this: never agree to multiple identities or travel on false papers. For the most part, only criminals/drug dealers have these.'

19

AN UNDERGRADUATE'S VIEW OF SIS

I saw my father's SIS life in terms of his case officers. As a result, I built my opinions around the men, rather than what they did. The word 'espionage' was never used. Then, along came Alexis Forte, who mentioned it all the time.[1] He was the sort of man who took up all the oxygen in the room.

By the time I met Forte in 1973, I was 18. By then, I had had five years' experience of SIS case officers and had the benefit of comparison. In addition, I had been in the country for eight years and, after changing schools three times, was about to start my second year as an undergraduate at the School of Oriental & African Studies (SOAS), London University. (One of the first arguments I had with Forte was when he said, 'In my day, it was called the "School of Oriental Studies". The school lost prestige when it added the word "African" to its name. Africa devalues the school.')

My father served with Forte from 1973 until 1977, when the diplomat became SIS station-head in France, as well as counsellor at the British embassy in Paris. Halfway through Forte's secondment, (Sir) Richard Dearlove, SIS's present 'Chief', arrived as first secretary. Dearlove was Forte's subordinate at the embassy from 1980 until Forte retired after the Falklands War. Forte died in 1983.

During the Falklands campaign, and as a personal friend of the head of French Intelligence, Pierre Marion,[2] Forte's work was outstanding as he ensured French Intelligence co-operation during the crisis.[3]

A personal friend and former adviser of the Shah of Iran, Forte was a White Russian and an acknowledged SIS hero who 'established a reputation within SIS as a fearless case officer and was particularly admired because of the time he had spent living with Kurdish hill tribes in Northern Iraq'.[4]

In *MI6: Fifty Years of Special Operations* by Stephen Dorril, Forte is quoted as being an 'ace agent runner'.[5] On the other hand, Tom Bower, in his biography of the former head of MI5 and SIS, Sir Dick White, strikes a more cautionary note.[6]

Describing a three-day SIS conference in summer of 1960 when Alexis Forte, Norman Darbyshire and others were present, Bower writes, 'The tone was set by Forte who, while chief in Baghdad in 1958, had failed to anticipate the overthrow of Britain's protégé and was renowned for sending agents across the border into Russia on missions from which they never returned.'

My family's view of Forte chimes more closely with that of Tom Bower. However, I should add that Bower also concludes: 'Forte's reputation had recovered in Teheran where, every week, he spent 30 minutes in private audience with the Shah.'

My father, who had little respect for the British diplomats who served in Baghdad in 1958, had doubts about Forte from the start. He was outraged that the SIS diplomat who had failed to anticipate the toppling of the Boy King of Iraq 15 years earlier was to be his case officer, and the filter by which all his Middle Eastern intelligence would reach Whitehall.

I had problems with Alexis Forte too. In fairness, this may have been no more than to be expected, in view of the fact that Forte was childless and may not have been comfortable with the strident attitudes of teenage students, particularly when they differed from his own. A divorcé, he was very proud of his young wife, his former SIS secretary, and considered her younger sisters to be the daughters he never had. Although I never met his sisters-in-law, it was clear from fairly early on that I did not reach the standards they, wholly blamelessly, set.

It is also fair to say a daughter, even a young one, can influence her father. Although I was initially taken with Forte – he was a wonderful raconteur – I came to loathe his political views. This meant that I came to loathe him too. I did not hide this from him or my parents.

My parents had more personal qualms. For a start, they disapproved of middle-aged diplomats who divorced their first wives in order to marry their much younger secretaries, as Forte had. My mother, who was expected to strike up a friendship with Forte's wife, was especially uncomfortable. She considered Mrs Alexis Forte 'A sweet girl, young enough to be my daughter, with whom I have nothing in common, nor would I wish to.'

This, inevitably, impacted on the relationship between the two men.

Some of my early disagreements with Forte were no more than minor irritations. These, had there been a better rapport, would have been quickly forgotten. For example, I resented being forced to apologise to him for suggesting that he picked 'rich sources so he could meet them in smart places'.

Other problems were more fundamental. My father was nervous of Forte's habit of talking frankly in front of me. This made the atmosphere at home tense whenever Forte was present, which was often. (He made mostly general SIS comments, with some colourful gossip thrown in, which I loved; as well as more specific references to which my parents profoundly objected.)

One of the first rows that I can remember was when Forte gave me detailed information as to why 'our spies have moved to Durham University', adding that 'the Kurds have gone to St Johns, Oxford' – explaining how SIS had moved its spy school away from SOAS. This particularly infuriated my father since Forte also volunteered details of an SIS meeting in Oxford my father was about to attend. Forte brushed aside my father's protestations by referring to my 'maturity'.

Far worse, Forte gave unsolicited information about the well-born divorced parents of a young medical student I was then dating.

Forte's conduct particularly worried my mother, who became concerned that he was encouraging me to consider myself an 'insider' with an unattractive appeal to my all too susceptible vanity. Seeing that my father was unable to control the diplomat, she took me aside and cautioned that such flattery could 'easily turn your head and is for a reason, or, if it is not, is because Alexis knows you like praise, which does not say much about you'. Since I was appallingly vain, my mother's words hit the spot.

To be fair to the man, he had every reason to think I was more espionage-aware than I actually was.

I had been told formally that my father was a spy in 1972 when I was about to start my first term at SOAS. I was 17. I met Forte a year later. Therefore, through no fault of his own, he assumed I was familiar with various SIS details when I was not. In extending what he believed to be an existing induction process, he unknowingly stirred up a hornet's nest within my family.

This was because not long after I arrived at SOAS, SIS had asked me, through my father, to recommend four fellow students who would make 'good intelligence officers'. My father willingly consented; my mother, however, was furious. She disapproved of any attempts to encourage me to take an interest in my father's work.

Struggling with the sophistication of SOAS's academic demands, I puffed up. I was enormously proud I had been asked to suggest possible SIS recruits and took every care in making my selection. Three of my recommendations were turned down on the basis of their race and/or class. (The one person I know SIS considered was not someone I would have recommended.)

It was particularly hard to be informed that my choices were a disappointment and a relief to be congratulated on my fourth. However, it was explained that SIS could not approach the latter because his father had just been appointed the British ambassador to —, and the ambassador had made it clear he did not want any involvement with SIS – this would apply to his son.

SIS did not tell me that it was not common knowledge that my friend's father had been appointed ambassador to —. Therefore, when I next saw the student, I was inadvertently indiscreet, asking whether his family were pleased about his father's appointment. My friend looked stunned. In showing awareness of where the ambassador had been posted, I had inadvertently identified my father.'

This, therefore, is the background to my first meeting with Alexis Forte and why I believe he understood me to be more espionage-aware than I was.

If I was initially flattered by Forte's genuine attempts at friendship, the constant arguments soon corroded this. His approval was too conditional.

He presented himself as an expert on Middle Eastern affairs, when in fact he was an Iranian specialist. He was profoundly disappointed I had no interest in Iran, preferring Egypt and Iraq as my area of study. To encourage me to consider what he called Persia, a country he adored, he told me to 'ask Nancy Lambton to tell you how we got rid of Mossadeq'.

Professor Ann (Nancy) Lambton was one of SOAS's most distinguished Iranian scholars, who taught me for a term. Twenty-odd years earlier, Forte had been her student when he had done a language course at SOAS. Previously of the British embassy in Teheran, Lambton had been closely involved in events leading to the downfall of Iran's democratically elected Prime Minister Dr Mohammed Mossadeq in 1953.

Neither my father nor I were sympathetic to Alexis Forte's views on Mossadeq. My father particularly disagreed with Forte's opinion of Mossadeq's character. (My father had had the same disagreement with his former case officer Norman Darbyshire, who had been similarly involved in the Mossadeq affair.)

Leaving Mossadeq behind, Forte next claimed, 'It was our duty to assist the Shah of Persia in the control of his people.' At the time he made the statement, rumours were sweeping SOAS about Britain's involvement in the training of the Shah of Iran's brutal secret police.

Forte tried very hard to shape my opinions.

Some respite from him was offered by 'Geoffrey Kingsmill' on his brief visits to London. However, on the few occasions I saw 'Kingsmill', he was very tired. Worry lines were etched across his face. My parents were always concerned about how hard 'Kingsmill' was working, and the strain under which he and his wife were living. He would visibly relax with them, and I have no doubt his affection and appreciation could not have been more sincere.

Unlike Forte, 'Kingsmill' never, in my presence, advanced a political opinion about the Middle East, far less interfered with any I held. He was merely thrilled I was enjoying SOAS, and interested in anything I had to say. He was curious when I informed him (probably erroneously) that the then president of Syria was married to the king of Jordan's sister. Looking surprised, he raised his eyebrows and said, 'Now that is something I did not know.'[8]

He loved undergraduate news. He chuckled non-commitally when I told him that on the eve of the Six Day War, President Nasser was reading RAND reports; and smiled when I also informed him that President Sadat of Egypt, pictured with his wife in a glossy magazine, was reading a novel by the regency romance writer Georgette Heyer.

However, 'Kingsmill' did not welcome all information. Some time after I graduated, I mentioned a woman journalist whose son, also a journalist, was at the time closely connected with one of my undergraduate friends. Because of their specialist areas, and place of residence, and thinking 'Kingsmill' might know them, I mentioned their names. 'Kingsmill' killed the conversation immediately.

On another occasion, I mentioned I had heard that a British diplomat, finding himself locked over a weekend in the cipher room of a British embassy, had had to send a message to London to get himself out. Annoyance flickered across 'Kingsmill's' face and he asked crisply where I had heard the anecdote.[9]

In maturity, I accept Alexis Forte felt excluded by the long-standing friendship between the 'Kingsmills' and my family. This did nothing to improve relations between him and my father. He was bitterly hurt that my father constantly compared him to 'Kingsmill' – I cannot remember the number of times Forte said despairingly, 'I am not "Geoffrey Kingsmill". We work differently.' He was equally hurt that my father complained about him to 'Kingsmill'.

The most damaging information Forte mentioned were the student files compiled by Special Branch. I had no idea such things existed. He no doubt meant well when he cautioned, 'We have a record on every single student signing up to dubious societies at London University. We hope you are careful about your friends,' but it chilled me. I found the whole thing shocking.

Emphasising that I must not say anything about the files to my fellow students, Forte advised me not to join specific student groups and societies, 'since this would be bad for your future.' (On another occasion Forte remarked, 'Not even the SOAS Drama Society is safe. Those interested in theatricals can often come in useful.') One file was created on one of my contemporaries merely because 'he wore a Green beret' (a sign of possible IRA sympathies). As a result, I grew up with the knowledge of the student files. My father specifically warned me not to give the intelligence services any opportunity to build up an independent file on me since he would not have been able to control its contents.

My father said some PhD students were in a particularly awkward position if, for example, they had left-wing supervisors. This was because, in order to progress their careers, the students sometimes had to join various societies favoured by their tutors. As a result, a file on the student was 'automatically created'. This, my father said, 'is a nonsense, not least because a politically active mature student does not have the time to join societies. Therefore, we are most likely missing the key ones.'

My father was also concerned 'about the influence some mature students from overseas can have on young British ones'. He continued, 'Generally speaking, our students are much younger, and therefore more easily manipulated by those from abroad. For this reason, the files can help us, via some tutors, protect the cream of our young people at our universities from coming under the influence of malign personalities.'

The files were exceptionally detailed. On the strength of a description alone, SIS were able to identify a homesick and warm-hearted Middle Easterner who invited me to join his wife and himself for an Arab meal. SIS refused to allow me to accept the hospitality, because 'there [was] a problem with a relative of his' who was studying in another Western country.

As always, I was given no assistance as to what reason I could offer, without giving offence, to turn the invitation down. Nevertheless, it was made clear: 'Whatever reason you do give, on no account are you to mention your father.'

NOTES

1   Alexis Kougoulsky Forte OBE was born in 1925. He joined the Foreign Office in 1950, becoming third secretary in Teheran the following year. He became Vice Consul in Basra, Iraq, in 1952, moving to Port Said two years later. He was first secretary at the embassy in Baghdad in 1957, becoming Teheran SIS Station Chief two years later. His other postings included Saigon and Nairobi. He served as counsellor at the British embassy in France 1977–82 and died in 1983.
    Source: 'A Who's Who of the British Secret State', *Lobster* special (1989).

2   Following publication of Pierre Marion's controversial autobiography, *The Sunday Times*, 25 June 2000, wrote: 'It is difficult to imagine any senior British official publicly admitting to planning the assassination of foreign diplomats, yet that was only one of Marion's revelations from his time as head of the Direction Generale de la Securite Exterieure (DGSE), the French counter intelligence agency. After a successful career as an aerospace executive with good security contacts, Marion was recommended to Mitterand in 1981 for a job that none of the new Socialist President's left-wing supporters would touch.'

3   West, N. (1997) *The Secret War for the Falklands: The SAS, MI6 and the War Whitehall Nearly Lost.* Little, Brown and Company: London.

4   *Ibid.*

5   Dorril, S. (2000) *MI6: Fifty Years of Special Operations.* Fourth Estate: London.

6   Bower, T. (1995) *The Perfect English Spy: Sir Dick White and the Secret War 1935–90.* Heinemann: London.

7   I assume my student friend warned his father. For this reason, I was amused to read in Stephen Dorril's *MI6: Fifty Years of Special Operations* that the man concerned 'Would not permit even the limited MI6 presence to use his embassy for spying.'

8   This could make the present king of Jordan and the present president of Syria first cousins. However, the information I had as a student could have been wrong.

9   The story, and the diplomat's identity, is now widely known. At the time, when I heard it from a friend working at 10 Downing Street, this was not the case.

20

A RACIST SIS DIPLOMAT

Alexis Forte particularly loathed Arab students. He was wholly unconcerned that some, in order to protect themselves and their families from specific threats – which the police would not take seriously – were carrying hand-guns and had rosters of British friends who would sleep at their houses to protect them. I was ashamed of Forte's comments, in particular those he made about the British young people, one of whom was a close friend of mine, who were courageously trying to help the Arab students.

Forte's attitude made things difficult for my father, who was concerned about the safety of the wider Iraqi community living in Britain. My father was especially worried about how much those having to pay for their own security were being charged. He remarked scathingly, 'Some are not even on a "hit-list". They have been frightened into paying for security.' He was particularly upset there were no fixed prices. 'People can be charged one thing one day, and another the next.'

Forte responded, 'I would not start handing out insults or questioning Special Branch methods if I were you.'

One family was subjected to an utterly vicious campaign of harassment. This, my father knew, was not the work of Iraqi hit-squads, but of 'moon-lighters' from the police, trying to put up their protection price by pretending to be from the hit-squads.

I found it particularly difficult to deal with Forte's racism. He was almost an apologist for the Nazis (until he remembered he was a Russian!). He was cruel about the high-born continental wife of a senior SIS colleague much loved by my family because of her 'Moroccan connection'; said '*Sale Juif* [dirty Jew]' every time he paid an East End taxi driver; and, referring to my mixed race, told me I was 'lucky to look French'. (To which my mother icily inquired, 'Would she have been "unlucky" if she had not looked French?') Getting himself into a bit of a fix, next he told my father that he was, 'Fortunate your father was an Indian, because all Indians are Aryans.'

Other Forte 'gems' included:

- 'The Arab is not an instinctive learner.'
- 'The Jews did not die in the Holocaust because they are all running Israel today.' (When Iraq's Revolution Command Council adopted a decision in November 1975 stipulating that Iraqi Jews 'Who have left Iraq since 1948 have the right to return . . .' Forte gleefully suggested, 'Shall we put the word out, so we can get rid of all our Jews too?'
- 'We need to send the explorer Wilfred Thesiger to Iraq to provide the Marsh Arabs with malarial tablets. They would be in hock to us for ever more.'[1]

Forte's knowledge of Iraq, which stopped at the Iraqi monarchy, which he wanted restored, was laughable. He would go red in the face when reminded that the king had been dead for 15 years, and Iraq had moved on. He was always mentioning a well-known Iraqi monarchist, living in Europe, apparently unaware that the man, however distinguished, was no longer well placed to know what was going on in the country.

All of this infuriated my father, who complained, 'If I am stuck with Alexis for much longer, the British will completely lose the initiative in Baghdad. Because he knows nothing about Iraq, he gets nasty. Every time I say something, he mentions Teheran. I keep having to remind him that Teheran is not Baghdad.'

Meantime, Forte talked constantly about friends I had never heard of, marking me down because of it. His legendary name-dropping included a mix of British aristocrats, as well as senior SIS officers. He had been in SIS for so long that he knew them all personally. Furious, my father said, 'Of course my daughter has not heard of these men. I have not heard of these men. How can you expect her to? Leave her alone. These things are not for her to know.'

Rather than heeding my father, Forte, instead, upped the information he was giving me. This was both dangerous and too much, as well as being a source of endless rows with my parents. They believed he had been trained to cause dissent and could not stop himself from doing so, even in a family situation.

He hinted at the homosexual relationship between the explorer Wilfred Thesiger and travel writer/*Observer* journalist Gavin Young,[2] before commenting on the academic Steven Runciman,[3] who was 'a personal friend of the Regent of Iraq'. This gave him the opportunity to mention (yet again) what a good friend of the Shah of Persia he had been.[4]

He hated Communists and never missed an opportunity to boast that he was a 'White Russian'. He said it so often that eventually my father remarked, 'My family would not have mistaken you for an African one.'

Forte's constant references to his White Russian background meant, by implication, although he never actually said so, that he considered himself an aristocrat. This annoyed my father even more. 'Those of us from the Middle East, of a certain age, do not always have a good opinion of the White Russians,' my father remarked – an allusion to those who drifted into the area, in straitened circumstances, following the Bolshevik Revolution. (Today, these might be called 'asylum seekers'.) Forte was furious. It was like a ping-pong match as the two men hurled insults at each other.

Much of what they were arguing about went over my head. However, I was comfortable with my certainties. Therefore, I was happy to disagree with Forte when he said that even the possibility of Communism was the biggest evil in the Middle East;[5] and I could not believe his reaction when I mentioned that a schoolfriend's father, a distinguished academic of world-renown, and a governor of SOAS, had fought with the International Brigade in the Spanish Civil War. ('A Communist!' he spat.)

The diplomat loathed homosexuals, Jews and trades unionists. When I remonstrated with him, he concluded his conversation, 'You are playing a dangerous game. You had better watch yourself. Such views are not tolerated in our society.'

My father was furious, shouting at him, 'My daughter's opinions are her own. They prove I have been a good father and have raised her to think freely. This is why I sent her to a free country. I thought this was the cause we both served.'

On every occasion, Forte tried to bend me to his opinion. He was uncomfortable with, and tried to change, my childhood recollections of Iraq. He was contemptuous when I spoke affectionately of my Polish friends in Baghdad – whom he dismissed as 'peasants' – and was amazed I had 'liked the Hungarians', but had no feelings either way for the Russians. He took the last to be a personal insult, since he despised the Poles and Hungarians, but was proud of the Russians.

More than anything else, he was dismayed that none of my friends in Baghdad had been the children of the monarchist regime. (The one exception was a family I met in London. On discovering I knew them, Forte dropped heavy hints that he wished to meet them, not least because one of their relatives was well connected in several parts of the Middle East. I refused. Meantime, my father told him, 'You are not permitted to do your job on the back of my teenage daughter's friendships. Nor, at any time in the future, do I permit you to question my daughter about her social circle.' Nevertheless, as a precaution and of my own volition, I never saw the family again.)

Another problem my family had with Forte was that we did not share his sense of humour – an essential espionage bonding ingredient. On one occasion he arrived at my parents' home giggling. 'The boys have arrested a chap behaving oddly in the Kings Road wearing his dish-cloth. They threw the Arab in the cells,' he said, expecting us to laugh. It was subsequently discovered that the man had suffered a nervous breakdown in his home country and was in the UK, with his family, for medical treatment.

I was similarly unimpressed by Forte's hints that he was 'in the know'. I particularly remember him going off like a fire-cracker following events in Malta and Cyprus in 1974.

Nor did I like the assumptions that Forte made about me. He believed my mother and I found SIS and espionage exciting. In fact, having had so many years of it, we, particularly my mother, were fed up with it. As for myself, I wanted to lead a normal life because it not only curtailed me, but locked me in too tightly to the adult world.

Forte's other opinions included:

- 'Holidays are for the employer. Workers are likely to fall prey to Trotskyists if they have time on their hands.'
- 'Eccentricity is for the top. If we allow our subjects to take an independent line, we are opening the door to anarchy and Trotskyism.'
- 'Education is for the few. We maintain the value of our own type, if we limit higher education.'

The latter particularly upset my father, who said, 'As a young boy, I dreamed of being able to complete my education in the West but, following my father's bankruptcy, this was no longer possible. This is why I dreamed of England. I knew education was free in England and it was a fair society. I had no idea that in reality the British deliberately limited higher education to the lucky few.'

Finally, I was embarrassed by the way Forte treated one of the nicest of my student friends, for no better reason than the young man's modest background. They met at a drinks party hosted by my parents to which two of my friends had been invited to keep me company. Finding out what my friend's PhD thesis was on, Forte, considering himself the expert, was obnoxious. Moving the conversation on to Iran – having quickly found himself out of his depth in my student friend's specialist field – he fell over himself to impress upon the student that he worked for HMG. Next, Forte repeated that he had been a personal friend of the Shah and was, he said, therefore, 'In a better position to judge the Shah and modern Persia than you are.' He then once more proceeded to defend the Shah's secret police.

Forte's boast that he worked for HMG confirmed to everybody present, including two people from the Middle East, what he did for a living. Consequently, it drew attention to his connection with my father. Their relationship disintegrated into four years of slanging matches.

During one argument, I was so incensed by what Forte said that, in front of him, I got out my notebook and started writing everything down. My father made endless complaints and requests for a new case officer. These were ignored. Instead, SIS told my father to 'persevere'. After one particular row, my father noted in his diary, in bold capital letters, that Forte had referred to him as a 'thick dark fog'.

It was never SIS's best idea to run a White Russian racist with a brown-skinned spy.

NOTES

[1] A variation of this story was quoted by Nigel West in *The Secret War for the Falklands*. In this, Forte explained, 'We could defeat Qasim by sending Wilfred Thesiger to the southern tribes of Iraq. He should distribute Mepacrine anti-malarial tablets to the tribesmen. They'd be in hock to us for ever more.'

   I heard the comment, on several occasions, at first hand. It is a story that may amuse a British diplomat. It had no amusement value for a family raised in Iraq.

[2] Gavin Young's *Times* obituary, 19 January 2001, said he had 'A nodding acquaintance with MI6'.

[3] Steven Runciman was a specialist in the Crusades and Byzantine Empire, who had once taught at Al-Hikma University in Baghdad.

[4] Forte was profoundly put out that my family knew SIS diplomat Norman Darbyshire well, who, as a young man, had also been a friend of the Shah of Iran.

[5] The irony, of course, is that Islamic fundamentalism, brought to Western attention by the tragic events of 11 September 2001, was encouraged as a buffer against Communism.

21

OPERATIONAL DISAGREEMENTS

One reason why the working relationship between my father and Alexis Forte was so bad was because the latter did not understand that political and/or commercial intelligence was not the same as intelligence on armament supplies. My father complained, 'Because Alexis knows nothing about the Middle East, he marginalises anybody who does. As a result, "intelligence" as I know it is of no consequence. He tells me that I am out of date and will have to "modernise" but has no answer when I ask how political and commercial intelligence can ever be out of date, if it is the most recent.'

My father continued, 'He tries to use business phrases he has picked out of the *Financial Times* to impress me but does not understand hard commercial intelligence which has political significance. For example, the implications for our country if Middle Easterners continue to buy into British companies. There are such serious things going on and yet his butterfly brain cannot concentrate. He is also difficult to work with because his views are all over the place. Sometimes he is pro-Israel, the next minute, he is anti-.'

What particularly hurt my father was the fact that Forte would pass off other people's ideas as his own, thereby getting all the credit. For example, my father devised —, and handed it to Forte for SIS development. A couple of weeks later, Forte, claiming its success as his own, showed my father the results. My father was so angry that he wrote in his diary, 'Alexis expected me to congratulate him on my own work. I praised the dummies as they deserved.'

Another serious disagreement was over the false identity my parents were expected to sustain at the SIS Dolphin Square apartment. Since it was next to the Thames, they kept bumping into people along the river whom they knew. My mother said, 'Alexis seemed to be unaware that London is not the easiest place to live in, in disguise. We were not exactly unknown. As for bumping into — and his wife, it would not have been so bad if your father had not been wearing his new "wardrobe". Your father was a complete embarrassment, dressed as SIS expected a flashy Arab to dress. Our friends looked at us in amazement. I think they thought your father was going through his second childhood.'[1]

My parents also worried about bumping into my brother or myself. Needless to say, we thought the whole situation hilarious.

My father was also uncomfortable at having to act with an SIS 'mistress'. (My mother was similarly asked 'To pretend to be your husband's bit of stuff', to which she replied, 'I have no requirement to pretend. I am his bit of stuff.')

Then there was Alexis Forte's jealous refusal to allow my father to take up with his old pal Colonel Michael —, formerly of the Soviet embassy, Baghdad, and, by this time, at the Soviet embassy, London.[2] My father said, 'When I told Forte the Soviet Colonel was my friend, he immediately replied, "That's the job of the other lot." He could not bear the idea that I knew the man. As a result, Alexis vetoed my proposals. In view of other things going on, his jealousy, as a White Russian working for the Crown, was not only self-serving but contrary to the national interest.'

Some years later, my father said, 'I should have disregarded Alexis' veto. I advise any spy who has no respect for his case officer to follow his own instincts. At the time, nobody in London seemed to know anything about the Soviets, far less be able to mix with them. All we were concerned about was identifying the KGB in London, keeping a watch on them and/or throwing them out. Nobody was fraternising.

'It was just like Baghdad all over again – i.e. SIS diplomats completely ignorant of Eastern European/Soviet Bloc personnel. This was always my value because I did mix with them. Alexis could not stand it. For his own ego, nothing else, he blocked me when the country needed the sort of assistance I could offer. What sort of fools were running our intelligence services that they could allow the vanity of a dated White Russian SIS officer to dictate policy?'

The personal hostility between Forte and my father became so bad that my mother and I turned their relationship into a weather forecast – 'expect thunder, with a few bright spells'.

There was fault on both sides. Today, I blame SIS for continuing to run the two together, even when it was obvious their relationship was non-existent. How they did not kill each other I will never know. Apparently they were stuck with each other because nobody else as senior as Forte was available. Therefore, retrospectively, I feel sorry for both of them. At the time, I wholly condemned Forte.

Forte's jealousy of my father went so deep that my father even found him skipping things in reports. On three important occasions, Forte failed to pass vital information to the relevant personnel at the Ministry of Defence. In addition, he did not even pass on minor warnings my father was giving, for example my father's anxiety at the number of requests he was getting to help place young men from the Middle East on training schemes in the British aircraft industry.

Forte was particularly panicked when a senior official of a British organisation representing a geo-political area asked my father, a fellow freemason, to participate in a group connected with Parliament. With the exception of the official, the representative organisation was staffed with enough retired misogynist SIS officers (all of whom were Forte's friends) to start a revolution.

The request for my father's help came via a non-SIS senior British diplomat who was anxious about the way some members in the House of Commons and Lords were conducting themselves commercially, and in respect of other overseas matters. The diplomat, the official from the representative organisation and my father believed there was major fraud involved.

Forte refused to allow my father to take things further on the basis that, he explained, 'We do not interfere with Parliament. Nor are we policemen.'

My father argued, 'The conduct of these men is damaging the United Kingdom's reputation.' He always believed Forte was protecting people he knew, especially in the House of Lords.

Forte also jeopardised other people's security. On one occasion, my father took a telephone call from a Middle Eastern Jewish friend in America who gave my father chapter and verse of a discussion Forte had had with a non-UK journalist, known to my father, who was rumoured to be working, at alternate times, for the CIA and SIS, as well as other agencies.

My father said, 'Alexis was dazzled, absolutely dazzled by this "journalist". I have no doubt in order to impress him, and find out what the CIA or others were up to, including his own side, he was feeding him "tit-bits". I later found out that I and my source were one of those tit-bits. Alexis was not aware the information would come back to me, and certainly not so quickly. He was prepared to jeopardise two lives in order to look good himself. He needed everybody to know that he was a "master spy" with countless "informants" at his beck and call.

'I pointed out to Alexis that I was not an "informant" and told him to learn to keep his mouth shut.

'Alexis was playing so many double games for his own amusement that he was creating conspiracy and danger where none existed. He needed the "fix" that he was running a million spies, each one expendable. He was a "junkie", and should have been treated for such addiction as if it were heroin. I thought all SIS diplomats were like "Geoffrey Kingsmill". No one prepared me for the scandal of Alexis Forte.'

To my knowledge, my father received two specific warnings from overseas friends concerning Forte's indiscretions. My father also had evidence of a third when he received a request to help someone in the Iraqi Jewish community with his papers with the Home Office. 'I was very happy to assist,' recalled my father. 'However, it told me to what extent Alexis had blown my cover and via which avenue.'

My father was also saddened by Forte's attitude to potential sources who 'did not come over, after all'. My father said, 'I had one similar experience with

"Geoffrey Kingsmill". The difference was that "Geoffrey" behaved like a complete gentleman. He said that it was a contact's prerogative to change his mind, and there was the end of it. We left the man alone. Nor did we claim back the money the Crown had paid him, although he offered it. However, when similar circumstances arose under Alexis, he wanted me to blackmail the man. It was a disgrace. I refused.'

My father also believed that Forte compromised his life when he was on an SIS visit to Brussels. My father refers in his diary to a 'tasteless and unpleasant incident'. Subsequently, nearly every SIS trip my father undertook had some peril or upset. He commented, 'Eventually, I realised Alexis was so jealous of my contacts, he was trying to stop me from travelling to meet them, in order to undermine my career. To do so, he was prepared to endanger my life.'

When my father did travel, it seemed as if Forte was making the trips as uncomfortable as possible, for example, insisting my father visit Saudi Arabia in the middle of the summer, the hottest time of the year. 'The real problem was that Alexis wanted to stick with what he knew, in order to remain "top-dog" – never mind he was living in the last century,' said my father.

In due course, nearly every time my father prepared for an overseas tour, Forte rang up at the last minute to cancel it. On one occasion, my father had already left for the airport. Forte cancelled one of my father's trips (to New York) four times and eventually went himself, saying, 'It is better if I go, I have the better contacts.' (He reddened when I commented, 'In which case, you cannot be meeting the same people as Daddy, since you do not speak good enough Arabic.')

Not everything was Forte's fault. A letter from my father, dated 21 August 1976, to a British company, which he was assisting on SIS's behalf, gives an idea of other problems arising:

> Instead of the period of ten days I was expected to spend in Jordan, I spent only four days and returned to London on 12 August because I found Amman in a state of complete chaos and confusion as a result of thousands of evacuees and refugees who had poured into Jordan from the Lebanon. In the circumstances, I was unable to attend to business. I understand that the same situation of turmoil applies to many neighbouring countries in the Middle East.

When my father was out of the country, it sometimes appeared as if Forte was going out of his way to upset my mother. On one occasion, when my father was on an SIS trip to Vienna, Forte telephoned in the middle of the night to ask her what hotel my father was staying in 'because there are two Nasties at the Hotel Bristol'. (Forte later said that the warning had come from Helsinki. Through no fault of his own, it turned out to be a hoax.)

On his return, my father made a formal complaint 'because my case officer should have known in what hotel I was staying. My wife had a sleepless night and was sick with worry. Our daughter gave him hell the following day. He told her off because she lost her temper with him. The next thing she knew was he was telling her that if she "did not pull her socks up", it was going in her file.'

Forte's other favourite trick when my father was away was turning up unannounced on our doorstep. My father said, 'This was something "Geoffrey Kingsmill" would never have done. When I was abroad, "Geoffrey" always kept in touch with my family by telephone. Usually these calls were made by his wife. I always appreciated this courtesy.

'Alexis, however, insisted on visiting. When I tackled him about this, he looked hurt and said, "I am only looking after the wife and daughter of a colleague." In fact, it was an attempt to develop a relationship with my family, most especially my daughter, who called him "Biggles".'

My mother said, 'It was quite clear that Alexis was seeking to win our daughter's confidence. When her father objected, he was arrogant. He told him, "If I wanted to, I could arrange for your daughter to be contacted directly. You would not even know it, and she would not tell you. She is over 18 and an adult." Your father went mad. In fact, we both did.'

Eventually, my mother banned Forte from having 'any contact with my daughter unless either I or her father are present.'

This followed Forte's persistent questioning of me, under the guise of social chit-chat, as to what I knew about a well-travelled musician friend of the 'Kingsmills', and the musician's wife, both of whom I had met on a couple of occasions. So far as I was aware, the musician had refused to work for SIS, although 'Kingsmill' had tried to recruit him.

Forte's inefficiency also infuriated my father. Contrary to all rules of espionage, Forte would arrive late for meetings, forget a meeting had been arranged, or turn up in the wrong place. He would confuse the Travellers with the RAF Club. As a result, standards slipped and subordinates followed Forte's lead.

My father said, 'I found if I was expecting a source at my house, I would be telephoned by countless people asking to give my source a message. Under "Geoffrey Kingsmill" this would never have happened. He was always careful about what was said over the telephone; and never informed people about my source's movements unless there was a good reason for them to know.'

On other occasions, Forte would call meetings with my father's sources, which, at my father's request and despite the risk to themselves, the sources attended. My father said, 'When we got to Alexis, we would find all he wanted to do was shoot the breeze. Or, he would leave immediately, as if ours was merely a social call we had instigated, rather than as he had demanded. He would then push off for lunch at L'escargot or go on holiday.'

It seemed Forte spent most of his life on holiday, whether or not my father was overseas, or, at SIS's invitation, expecting a visitor from abroad. This was ridiculous since the one thing a spy needed was continuity. One year, when there were significant political changes, Forte was off again within days. On the day the Basrah Petroleum Company in Iraq was nationalised, my father's diary reads, 'Alexis away. Says it will keep until his return from holiday.' My father's diaries are littered with comments such as 'Alexis on holiday. Cannot discuss Mosul proposal until his return.'

Other diary inclusions reflect the escalating problems in the Middle East. For example, one reference begins, 'Alexis returned from holiday. He telephoned to say he understands that Sandy had suddenly left Beirut for Cairo and that his office is closed down owing to the troubles in Beirut . . .'

Back in the office, Forte was disorganised. He would ask my father for specific information. When my father provided it, having gone to enormous trouble to obtain it, Forte had forgotten that he had asked for it in the first place, let alone why it was so important.

My father said, 'Once, Forte wanted some highly sensitive information. When I brought it back, he commented, "It's rather thin." He then told me to go back to my source (thereby putting my source at risk) and get better information. Had there been more information available, I would already have got it. Moreover, the intelligence I obtained was first-class. Nobody else could have got this much.'

If Forte was lax about safety, he was even more negligent about my father's non-espionage commercial contacts. These he tried to 'contaminate' by approaching them directly, using my father's name as an introduction. As a result, he jeopardised my father's life, as well as others'. These, hardly surprisingly, became frightened. Eventually, they ceased all contact with my father.

Forte even tried to involve/meet my father's relatives whose network was spread across three continents. Enraged, my father made his position clear, 'My family is sacred. You do not go anywhere near it.'

(At a later stage, my father introduced one member of his family, at his relative's request, to various SIS Whitehall civil servants. The relative had information relevant to the national interest. My father came to regret the introduction because he did not feel it had been in the family member's best interests to report it. In due course, my father became so anxious about the safety of his wider family, he cut off all contact. He ordered me to do the same, which I did. His anxieties arose following various, specific, SIS comments pertaining to the 'usefulness' of individuals, as well as derogatory comments about others.)

Forte also tried to force my father to travel on false documents. The suggestion was as ridiculous as it was hazardous. Firstly, my father was known in the Middle East. He had already been forced to snub a friend whom he had bumped into at an Arab airport, and this was when he was using his own papers. (The incident caused immense grief since my father was never able to explain the reason for his behaviour to his friend, or his friend's family.)

Secondly, my father had relatives in the region, who could similarly have identified him.

When my father refused to use a false passport, Forte aggressively tried to change his mind. My father said, 'This was sad for me. In all the years I travelled for SIS, I always trusted my colleagues to put my safety ahead of all other considerations. Alexis broke this trust. He wanted to play ill-conceived games. I believe he would have been a danger to any spy travelling into volatile situations, especially an inexperienced one, which, luckily, I was not.'[3]

On another occasion, Forte wanted my father to pretend to be a journalist on an obscure so-called English-language Arab magazine. My father told him that, since he was a businessman, he knew nothing about journalism and could not pretend to be a journalist, not least because in the Middle East he was known as the businessman he was. He had never heard of the magazine, which he should have done since it covered his area of knowledge.

When he asked to see back copies, none were produced. Eventually Forte said it was not a news magazine but a news agency. My father asked me about this and I checked with student friends. He could not believe how good their information was. I told him not to touch the 'news agency' with a barge pole, so he did not. I also gave him one specific detail which astonished my father and which Forte confirmed.

Finally, my father and Forte fell out because of their different views on the handling of sources. 'On one occasion,' remarked my father, 'Alexis rang to say that he would be unable to attend a meeting I had arranged with a potential and well-placed source. He said he was off to the country to go beagling. I blasted him. In the end he turned up but he was wearing country clothes and my guest fell apart laughing. He could not take him seriously. Because he was laughed at, Alexis refused to allow me to develop the source, who, in my opinion, could have been useful.'

Forte's attitude to my father's existing sources was similarly upsetting. In an attempt to play one off against the other, Forte thought nothing about approaching them behind my father's back. Without exception, they were loyal to my father because they did not trust 'an Englishman who says he is a Russian'. When they refused to be handled by Forte, he ordered my father to drop them.

Nor did Forte rate anecdotal information provided by superbly qualified patriotic British civil engineers, reporting to their companies about political instability/local power-brokers, in the countries in which they were working. He gave as his reason: 'The ambassador's good lady does not want to have to be polite to their wives at the Christmas Bazaar . . .'

This was frustrating for my father, who rated information on its quality, rather than the 'class' of the informant. Moreover it was the same arrogance that had annoyed him in 1960s Iraq when the British embassy had been so rude to the Irish, Scottish and Welsh contractors. It was as if Forte was stuck in a time-warp and had not moved on.

Forte was only comfortable with sources who accepted payment. This, again, put my father at a disadvantage since two of his senior sources refused all inducements, including money. As a result, Forte ordered my father to 'run down' the relationships. Forte described one source, in particular, as 'too rich'.

My father was furious, saying, 'Alexis would rather deal with those who have a price than with a man who cannot be bribed. It is ridiculous. The man is a man of honour.'

He continued, 'I told Alexis that Americans buy sources. SIS do not. Not only can we not compete – the Americans have more money than we do – but information that has a price can be sold several times and can be made up. Therefore, it does not always have a value since it cannot always be trusted.

'This meant nothing to Alexis. He wanted paid "informants". He used the term pejoratively. (There is an enormous amount of snootiness in whether a source is called a "source", "contact", or "informant".) He did not want me to have sources. Moreover, he was offended that I, who was not a British diplomat, had my own sources who would not report to him. He felt devalued that he was running informants, irrespective of their sometimes high social status and wealth, whereas I had very good sources.

'Then he began to take an interest in the Masonic Lodges of the Middle East and Eastern Europe. Turkey, in particular. I told Alexis to go to Grand Lodge if he wanted this sort of assistance. I was not prepared to give it. He did not care about endangering other people's lives. It meant nothing to him that freemasons were being slaughtered everywhere.'

NOTES

[1] SIS considered the first 'wardrobe' my father purchased, paid by the taxpayer, 'too discreet'. He therefore had to buy, also at the taxpayers' expense, 'a more vulgar wardrobe'.

[2] I have always been surprised that neither Colonel Oleg Gordiefsky, nor the archivist Vasili Mitrokhin, have ever referred to my father's Soviet friend Colonel Michael — . In case there are remaining sensitivities, I have similarly not named him.

[3] Former SIS staff officer Richard Tomlinson, in his autobiography *The Big Breach*, published by Cutting Edge Press in 2001, mentions that he travelled on a false passport on many occasions. Therefore, the Crown places staff and spy equally at risk. Civilian spies like my father, however, may not have the special forces training available to those like Tomlinson.

22

SOLD-OUT BY AN SIS CASE OFFICER

As the relationship between my father and Forte disintegrated, Forte suggested that my father offer his services to the CIA – something that a senior SIS agent would never agree to. Forte was attempting to imply that not only was my father simply an informer rather than an agent but also that he was not a patriot. To my mother's horror, Forte continued, 'The CIA would pay you exceptionally well. Nor would HMG mind. We would pop you straight in at the highest level. We would continue to pay you as well.'

My father replied, 'If I had wanted to be a CIA millionaire, I would have become one. There were always sufficient opportunities for me to do so. I work for my country. Her Majesty the Queen is my boss.'

He continued, 'This was a disappointment to Alexis. He was so rude about the Queen, whom he considered "bourgeois", that I replied, "I, too, am bourgeois, like my Queen." He looked down upon the Queen not because he was a Republican, he was not, but because of her class. In addition, he despised her belief in the Commonwealth.'

Forte wanted my father to become a mercenary. He hoped that my father would meekly fall into agreeing to work for SIS, CIA and probably the Iraqis or Israelis as well, so he was not a spy, but an 'informant' going to the highest bidder. Crucially, Forte did not believe that a brown-skin spy (my father) could be a British patriot. This caused my mother, in particular, untold anguish.

On one occasion, after I had complained about his treatment of my father, Forte told my mother mockingly, 'An Iraqi child always avenges the father.' The comment outraged her. It, rightly, recognised my pride in Iraq, the country where I was born. However, it also insulted my English blood, and her equal parentage.

He insisted that my father join the CIA to extend his shelf life. My father believed, 'What this actually meant was that either Alexis owed someone a favour, which he probably did, or, in his opinion, I would be killed sooner or later so I might as well make myself personally useful to him beforehand. When I refused to even consider working for the CIA – I am British, not an American, although I wish the United States well – he told me, "In which case, this is the end of the gravy train." But I had never been on a gravy train.

'I was livid. He kept telling me he had run spies all his life. This was probably true but my suspicion was that these, poor fools, were expendable. I do not know how many lives he had on his conscience.[1]

'He saw spies as pawns, not as colleagues, and wanted their loyalties and reputations confused so that they could be passed from one espionage service to the next, to his greater glory. He did not realise that there was such a thing as a Brown Englishman, which is how I saw myself, and thought only a white man, preferably an aristocrat, could have the honour to be a British patriot.

'He found my love for my country an insult to it.

'He told me he was "offering me such chances", as if I ought to be grateful to him. What he was offering was a one-way ticket to the graveyard. I told him that if he was so keen on triple agents, which can be the grander word for 'informants', working for many masters, and if such work was so important to SIS, he should offer his services to the Soviets since he was a Russian, and become a triple agent himself. Alexis went mad and said, "How dare you say this. I am a British diplomat. We do not do that sort of thing. There would be an international incident."

'Unlike the other SIS men with whom I served, who shared all the risks with me, and in "Geoffrey Kingsmill's" case, took greater risks, Alexis did not risk his own life, only other people's. If I can offer any advice to a new generation of spies, it is this: only work with a case officer who values life, and shares all the risks with you.'

Shortly afterwards, my father hosted a military delegation from an Islamic country whose members were stopping in London before flying to Paris. His work involved giving all-day lectures, 'including one on The Service'. In the evening, he took some of its members for dinner at the Serpentine in Hyde Park. The following day, he offered a similar lecture programme, 'with a break for lunch at the RAF Club where Alexis arrived late when he should have been there to meet them'.

My father was disgusted because it was an insult to the country concerned, and commented, 'This sort of behaviour could cost the UK a commercial contract.' By the end of the week, and having torn Forte off a strip, my father noted in his diary that the delegation's final meeting with the diplomat went well. Forte, he said, 'was on tip-top behaviour and very good'.

Forte tried to exercise power in petty ways. For example, he expected my father to fund personally SIS trips overseas, saying that 'The Office' would sort things out on my father's return. My father refused, forcing Forte into a climb-down. Far more serious was the fact that Forte was responsible for my father's salary, and denied him all pay increases.[2]

In the end, my father was in the ridiculous position of paying his own sources, whose pay increases he negotiated himself, substantially more than he was being paid. When he pointed out to Forte that 'Geoffrey Kingsmill' had pegged his salary to the appropriate civil service grade, Forte denied all knowledge of the agreement. This had serious implications for my father's rank, salary and pension.[3]

I wanted my father to tackle the problem immediately but he was too embarrassed to do so. He thought that it would have looked as if he was begging. As a result, he never made up the lost ground. My mother, on the other hand, wanted him to 'shut the chapter', as she put it. She was disgusted and wanted nothing more to do with Forte or SIS.

Forte's refusal to pay my father appropriately did not stop him from asking my father, on behalf of a friend, to prepare a detailed report on an industry my father knew well, most especially the relevant markets overseas. My father was so shocked by Forte's brazenness that he replied, 'If one of your cronies wants a market report, Alexis, get him to pay for it.' Forte never asked again.

However, Forte got his revenge by mentioning the amount SIS was paying a man now based in the West whom my father had recruited in Iraq in the 1960s. Forte claimed the man was 'productive'. He could not have hurt my father more, first, because my father was a patriot, when the man was not, although he had been given British nationality; second, because the implication was that my father was not 'productive'.

My father said, 'Although the man had indeed been "productive" when I was running him, he was now no more than a very wealthy crook. Alexis knew this even better than I did. But then, Alexis preferred crooks to patriots.'[4]

'My wife and I were scandalised. Not for the first time, we were sad that "Geoffrey Kingsmill" was still overseas. This sort of thing would never have happened if he had been around. He was completely scrupulous in all matters financial.'

The final collapse in the relationship between my father and Alexis Forte came as a result of the UK's change of policy in Iraq, when the regime in Baghdad started buying Western technology (having stopped buying from the less-advanced Soviets). One evening in 1975, my father came home shattered, telling us 'SIS is happy with Saddam Hussein. HMG wants to encourage him.'

One of the results of this change was that HMG ditched the Iraqi Kurds, on the basis that 'The Crown cannot sacrifice billions of pounds' worth of trade with Iraq for the Kurds.'

At the time, Saddam Hussein was powerful in the Iraqi government but not yet president. (Although the British press date President Hussein's rise from the start of his presidency in 1979, my father, and in consequence SIS, had been charting it immediately following the second Ba'ath revolution in July 1968. I believe that of all the foreign intelligence services, SIS's knowledge was the most sophisticated and informed. From the late '60s onwards, I grew up knowing that Saddam Hussein was the 'strongman' of Iraq.)

My father had heard from his sources that the Crown was now in favour of Saddam Hussein, but had not believed them. The realisation that they were correct came as a profound shock. He said, 'What sort of intelligence service was SIS running when I heard the facts from the men I was running and not from my colleagues? When I queried HMG's attitude towards Iraq, Alexis informed me it was not my business to determine service policy or to jib.

'He made it clear that my anguish was of no interest. I felt totally confused and without an identity any more. All the work I had been doing had had one goal. To get rid of Saddam Hussein and the regime in Baghdad. I had no idea that either this was never the goal or it had changed. SIS's heart had turned to stone.'

HMG's change of policy was one of the many bitter blows that accompanied my father's increasing disillusionment with the service he had once been so proud to serve.

What particularly upset him was that he was made 'to look duplicitous with my sources. Alexis did not seem to realise that we had let people down who trusted us. Lives were meaningless to him.

'I wrote a detailed report setting out my anxieties about HMG's reputation, in the long-term, if we reneged on the promises we had made to the Kurds. No government can hope to influence a region if its intelligence services cannot be trusted. Alexis did not know what I was talking about. This was not surprising. He never understood the Middle East, despised Semites – be they Christian, Jew or Muslim – and had no interest in the direction in which the Middle East was headed.[5]

'He thought things should be the same as in Iran, when he advised the Shah how to control the people. He thought the Shah of Iran was a model for the rest of the area.'

NOTES

[1] An anxiety echoed by Sir Dick White, as told to Tom Bower in *A Perfect English Spy: Sir Dick White and the Secret War 1935–90*, published by Heinemann in 1995: p. 236.

[2] All prospective spies could keep in mind that there are enormous conflicts of interest inherent in the system, i.e. the intelligence services combining the role of agent, while commissioning agents' services, while being advocates for individual agents, while being a commissioner of services.

[3] When my father retired and was in poor health, I tried to argue with SIS that his pension had been calculated from far too low a base. I tried again, after his death, in an effort to have my mother's SIS widows' pension raised. I was unsuccessful in both attempts. Because of the Official Secrets Act, I was not allowed independent professional advice, any more than my father had been; nor, prior to 1994, was I allowed a lawyer, or to be accompanied at any meeting with SIS. (For more on pensions, see Part Two, Chapter 27 and Part Three, Chapter 34.)

[4] In espionage, a crook can be a fearless, patriotic and intelligent source, as well as being a capable all-rounder. My father came across one such man during his SIS career and was proud to deal with him on behalf of the Crown. He came across others, however, whom he advised the Crown to avoid. It did not do so.

[5] Alexis Forte said, 'The only good thing about the Kurds is that they are Aryans.' He swung between calling them 'peasants' or thinking of them as 'noble savages'.

He was furious when I said, 'Given my grandmother was Kurdish, which category do you think I come under?'

23

THE SIS 'NO NAMES'

At about roughly the same time as my father was shattered by his discovery that
SIS was backing Saddam Hussein came the introduction into his working life of
the 'No Names'. These were SIS officers who staffed a joint SIS–MI5–Special
Branch section responsible for tracking Middle Eastern terrorists.[1] My family
called them the 'No Names' because they had aliases. Alexis Forte took great
pride in telling my father that, 'As a diplomat, I am allowed to know who they
are. You are not.'

My father protested about working with them – 'I work with diplomats and
civil servants whose identity I can verify' – but could do nothing about the
situation.

The relationship with the No Names was problematic from the beginning.
My father described them as 'hyperactive young men, wanting to prove
themselves, with nothing to do, and no one controlling them. Their ignorance of
the Middle East was equal to that of Alexis. In addition, they had no respect for
age or experience, and did not want to learn anything.

'I could not believe SIS's Middle Eastern expertise had come to this. After all
my years of service with SIS, and our once-superb Middle Eastern capabilities, it
now boiled down to Alexis and vicious puppies learning at his feet. Like him,
they despised anyone who was not a white man.'

This, my father believed, turned SIS's one-time cosmopolitanism on its head,
plunging it into right-wing supremacism. In his opinion, Forte and the No
Names, whose conduct the diplomat encouraged, collapsed SIS's international
prestige, so essential to quality recruitment. It broke my father's heart.

(It is worth remembering that during the '70s, especially during the strikes
and the four-day week in 1974, there was considerable anxiety about left-wing
militants in Britain working to overthrow democracy and capitalism – a situation
that was to contribute to Thatcher's rise to power in 1979. For this reason, it is

possible to understand why SIS recruitment during the '70s was predominantly from the right wing – including the extreme right – and in retrospect looks like a knee-jerk reaction to the militants on the left.)

The No Names were jealous of my father's business career, and his overseas work on SIS's behalf. They did not understand that they were in secure employment when a businessman was not; nor that my father was sent abroad, with all the attendant risks, because he had the contacts and necessary skills, including a knowledge of the Arabic language, which they did not.

No allowance was made for his age – he was 56. As a result, the No Names could not understand why he refused to run around in London nightclubs and similar places in Soho frequented by young Arab men. Instead of backing up my father, Forte accused him of being 'obstructive'.

My father held his ground, telling him, 'With my grey hairs, I am not the age for this sort of work. You require young men to haunt the dives other young men frequent.' He added for good measure, 'Since you have such a young wife, and are used to her age-group, the job would suit you admirably. Particularly as you are at a loose end.'

My father's skills were particularly needed to sift through visa applications in order to spot the 'Nasties'. While recognising the importance of this work, he felt that he had gone from, under 'Geoffrey Kingsmill', producing sophisticated political intelligence well received by Whitehall, and knowing all the senior civil servants concerned; to, under Alexis Forte, doing police work with men he could not identify, who were not his age, had no respect for him and whom he did not like. Nevertheless, often in poor health, my father worked, hour after hour, analysing thousands of visa applications to protect Londoners from terrorism. In this work, he was sometimes ably assisted by one of his most respected sources.[2]

My mother and I were appalled at the way Forte was treating him. We felt that it was stupid for Whitehall to waste his age and experience – which is how the Arab world functions – and Forte knew it. He kept assuring us that my father would go back to Whitehall work eventually but we knew that this would never happen. Forte had wanted to marginalise my father and had succeeded.

Nor did Forte accept that while my father was scanning visas, he could not run his own business – the process is exhausting not least because it is so labour intensive and tedious. Whenever my father mentioned this, Forte made snide remarks about my father's patriotism being suspect.

Eventually, the two men had another big bust-up. My father said, 'I made it clear to Alexis again and again I did not wish to work with the No Names, but he was exceptionally nasty. The next day, the visa pile was even bigger.'

Yet again, Forte refused to give my father a proper pay-rise – I challenge SIS to release details of his salary during this period. The No Names, who, as staff, were on full salaries, did nothing. This was not surprising since they did not know anything about the Middle East so could not spot people anyway.

In addition, their racism, coupled with that of Forte's, ate into my father. Only those who have themselves been on the receiving end of this will understand its impact. He was exhausted and over-worked; it destroyed him.

I regarded Alexis Forte with a contempt I can still remember. He could not meet my eyes. I had been raised in this country – I knew the stunts he and the revolting group of young men who surrounded him were playing. My father was frightened of the No Names. It was as simple as that.

They had absolutely no respect for anybody's culture, education or history. Faith meant nothing to them, whether a man was a Christian, Jew or Muslim. They praised the vain-glory of a British bishop who preferred the company of rich businessmen, politicians and generals to that of his flock, because the bishop was famous. However, the Church he represented so godlessly meant nothing to them.

They defined those from overseas under religious 'labels' such as Sunni or Shiite, without knowing anything about those they 'labelled'. (Not all Muslims define themselves by religious identity, any more than Christians or Jews do.) Nor did they know anything about the simplicity of faith or a Muslim's code of conduct.

'For example, the Muslim's have a beautiful system of asking for "Sanctuary",' explained my father. 'This means that if a particular request is made, it cannot be refused. I used it once in my SIS work, and once in a personal matter, on behalf of a relative. It is a system full of honour, humanity and dignity. The No Names had no respect for it. They had no desire to learn anything about other people, even though I was happy to teach them.'[3]

'Many years later it was explained to me that the poor calibre of staff in SIS and MI5 at this time was because it is only in wartime that good people sign up.' (This is why MI5 started employing women from the 'traditional' families, i.e. to take the jobs their brothers had spurned.)

'The No Names knew so little about the Middle East that they had the idea if an Arab put on a tie instead of wearing his traditional Arab robes, he was Westernised! These were supposed to be trained intelligence officers! I politely pointed out that the most sophisticated and pro-Western Arabs could also wear traditional Arab robes; while the most anti-Western, especially anti-British, might not only never wear traditional Arab dress, but have his entire wardrobe made in Paris.'

My father was also uncomfortable with the No Names' attitude to women. On one occasion, he heard that they had employed people to go through rubbish bins to find out whether a man's wife was using the contraceptive pill. (This gave an indication as to how modern or Western an Arab husband was.) The man also had teenage female relatives with him. My father found the No Names' speculation about these young girls distasteful.

Nor did they have any understanding of the Islamic sense of honour. For example, the Muslims had a system of exchanging money from one part of the world to another, and everybody from the Middle East was aware of it. It was based entirely on trust. 'The No Names,' said my father, 'thought that only an English gentleman understood the expression, "My word is my bond." That only the British knew how to be honourable. Then they twisted what I said as if, by using the system, all that people were trying to do was get around exchange controls. They could not accept virtue in others. When confronted with it, they had to dirty it.'

My father was particularly concerned that SIS was no longer receiving appropriate Middle Eastern political analysis. 'It was as though the British, who had once been brilliant analysts and strategic thinkers, were no longer interested in what was happening in the world, but only in terrorism,' he remarked sadly.

To this extent, the terrorists won. The focus was hardly surprising – young men are much more likely to be excited by terrorism than learning about people.

My father said, 'I told Alexis again and again that the Middle East is not run by young men, even if the Foreign Office was trying to develop the careers of a new generation of British diplomats, including SIS ones. In response, Alexis said that SIS had "As much information as it can cope with" – most of it commercial. This was not, and never was, the political information that the Crown needed.'

Possibly because they knew that my father was criticising them, the No Names continued to give him a hard time. My mother and I never forgave SIS, particularly 'Geoffrey Kingsmill', for abandoning him to them and Forte. Whenever we saw 'Kingsmill' he told my father to 'Give Alexis time. Scratch the surface of the man and you will see how good he is.' If he really thought that, he was a fool. As for the No Names, 'Kingsmill' never made any comment about them except to say, 'This is the new system.'

My father particularly disliked having to socialise with the No Names. 'Alexis loved it,' he said, 'because they made him feel younger. I, on the other hand, had no desire to feel younger. I liked my age and maturity.

'On one occasion, Alexis complimented me, ostentatiously, in front of these men, on my beautiful daughter. Next – later he called it "only joshing" – he said to one of the men present that he should ask for my daughter's phone number. I lost my temper. He had no business mentioning my daughter in the company of these men. Alexis' response was that I was being "Too protective. Your daughter is in a free country and must go out with whom she wishes. This is not the Middle East, you know."

'I replied, "I know that this is not the Middle East. I moved heaven and earth to get her out of that hell hole. I did not send her to England, however, for a British diplomat to be her pimp with British policemen." He flushed to the roots and apologised immediately. When I got home, I told my wife what had happened. The next morning she telephoned Alexis and told him to visit her at his earliest convenience.

'He came immediately. My wife did not even invite him to sit down. She wiped the floor with him. By the time she had finished, Alexis was almost weeping. After this, my daughter was never mentioned in front of the No Names again.

'Subsequently, a female No Name became involved. She was introduced to me as "Wave". As always, I was not allowed to know her real name. She was the liaison between SIS and MI5 and Alexis regarded her as something of an "office pet" – his expression, not mine – not least because her father had been in the service. Some years after I retired, she drove past my house when I was working in my garden. She stopped and chatted for about half an hour. In the course of this, she identified herself as Wave — . She also gave me her address, which was only seconds from where we lived. She retired in 1984.

'The introduction of the woman No Name, in many respects, made the situation worse. First of all, she knew even less about the Middle East than did Alexis and the male No Names. Second, presumably as instructed, she kept trying to insert herself into my family.' Forte apparently was particularly insistent on this one. He kept suggesting to my father, 'Invite her for tea this weekend, I know she is not doing anything. She would so much like to meet your wife and daughter.'

This particularly upset my mother, who did not want 'either an SIS diplomat or a woman No Name to have any influence over my daughter'. Her anxiety was based on the fact Forte had again told my father that SIS could 'always approach your daughter without your knowledge. She is over 18 and an adult.'

My father refused to allow the woman No Name anywhere near my mother or myself. Forte was insisting that my father introduce his family to a woman whose name he did not even know. In addition, he was specifying that I be included, which caused huge rows with my mother. It was the final straw.

NOTES

[1]   The office was closed by Dame Stella Rimington, then head of MI5, in 1994 on the basis that it was concentrating too closely on political information rather than on terrorism. Also that year, the late Sir David Spedding, who had been closely involved with it, became SIS Chief. My father believed that in his day the reverse was true, i.e. it did not concentrate on political information at all.

[2]   Dame Stella Rimington, in her autobiography *Open Secret*, published by Hutchinson in 2001, omitted to mention the 1970s fight to clear Iraqi hit-squads off the streets of London. Had she been able to mention this, I am sure she would have paid tribute to the work of those like my father and his source, and been frank about the poor calibre of the then staff.

[3]   Post-11 September, I believe that had the American government couched many of its pronouncements in dignified Islamic terms, rather than the language used, and, in particular, shown awareness of the system my father described, some of the unhelpful polarisation could have been avoided.

24

'NOBODY RESIGNS FROM SIS'

At my mother's instigation, my father submitted his resignation to SIS for the second time. Forte was ashen-faced when he finished reading it. He said, 'We can sort this out.' But my father refused.

That evening came a whole series of nuisance calls. One was from someone who, apparently, thought my father had a lock-up garage available. We did not connect this until the following morning, when the local police telephoned to say that my father's car had been found. We did not even know it was missing. Apparently, it had been stolen from my father's lock-up garage, at the bottom of his garden, which had been tidily relocked, his car's disappearance and whereabouts then reported to the police.

'The police informed me that it had been taken to Dagenham, where the Ford Motor Car company is,' said my father. 'It took me hours to get there. When I arrived, apart from row upon row of cars, the place was completely deserted. As it was so isolated, I was anxious about my safety. Anything could have happened. When I found my car, I was expecting the worst. In fact it was in perfect condition and, additionally, had been cleaned and was full of petrol.

'The following day, Alexis telephoned as cool as a cucumber about a meeting with one of my sources that had been arranged before I had handed in my resignation. I attended the meeting. I had learned my lesson. As his predecessor "Geoffrey Kingsmill" had once said, "Nobody resigns from SIS".'

The harassment that my father endured, which started in the mid-1970s as an attempt to stop him resigning, went on, in bursts, until he died in 1986. For example, one day he went out for a walk with my mother. Returning home, he found a poster of a mad dog on his desk with the caption, 'Keep Rabies out of Britain'. He was shattered.

Other problems were constant. Our telephone echoed non-stop, and there were all sorts of clicks and buzzing. Sometimes snippets of conversation referring to HMG could be heard. Every time my father complained, something else happened – the heavily weighted birdcage in his high-walled garden was transported from one end to the next; a stranger, having made it known that he had gained entry into our house, left, relocking the front door with his own key. On the first-floor landing, we found a carefully arranged display of hard-core pornography. The security in the house had been put in by SIS.

My father said, 'These were dreadful times for my wife, daughter and myself. It cut us off from our civilian friends to whom we could not explain what was happening. As a result, we were thrown back in on ourselves. Only we knew what was going on. To this day, I do not know how we remained normal. Actually, I did not remain normal. I think I slowly began to go mad. But my wife and daughter were always normal. They were wonderful. Always giggling and laughing as if they did not have a care in the world. Real life, they said, goes on. All of this meant, of course, that our daughter did not leave home as early as her other friends, when we knew she wanted to. She was her mother's best friend and could not leave us to it.'

My father made endless complaints about what was happening. Forte laughed, not unkindly, and said, 'Oh ignore it, it is only a try-on. I'll mention it.' His feeling was, 'They are only being boisterous, having a bit of fun.' He said my father did not understand their 'boyish camaraderie'. On a different occasion he said, 'It must be some swain your daughter has rejected.' Forte, it is worth noting, had the power to stop the harassment at any time if he chose to do so.

Then came the repeated anonymous telephone calls as to whether my father had any guns in the house. 'Of course I did not,' said my father. 'The one and only time I had asked for one, "Geoffrey Kingsmill" had refused.' Next, Forte kept offering him a gun. When my father said that he did not want one, it was as if his manhood was in question. Guns were literally being chucked at him. Then came the phone calls, asking if he was 'All right'. My father replied, 'Of course, why shouldn't I be?' Finally, came the messages asking if he needed any protection for his wife and daughter.

My father said, 'My wife went mad. She was petrified something was going to happen to our daughter. Once I caught her crying. It broke my heart. In all our married life, this was her only reproach to me. I went to see Alexis. He flatly denied what was happening. He said we were inventing things or "getting paranoid".

'On the spur of the moment, I said that I wanted my daughter to join SIS. It was the only thing I could think of, to protect her. When I told my wife, I saw her spirit break. Alexis replied, "Your daughter does not meet SIS criteria."'

(Forte had mentioned 'SIS criteria' when I was still a student. He told me SIS candidates had to be 'The sort of people who walked up escalators.' This, he said, 'Showed a sense of purpose' and made it difficult for women 'because of their high heels.' He was less than amused when I pointed out that he would not know what an escalator looked like since he always took taxis.)

My father continued, 'Alexis had spent all those years chasing after my daughter, only to insult me. He added that SIS would consider her "untrustworthy" because of her mixed race. As if he was a "pure" Englishman himself, when he was not. When I said that this was not what "Geoffrey Kingsmill" had said, Alexis responded, "'Geoffrey' is wrong. Besides, there is a question mark over his children too, because of their foreign mother. You must have misunderstood him."

'Alexis continued, "Your daughter would be treated as a second-class citizen. We can take her passport at any time. She was not born to it. Only her mother is entitled to her British passport. Your daughter is not the sort of candidate to interest SIS."

'But I had not misunderstood "Geoffrey". He had made it clear he was interested in my daughter for SIS. I had not told her, however, principally because I did not want her involved in it. "Geoffrey" had himself admitted that he did not want his own children signing up. Since it was not good enough for them, I did not see why it should be good enough for mine. Besides, I did not like the idea of young girls being sent to inhospitable places.'

My father was aware of the latter because of the fate of one of my academically gifted older schoolfriends, who had joined the diplomatic service after university. Another reason why he had not mentioned 'Kingsmill's' interest was because he believed that some espionage-children could be encouraged to consider SIS as a career, so that if things went wrong with their parent's employment, the father could not complain because of embarrassment or threat to the child's future career prospects. 'This way,' he said, 'SIS can control the family, not only for the present, but the future. Things have changed. The British diplomat is not what he used to be. He can recruit a child, turn it against his family and destroy both.'

Nevertheless, to make his point, he submitted a formal application to Forte on my behalf:

> In January this year, while in private conversation with 'Geoffrey' the idea was put to me that on her graduation from SOAS, my daughter might possibly wish to join the firm and it was suggested that either I tell her or, if I so wished, the firm could arrange a direct approach to her for recruitment [. . .]

My father said that I was enthusiastic

> [. . .] because of the atmosphere at home and her awareness of my own activities, past and present [. . .]
>
> [. . .] I fully appreciated your very discouraging attitude and remarks of her expecting to be treated as a 'second-class citizen' without any hope of seniority because of her sex. I would like to point out that in our private discussions last January, 'Geoffrey' was reassuring in respect

of sex when he pointed out that many ladies had attained high positions and were even decorated for their services in the firm. These conflicting attitudes would indeed be very confusing to a young girl who thinks of herself as *very English and a first-class citizen in the UK irrespective of her sex or foreign birth.* At any rate, please accept this as a formal application [. . .]

My mother was white-faced when he told her what he had done. He said sadly, 'My wife considered it to be a betrayal of her and our 20-year-old daughter.'

To reinforce the application, my father also telephoned a retired SIS diplomat with whom he had worked in Iraq, Keith Womersely, and asked him to go and see Forte. So far as I am aware, he did so.

In due course, a letter arrived from a government department stating, '[. . .] I understand from a mutual friend of your father that you are at present seeking employment and would be interested in a discussion of career possibilities [. . .]' Although I had no desire to join SIS, I went along with what was happening in the hope that it would protect my parents and stop the harassment. A short while later, my father saw Forte again.

He said, 'Alexis was evasive about the level of harassment I had been enduring. However, he was absolutely adamant my daughter was safe. I believed him. He knew what a storm I had kicked up. He also knew that I would kill him if anything happened to her. When I got home, I told my daughter to write to the government department concerned to withdraw her application, which she did.'

Several months later came the celebration of my 21st birthday at a private nightclub. My father said, 'Alexis wanted to come to my daughter's party with his young wife. He dropped so many hints, it was embarrassing. I am sure his wife had no liking for our company, far less for that of my daughter's student friends. It was all Alexis. In the end, I had to tell him the truth, which he resented – i.e. I did not want a middle-aged diplomat at my daughter's party.

'Eventually, my wife and I invited the Fortes to dinner at a separate venue, and joined the young people after midnight, which I thought was a good compromise.'

By the time Alexis Forte was posted to Paris in April 1977, the two men were scarcely on speaking terms. Forte left my father before a new case officer had been appointed. As a result, my father reported to a woman No Name who knew absolutely nothing about the Middle East and vetoed an SIS visit to West Germany 'Without having even a minor understanding of what was at stake.'

Eventually, my father's final SIS case officer became available. In July 1977, Forte returned from Paris to hand over and introduce them. The three men had dinner at the Poissonerie in Chelsea. My father noted in his diary, 'Dreadful evening. I walked out on them as Alexis was rude to me. He phoned at 1.15 a.m. to apologise.'

A few days later the three men, plus a source, met again. My father wrote in his diary, 'It was at first tense between me and Alexis but he kept offering his apologies. The air was finally cleared and we parted as friends.'

They never met again.

25

A FIRST-JOBBER'S VIEW OF SIS

By the time Forte left the country, I was 22 and, at long last, planning on leaving my parents' home as soon as I could support a mortgage. One consequence was that I knew my father's final SIS case officer, Ken Boswell, and his wife, the least.[1] In addition, following the disruptive years of 'Life with Forte', I distanced myself from my father's new colleague, and refused to be present on various occasions.

However, the few times I met Ken Boswell, I liked him. My father did too. In his diary, he described their first business meeting after Forte had left the country as 'delightful and constructive'. They met at the Ritz with one of my father's sources.

Although eventually there were criticisms on either side, Ken Boswell, while coping with his own anxieties and disappointments, did his best to restore the trust that Forte had betrayed. I believe, however, that the breakdown in the relationship between my father and SIS had gone too far by the time Boswell took over for him to be effective. (In espionage, trust takes years to develop. It can be undone in minutes.) Therefore, Boswell had an impossible task. I am proud to record my memory of him in warmest appreciation of what he tried to do.

He was particularly kind when my father went into hospital – when, incidentally, SIS is always at its most humane, providing the finest care and hospital consultants. My father was able to keep on working and good facilities were made available so he could continue to meet his sources. At the time, he was grooming an important new one. This person, SIS hoped, would replace another of my father's sources who had had a heart attack. My father's diary is full of meetings and events. There was a great deal going on.

There were four things about Ken Boswell that I liked.

First, he was happy in the company of women. Second, he understood young people brought up in 'town' as opposed to 'country' and was not arrogant about the divide. (I believe it is this divide that cut off the majority of SIS personnel from reality. For the most part, they looked down upon those who were 'urban'. This tendency was exaggerated after an overseas posting.)

Third, he was not snooty about sources. Unlike Forte, he never referred to them as 'informants'. Nor did he use other pejorative terms.

Fourth, and again unlike Forte, he tried to get on with everyone.

Nevertheless, the harassment to which my father had been previously subjected – which had nothing to do with Ken Boswell – returned. When my father reported it to an SIS civil servant responsible for looking into such matters, he noted in his diary that the civil servant responded, 'If it is happening, it is not organised. It is at an individual level.' I believe this attitude allowed SIS to condone the harassment, while pretending to be at arm's length from it; or, if not condoning it, allowed my father's colleagues to escape the bother of doing anything about it.

Soon after came the accusation that my father had harassed an SIS secretary.

'I was waiting for this one,' commented my mother.

The young woman was never produced; moreover, my father's poor health made the type of accusation unlikely. As my mother dryly observed, 'The young lady [maiden and married name withheld] still managed to arrange collection of her wedding present.'

Of the many things SIS did, this accusation was one of the worst. My father was so distressed about it, he telephoned my mother from a call-box to come and meet him, because he could not concentrate on his driving and was frightened of having an accident. That night, and already a sick man, he sobbed until dawn. A week later 'The Office' reported, 'Oh, let's forget it. There was probably a misunderstanding. In fact, it might have been another chap.'

What SIS so airily dismissed – having caused, because of the injustice, maximum anguish – continued to play upon my father's mind. As always, my mother and, to a certain extent, myself were left to pick up the pieces. (In espionage, middle-aged and/or elderly men can spend long periods with young SIS women, in hotel rooms, apartments and cars. These, along with young people everywhere, must be protected from unwanted advances. However, I believe that there should be a formal procedure so that, if an accusation is made, a man is able to clear his name. This would have avoided the devastation that it caused in my family.)

A short while later, my father was advised that he would be retiring in six months. However, for whatever reason, 'The Office' soon changed its mind. This happened several times and we did not know where we stood. Eventually, it was confirmed that 'The Office' wanted my father to continue. Nevertheless, he had to hand over one of his key sources. He did so, despite warning SIS that its staff were not the most appropriate to handle sources from the Middle East, not least because they did not speak sufficiently good Arabic.

The handover took place at the Great Western Hotel, Paddington. My father said, 'My source was astonished. Middle Easterners have no understanding of Whitehall's culture of retirement. As for Whitehall, it has no understanding of espionage. Civil servants retire; spies do not. Not least because their sources are not parcels to be passed from one man to the next.

'My source watched in astonishment as, having handed him over, I made my excuses and left. I was no longer allowed to be privy to discussions. This was not only humiliating, but silly.

'I felt, but I could be wrong, that SIS was trying to bring everything in-house to be handled by the staff. This can be sensible. However, the source that I handed over, who was polite but bemused, subsequently came to see me. He could not work with Englishmen – which I always knew would be the case – had made his excuses to SIS and ceased contact. It was a great mistake on SIS's part.' The source was subsequently lost altogether.

Having handed over his source, SIS suggested that my father 'break into a new field'. He considered this but, after discussing it with my mother, excused himself on age grounds, and the fact, 'I might become even more exposed and vulnerable than I already am. Safety standards are not what they once were.'[2]

My father had also been unsettled by the accusation of sexual harassment and did not feel that he could trust SIS any longer. ('If they are prepared to do this, what else can they do?') More importantly, he was worried about the fact 'There are too many No Names operating. These believe taking risks with a spy's life is what espionage is all about. These men are cheap. They crave excitement. They think they are spies but devalue the career.'

SIS accepted my father's refusal with great reluctance. A considerable effort was made to try to restore his confidence. However, because SIS had not tackled the internal problems my father had encountered when he first reported them, he had lost faith in them. He had had to cope with it all, unsupported, for years.

Eventually realising that he was not going to change his mind, SIS urged my father to develop his business. This infuriated him. Returning from another long meeting, he told my mother, 'SIS do not seem to realise that I have been sucked dry under Alexis, and have lost my business. If it was this simple, do they not think that I would have done it already? Now, every time I am in contact with businessmen from the Middle East, they run away from me. It is so well known that I have been working for HMG they are frightened of "contamination", and who can blame them? Unlike SIS, I have a conscience and will not endanger the lives of others.'

As a result, far from developing his business, and despite the fact that his accountant did all he could to dissuade him, my father closed his company. Meantime, problems pertaining to the Middle East escalated.

Death threats in London, including those made against my father, became a sinister and regular occurrence. A short while later, a source complained about an article in a British newspaper. It was detailed, endangered life and the information it contained could only have come from someone within SIS.

My father raised the matter with his colleagues. The following morning, his car disappeared again from his locked garage. As per the usual pattern, the local police telephoned to say where it had been located. As always, he had not reported it missing.

He commented bitterly to my mother, 'I make a legitimate criticism, on behalf of my source, at a very tense time, and this is what happens. How can they be involved in this sort of nasty rubbish, when there are so many serious things happening? All my warnings are going unheeded.'

Nor was my father impressed by SIS personnel overseas. He was astonished when Ken Boswell sheepishly reported that one of my father's overseas suggestions had been vetoed by 'the man on the spot'. The latter had concluded a particular nightclub, which had formed part of my father's submission, was 'a place of ill-repute'. This was not only rather the point, the nightclub concerned was no more, or less, 'a place of ill-repute' than the grandest anywhere in the world.

At the time, I did not know that 'the man on the spot' was (Sir) David Spedding, later to become SIS Chief, although my father did, making the comment, 'The plan has been sabotaged by that pip-squeak who was in Beirut.'

There would have been several reasons why David Spedding, who died in 2001, exercised his veto. The ones I know about, confirmed by the case officer, did him no credit. Moreover, he was wrong and wholly misjudged an important matter. In societies where power rests with age, those like Spedding (in 1978, Spedding was 35) do not always have the judgement to understand the subtleties of political information and/or contacts, from which circle in any event they are often excluded. Especially if they are British diplomats. This is where spies come in. Or ought to.

(In one of life's amazing twists, Spedding subsequently became responsible for Middle Eastern intelligence during the Gulf War (see Part Three, Chapter 33.) Although my father died nearly four years before the war, he left clear instructions for the handling of information he knew would arrive after his death. Spedding's officers failed to progress the intelligence.)

In due course, Ken Boswell, nearing the end of his own career, went on holiday for six weeks.

Despite it being 'a very busy period, requiring sophisticated knowledge', my father was left to liaise with a woman No Name from MI5 whose knowledge and professionalism he did not respect. On his return, a furious Ken Boswell 'suggested a one-year sabbatical, which I turned down, because of the poor relationship with the woman'.

To his credit, Boswell had been concerned about my father's chauvinism. However, sometimes chauvinists can be right. Certainly, the complaint detailed in my father's diary is one I would have upheld since I knew all the circumstances. In Boswell's long absence, my father had made his objections about the woman No Name concerned to another, more senior woman No

Name called 'Stella', also from MI5. His diary reference begins, 'Had a meeting in my car with Stella. We discussed —.' I have always wondered whether the 'Stella' to whom he made his complaint was Stella Rimington, who was to rise to become the head of the Security Services.

Despite the upset about my father's undeniable chauvinism, Ken Boswell soon told him that another 'interesting proposal' had emerged. My father was immediately excited about it. He said, 'I swung between wanting nothing more to do with "The Firm" and still wanting to be a part of it. Apart from my wife and children, it had been my life. In addition, I knew SIS needed my Middle Eastern expertise – in many respects more than when it first recruited me – because it had so few Arabists.

'However, when the proposal was put to me in detail, I declined. My wife and I agreed that although Ken fully understood my anxieties about safety, his superiors had not taken them on board. This was a disappointment for all concerned, including myself. Ken asked me "to sleep on things", but my mind was made up.

'In my early days, danger was not something that bothered me unduly. I had complete confidence in my SIS colleagues, from Sandy Goschen to "Geoffrey Kingsmill". However, by the time Ken came on the scene, I was not convinced SIS had the will to protect me. I was, you see, not an Englishman. This made no difference to Ken, who was a gentleman. His No Name colleagues, however, were not. By the tail end of my career, SIS had been taken over by those who believed a brown man could never be a patriot. Therefore, a brown man's skin was not worth protecting.'

A short while later, my father's Crown service ended in documented catastrophe for which SIS accepted full responsibility. It could do little else. My father had specifically warned his colleagues as to what was about to happen.

No amount of retirement lunches at Simpsons, or dinners at the Travellers and RAF Clubs, could disguise his grief at SIS's mishandling of serious matters.

It was a sad end to a long career in a service he had once been so proud to serve.

NOTES

[1] Ken Boswell was born in 1924. He joined the British Middle East Office in 1952, becoming third secretary at the British embassy in Baghdad the following year. He was promoted to second secretary in Djakarta in 1956. Four years later he returned to the Foreign Office in London, before being promoted to first secretary in Kuwait in 1961. He later served in Teheran for four years, 1963–67, before returning to Djakarta as first secretary in 1967. He returned to the Foreign and Commonwealth Office in 1970 and retired in 1978.
Source: 'A Who's Who of the British Secret State', *Lobster* special (1989).

[2] Safety standards are an issue in SIS and MI5. For example, a confidential MI5 report

in respect of Northern Ireland in the 1980s, quoted in the *Guardian*, 14 June 2001, states '[. . .] It is important to ensure that information provided by the person so recruited is handled in such a way that his value as an agent is not put at risk at an early stage . . .', i.e. the Crown places no priority on the spy's safety, merely his/her 'value'.

In an interview with the *Guardian*, 13 September 2001, Dame Stella Rimington talks of 'terrorism bringing a different level of risk – physical danger to the staff – but also, of course, the risk to members of the public . . .' She makes no mention of the danger to spies, who, according to her, are not 'staff'. ('[. . .] In the British system, agents are never employees of the intelligence services [. . .]', *Guardian*, 10 September 2001.)

I argue that a spy's life is always at risk, whereas the lives of staff are usually at risk only in specific circumstances, and more often than not, in common with us all.

In the mid-'70s, one of my father's greatest safety worries was an SIS 'safe' address overseas which was even known to local taxi-drivers. In addition, his case officer Alexis Forte was so indiscreet that, on one occasion, even the driver Forte organised to pick up my father from an international airport knew what my father was doing there.

26

SIS, IRAQ AND THE MISSING YEARS

There are considerable sensitivities about SIS operations in the Middle East and Iraq in particular. For this reason, most books charting British intelligence in the Middle East skip the Baghdad Pact countries in the period 1958–79. It is as if Iraq, with the murder of the Boy King, ceases to exist in 1958 and only re-emerges in 1979 with the modern phase of Saddam Hussein's dictatorship.

Particularly absent is commentary on SIS involvement in Iraq, Turkey and Pakistan. (Such is the sensitivity, a senior military civil servant, whose family I know well, skips all mention of his Crown service in Pakistan in his autobiography and in an otherwise detailed entry in *Who's Who.*[1]) And so, a crucial period in SIS/Iraq's history – 1958–79 – is airbrushed. The regimes of Qassem, the Aref brothers and the rise of the Ba'ath, is nowhere. This is despite the fact that there is a considerable amount of SIS material available post-1979.

My father served SIS throughout the 'missing' years. From the mid-'70s onwards, he was profoundly anxious about SIS's understanding of the Middle East. He said, 'In the 1970s, the collapse of SIS's sophisticated intelligence on the Middle East, and Iraq in particular, was due to the departure of "Geoffrey Kingsmill" overseas. Alexis Forte, who replaced him, was a Persian not an Arab specialist. Moreover, at the end of his working life (although he successfully managed to prolong this) Alexis was more preoccupied with his own future than anything else. I advise all spies to refuse to serve with SIS diplomats or civil servants who are coming up for retirement, irrespective of the diplomat or civil servant's prestige within SIS, because, for obvious reasons, they are more concerned about their own future than anything else.'

My father continued, 'Forte's appointment meant that he, as the person responsible for HMG's intelligence on Iraq, one of the key countries in the world, knew nothing about it, had no desire to learn anything, and did not know how to handle the intelligence coming in. On one occasion, he told me SIS could not produce an SIS officer who spoke proper Arabic. This was a request I had made when I knew he could not handle a particular meeting, not least because he did not speak the language himself. It was a nonsense. Although SIS had very few Arabic speakers, one or two were first class.

'I cannot emphasise more strongly how essential it is for a case officer to be fluent in a spy's first language. One of the many reasons why I enjoyed working with "Geoffrey Kingsmill" was because of his first-class command of Arabic.

'Because of Forte, years of knowledge on Iraq, which had been second to none, dribbled away. This fundamental flaw was masked from the mid-'70s onwards by HMG's changing emphasis. This is to say, its decision, in competition with America and France, to sell armaments to the country. This meant that Forte could get away with down-grading "pure" political intelligence and contacts because his superiors did not notice it was missing since there was so much other information and contacts coming in. This will come back to haunt Britain one day.

'Iraq became a marketplace. It is easy to be in a market – I was in it myself – when the seller wishes to sell, and the buyer wishes to buy. What is not easy, is the provision of intelligence in readiness for when the market, for whatever reason, collapses.

'As for HMG's attitude towards President Hussein, I learned too late this was all that was cynical. Had it not been for this cynicism, Iraq could still have belonged to us, with all the good this could have meant for both countries. It was not to be. A spy, on behalf of the Crown, cannot recruit good quality sources seeking to undermine the regime from within, if HMG is doing all it can to secure the status quo from without.'

If the large-scale arms trade masked Britain's information vacuum, which it did, legitimate anxieties about Arab terrorism made the problem worse. Crucially, a new generation of SIS diplomats, for example Sir David Spedding, learned their trade on the back of Arab terrorism. Unsurprisingly, they therefore did not know how to change focus: other than terrorism, oil and arms sales, the Middle East meant nothing to them.

Demands for self-determination, and civil and human rights were an embarrassment ruthlessly ignored; fundamentalism, other than as a sop to Communism, an irrelevance. This professional imbalance was not corrected. (Terrorism had greater appeal to young men than painstakingly acquired political/societal analysis.)

Commenting on David Spedding's handling of Gulf War intelligence, the *Guardian*,[2] said that he had 'instructed his officers, with limited success, to obtain first-hand intelligence on the Iraqi leadership'. Had SIS been doing its job correctly, Spedding would not have had to issue the instruction, not least because, courtesy of my father, information, along with the recycled codeword, was available. Regrettably, the No Names failed to process it.

My father excelled in the provision of such information and for two decades placed it at the Crown's disposal.[3]

NOTES

[1] So far as I am aware, espionage civil servants and diplomats are not entered into *Who's Who* until after they have retired. At this point, I understand, such mention is allowed because it is a vital marketing tool for those who intend to become commercially active. The exception is the new policy of naming the Heads of Services. Their *Who's Who* inclusion is automatic upon their jobs being announced.

[2] 14 July 2001.

[3] In an article for the *Journal of the Campaign for Press and Broadcasting Freedom*, March–April 2002, Stephen Dorril said: 'Good, detailed secret intelligence from Iraq is something the West, former CIA director James Woolsey told John Simpson, "Hasn't possessed since the 1980s."'

I do not know anything about the CIA. I do know about the SIS. The reason why it had an Iraq information vacuum from the 1980s onwards is because it was unable to replace my father.

27

A SPY ORGANISES HIS PENSION

My father retired from government service on 31 January 1979. Shortly before he retired, SIS organised his pension. This occurred in the aftermath of chaos and disastrous events for which SIS accepted responsibility. He was not allowed independent internal or external professional legal or financial advice. He was in no fit state to secure his proper entitlement and the Crown knew it.

He was advised in 1978 that, instead of having an SIS pension, he should accept a lump-sum severance of £31,000, to be invested in the London property market. I believe this could be about £500,000 today (October 2002) in London real-estate terms.

Aware of the influence I had on my father, attempts were made to appeal to my greed, in order to persuade him to accept the lump sum rather than the pension. Under the guise of social meetings, at which I was present, an SIS colleague suggested to my father that he buy me an apartment with the lump sum. 'You do not need us to give you a pension,' he said to my father, continuing, 'It is better for you if there is no SIS linkage in the future. Besides, if you buy your daughter a flat, there will be quite a lot left over for other investments.'

Having originally agreed to accept the lump sum, my father changed his mind, deciding to opt for an inflation-linked pension instead. He did so because he was worried that SIS could, at a later date, deny his career if he severed ties. He was not convinced that SIS would explain things fully to the Inland Revenue as to where the money had come from if he did so. This, my father felt, 'may not be a danger today, but could be in ten years' time. I was anxious that my wife and daughter could face problems with the Revenue after my death.'

My father's worries arose because, at the time of his retirement, the Inland Revenue had asked his accountants whether he had a 'private account'. He did. This was his SIS account with a high-street bank in the joint name of himself and my mother. This, SIS had previously and erroneously assured him, had already been declared to the Revenue and did not need to be re-declared via his accountant. Assuming it would be sorted, he left the problem in SIS hands.

When he died seven years later, I found out that it had not. As a result, there was interference in my father's personal bank account, also held jointly with my mother, and his deposit box, for which I secured full written apology from the bank concerned. Soon after, the No Names asked my mother to return all bank statements pertaining to my father's SIS account, held with another bank, in which all financial transactions, over a decade, related solely to SIS.

I refused on her behalf and placed the bank statements in safe custody, where they remain to this day. I made it clear that if SIS wanted them, the Crown would have to write to me formally. In addition, I closed my parents' personal account and switched my mother's into what had been the SIS account, so its existence could not be denied or used against her.

To SIS's credit, when I met its Foreign Office representatives in 1994, they made no mention of the bank statements. At my mother's request, I will destroy them after her death.

It could also be noted that my father was required to retain accountants, at his own expense, because of his SIS pension, on which he paid tax. After his death, my mother was similarly required to retain accountants, also at her expense, because of her SIS widow's pension, on which she paid no tax.

I have always argued that neither of my parents should have had to do so, since the retention of the accountants was solely for the purpose of the SIS pensions. I have similarly argued that the accountancy fees should have been refunded.

In April 1994, the prime minister's private secretary, William Chapman, responded in a letter that SIS '[. . .] is responsible for the correct discharge of funds from the Secret Vote [. . .]'. I interpreted this as meaning that a wrongly calculated pension, or the fact that a widow is obliged to retain accountants, at her own expense, cannot be refunded since this is not deemed to be a correct discharge of funds. Instead, charity is on offer even though what is being asked for is the correct reimbursement of funds owed by the Crown.

The situation was ludicrous because, although the accountants were retained, neither the source of the pension, nor the pension itself, could be declared. SIS Welfare were so unequal to the problems arising that they advised me to 'make something up for the benefit of the Revenue'. The pension itself, as SIS admitted, was 'derisory'.

Today, it is paid in cash into my mother's account monthly.

In 1978, my father, having opted for a pension, was placed under enormous pressure to change his mind. He resisted. Pressure included my mother being contacted separately by SIS, when she was requested to 'use her influence' on my father. She refused.

Next, SIS suggested that my parents 'allow HMG to change [their] identity' and relocate. It was made clear that this facility would not be available to me, because, as I was then aged 23, they said, 'Your daughter is an adult now. She does not need you.' I was told separately, 'It would be selfish if you did not let go of your parents. Let them disappear. It is far safer for their future. Besides, you need to lead your own life. You are too old to be a daddy's girl.'

My father never forgave his colleague for seeking to break up his family. He said, 'They want my wife and I to lose our identity and become dependent on them. In addition, they want to deny us any chance of seeing our children again, and, in our daughter's case, take control of her.'

My father refused 'to disappear with my wife'. He said, 'The whole suggestion was preposterous. Moreover, I could not change my identity or my address anyway, since I knew my home was a vital contact point. This SIS recognised.

'However, it hated admitting I would remain "live", as would my address.'[1]

Soon our lives were turned upside down again by long bouts of massive harassment. At first it was subtle. For example, during a long pension discussion, which took place in my father's garden, his SIS colleague inserted the phrase, 'The balloon might go up at any minute', inconsequentially, three times. Shortly before departure, the civil servant pointed to a tree at the side of the house and asked, with apparent innocence, 'What is that?'

Tied to the top branch was an aluminium balloon (long before these were widely available) that required a workman to retrieve. The workman later reported that it had been secured with correctly fastened nautical knots. It could not be seen unless the civil servant spotting it had known it was there already.

Other harassment, as well as sinister telephone calls – 'You are all on your own now' – continued for years.

During the pension discussions, my father was also introduced to SIS civil servant, Stephen —, whom, he was informed, would handle any intelligence arising in the future. Stephen — also took responsibility for, as he put it, 'Any safety anxieties you may have.'

The arrangement was tested rather quicker than anyone anticipated.

A few months later, my father received a parcel of Middle Eastern sweets. Suspecting that they could be poisoned (a well-established Iraqi habit), he telephoned Stephen. Much to his disappointment, the SIS civil servant responded crisply, 'What am I supposed to do about it?'

My father contacted Stephen on two occasions. The first time, the latter reluctantly agreed to have the contents of the parcel tested. These proved negative. On the second occasion, Stephen refused, remarking, 'If you suspect the confectionery to be poisoned, just throw it away.' As a result, my father had it checked privately through a friend using a university laboratory. It had indeed been poisoned.

The SIS civil servant, who refused to accept this had anything to do with my father's former work, advised him, 'You can go to the police if you want.' However, he would not allow my father to explain to the police his former

Crown service. (Following my father's retirement, his 'Special' status with the local police had been cancelled.) Therefore, my father did not report the poisoned parcel to the police because 'There would be no point if my hands are tied behind my back.'

Which was the reason for Stephen's conduct in the first place.

NOTES

[1] In her autobiography, *Open Secret*, published by Hutchinson in 2001, Dame Stella Rimington talks about the inconvenience of moving house. Nothing can emphasise the difference between spies and staff more. Spies do not move house. Nor do their widows/widowers. This is because it is the only address that decades of sources, contacts and informants, know.

28

SIS WIVES

Along with my father, two of his former case officers – Norman Darbyshire and Ken Boswell – also retired at the end of the '70s. Darbyshire went into business; Boswell returned to work for SIS part-time when, I understand, the commercial opportunities he hoped to pursue did not materialise.

SIS offered my father 'translation work', which, after discussing things with my mother, he declined, not least because of his anxieties about the No Names. This, he acknowledged, was a shame because '"The Firm" is in difficulty – they do not have enough Arabists. I have been telling them this for years.'

His refusal did not stop the 'translation work' from arriving on his front doorstep anyway. As he figured, it was equivalent to an entire Whitehall department's workload. He organised for its return, and instead accepted a job as a typist in a youth club, in an underprivileged area of London, run by a churchman, where he happily spent the last years of his working life.

As for his other colleagues, Alexis Forte was promoted, becoming counsellor at the British embassy in Paris. Nigel West wrote this was intended 'As a reward after so many arduous years in some of the world's most dangerous trouble-spots.'[1] Which just goes to show what a cushy bunk is offered by the Paris mission.

'Geoffrey Kingsmill', rightly, rose to senior Whitehall rank. He retired from SIS in 1982 due to ill health. (I understand, had his career not been cut short, he might have become SIS Chief.)

Had my father's four case officers been brands of soap, Norman Darbyshire would have been 'Imperial Leather'; 'Geoffrey Kingsmill', 'Wright's Coal Tar'; Alexis Forte anything from 'Mr Trumper'; and Ken Boswell whatever the kids left over.

I regarded all four as family friends. Anagrams for the word 'espionage' was a favourite pastime. The best – 'Oi! Espagne' – was dreamt up by the 'Kingsmill' children in celebration of their parents fondness for Spain. Others were 'Age n' Poise' – a description of Norman Darbyshire and his then young wife; 'Ego Pansie' – a reference to Alexis Forte, and his 'pretty flower' of a wife; and 'EEO! Gas Nip' – an affectionate allusion to Ken Boswell's articulate wife, who, first, did not always appear to leave her husband enough time to nip into the conversation; and, second, liked to chatter before nipping out to play golf with Norman Darbyshire.

Of the four, three had strong non-British connections, whether by marriage[2] or birth; two, under the influence of their wives, brought up children in staunch Roman Catholic households; one was thrilled his eldest son had married a high-born Muslim girl; none were freemasons.

Norman Darbyshire and 'Geoffrey Kingsmill' married 'foreigners' although, following the tragic death of his first wife, Norman Darbyshire subsequently married his SIS secretary, in much the same way as his other two colleagues also married Foreign Office secretaries. Which is to say, for the most part, they married each other – a mix, presumably, of opportunity, discretion and SIS encouragement.

Despite their exoticism and the foreign languages they spoke, I did not regard any of the men as cosmopolitan. With the exception of Alexis Forte, who frequently appeared rootless, they were quintessentially English, however uncomfortable they were when posted back to Britain, or pensioned off. All, in different ways, were arrogant; three were pampered; two were institutionalised by Whitehall. ('Geoffrey Kingsmill' avoided the latter problem by going out of his way to court friendships outside of his work.)

Alexis Forte was capable of breaking the law in this country and across national boundaries.

Ken Boswell had a sincerity matched only by his love for all who were 'foreign'. Norman Darbyshire had a 'Persian soul'. 'Geoffrey Kingsmill' was the most internationalist in outlook, with a deep commitment to the Arabs and the Middle East. Alexis Forte was a caricature of White Russian supremacists everywhere. He was, however, generous to a fault and, in the giving of beautiful presents, he enlivened many a Christmas with beautiful Gucci scarves, bottles of matured malt whisky wrapped in scarlet velvet and, from Fortnum's, enormous boxes of Marrons Glacés.[3]

All four and their wives knew each other. Of the four wives, one was highly educated and a linguist; two were anxious to create their own lives instead of subordinating them to their husbands; one was overwhelmed by the *deuxieme lit*.

Attitudes to wives, and women in general, varied. 'Geoffrey Kingsmill' told his wife 'enough about my work to keep her interested, but not in any detail'. My father said he 'told [his] wife everything'.

This was despite the pressure under which he was placed not to because 'Women are apt to talk'; or, depending on the speaker, 'It is for her own safety.' My father thought this was nonsense – 'My wife was born discreet' – and 'told her everything not least because she is English. She knows when her countrymen are pulling the wool over my eyes.'

My father was profoundly disillusioned by officialdom's attitude to wives, which deepened when he was working with the No Names who appeared 'to know nothing about married life, far less have a respect for it, or women in general. They despised men who would rather be home with their families, than go out drinking with them.'

He was particularly contemptuous of the way the No Names tried to interfere with the relationship he had with my mother. She had shared all the dangers of his working life when he worked undercover in Iraq and he was shocked by SIS's lack of respect for her in her own country. 'SIS have always known that my wife and I are a team. She is so discreet, even people who have known her for 20 years comment that they still know nothing about her. These young men think my reliance on my wife is a weakness. In fact, it is my strength.'

To be fair to the No Names, they were substantially younger than my father, which could explain some of the problems they had with each other. There were other problems, however, which could not be put down to a generational divide. These included their 'Little Englander' mentality and their need for 'action' – often creating it themselves – when my father's strengths were his ability to collect and analyse information.

Of my father's case officers, neither 'Geoffrey Kingsmill' nor Ken Boswell had a chauvinistic, let alone racist, bone in their bodies. Nor did Norman Darbyshire. (More traditional in outlook, Darbyshire was too influenced by his love for the women in his family to be a credible chauvinist although, at times, he had a fairly good stab at it.)

As always, Alexis Forte was in a league of his own.

All four of my father's colleagues were staunch Tories. They believed the Conservative Party was its political arm in government. Alexis Forte described it as 'HMG's political wing'. All believed the Labour Party to be dangerous. However, 'Geoffrey Kingsmill' was the most laid back. For example, a short time into Prime Minister Thatcher's tenure, he commented dryly, 'The Socialists are bound to get in again one day. I am sure we will manage to cope.'

Their SIS secretaries, to whom they were devoted, were even more conservative. These, with rare exceptions, were young girls in the company of older men completely cut off from the realities of life. They were all nicely brought up *gels*, but lacked the cosmopolitanism their work demanded. Buried in SIS, they were all anxious about their marriage chances.

Norman Darbyshire reflected a certain Foreign Office type. Immaculately dressed, with very good social skills – when he wanted to apply them – he stood out from the crowd. Alexis Forte was no more than a strutting SIS billboard. 'Geoffrey Kingsmill' and Ken Boswell could pass unnoticed in any social situation. They held back and analysed exactly what was going on before, if they chose to, joining in. 'Geoffrey Kingsmill' often managed to look as if he was asleep; Ken Boswell's preferred method of diminishing his presence was to show others off at an advantage.

I found Norman Darbyshire the most straightforward. Even if I did not like what he said, or the tone in which he said it, I always knew where I stood with him. He had a fund of interesting anecdotes. These were never about his service life but illustrative of espionage in general.

For example, he once said that those who had obvious distinguishing features (e.g. if they are very tall) could not become spies. He said, 'The British Bobby has to be over six foot, seven foot with his helmet on, so he stands out. A spy, however, has to merge into the crowd if, for example, he has to escape dressed as a woman. A tall man cannot do this. Therefore it is always best for spies to be of average height.'

My father also had some good espionage stories. He used to tell one about a woman who became an important man's mistress. For this reason, SIS was interested in recruiting her. It attempted to do so at a social event in an Arab country. Finding herself tapped on the shoulder, she turned around and said sweetly, 'Hello! Join the queue. Ever since I took — as my lover, I have been invited to more of these things than I have time for . . .'

Apparently, all the Western intelligence agencies had been hoping to bribe her into betraying her lover. She did not do so.

All four of my father's case officers were badly paid and found life in the United Kingdom a financial struggle. My father was very sad that 'the nation's servants were treated like this'. His colleagues were particularly worried that they would not have enough to live on in retirement. One, who had hoped a job with a Saudi prince would materialise (it did not), was forced to sell insurance.

They hated kicking their heels in London until their next posting. With the exception of Alexis Forte, who was loyal only to a class, all were patriots. One, however, was particularly bitter at what he considered the Crown's lack of appreciation for his work.

Overseas, they did not correct a romantic view of the United Kingdom. Unsurprisingly, this did not live up to expectations. One of those disappointed was my father, who had believed the myths. He was stunned when, a few months after he retired, Prime Minister Thatcher 'outed' traitor Sir Anthony Blunt in 1979. The privileges that Sir Anthony enjoyed for so long, despite his treachery being known to the Crown, hurt my father deeply.

If the Blunt affair opened his eyes to the scale of his own naivety, so did various books. These included founding CIA agent Miles Copeland's *The Game of Nations*.[4] This upset many in SIS, first, because Copeland had published at all; second, because it airbrushed SIS's contribution to the American intelligence effort. (Irrespective of what is said today, SIS did not have an enormous respect for the Americans. The feeling, apparently, was mutual.)[5]

Closer to home, my father was impressed by passing references to espionage in Joe Haines' *The Politics of Power*,[6] less impressed by Chapman Pincher's work

Their Trade is Treachery.[7] He died before Peter Wright's *Spy Catcher* came out, but profoundly disapproved of any crown servant writing his memoirs, irrespective of grievance.

(Surprisingly, 'Geoffrey Kingsmill', then a senior SIS Whitehall figure, encouraged my father to write his autobiography when he retired. Therefore, and for whatever reason, the rules on publication must have been less stringently applied in those days.)

My father read every book published on the Middle East and was always disappointed at the polarisation. 'You have to be a Jew or a Muslim,' he would complain. 'Nobody seems to realise that there are thousands of Christians in the area who have a view, and as many again who have no faith. These, however, do not exist. To conform to publishing standards, you have to be a bigoted Jew or a Muslim zealot.'

He was grief-stricken by the Iraq–Iran War, and the subsequent campaign against the Kurds. He was incensed at the lack of coverage of these events on British television and contrasted it, following the television documentary *Death of a Princess*, to the wall-to-wall coverage of the tragic execution of two young lovers in Saudi Arabia. While appalled by their suffering, he believed, 'The deaths of two who have broken their country's rules, cannot be compared to the thousands of young conscripts dying in the Iraqi and Iranian desert.' He blamed HMG for prolonging the Iraq–Iran War for cynical reasons; and believed that British television coverage of the war was censored.

He watched Alex Guinness' portrayal of Le Carré's 'Smiley' on television with initial interest but subsequent disappointment, saying Le Carré's portrayal of espionage was 'far too English. He does not appear to know that half of SIS is either married to foreign wives or born abroad. And this does not include spies like myself.'

He continued, 'Le Carré has obviously not been involved with espionage for many years. Besides, he is writing about espionage from the point of view of "The Office" rather than from the focus of SIS overseas. One of SIS's principal roles is to protect British trade and the oil supply. How can anyone portray SIS without knowing what it is for? Le Carré makes all spies seem tortured, agonised, and tired of life. In fact, we are the reverse. I think he is pretending to write about SIS when in fact he is describing staff who work for MI5.'

My father was even less impressed that SIS continued to take the fictional spy 'James Bond' seriously. He discovered this when, following a visit to West Berlin, he was given a present of a 'pen' which, when fired, drugged an assailant for 15 minutes. On his return from what was then West Germany, Alexis Forte wanted him to hand the 'pen' over for analysis. My father refused on the basis that he would not get it back. The 'pen' was commonly available in West Germany at the time.[8]

Forte was furious. 'Alexis was sore. Very sore,' recalled my father. 'He wanted my "pen" and was cross when I would not give it to him. He was also offended the West Germans were coming out with these gadgets and making them available to the wider public. He thought it devalued espionage in general and "James Bond" in particular.'[9]

'I told Alexis that if he really took James Bond seriously, he was an even bigger twit than I thought he was. He was furious and started shouting, "Even the Russians take James Bond seriously."

'In my experience, the Russians did not take James Bond seriously. They said so to flatter SIS's ego and to annoy the Americans because the CIA only got bit parts in the books. They were not wrong. James Bond annoyed the CIA for years, particularly when Hollywood turned him into a superstar. Nevertheless, they were pleased this brought in all the dollars.

'This, in a way, was what it was all about. Britain got all the glory; Hollywood got all the money. In those days, Britain did not mind. They looked down on money, which is why they looked down on the Americans and the CIA, and went for glory instead.

'This, all those years ago, is what meant so much to me. I thought working for the Crown was about glory, honour, patriotism. I do not know how or why it altered, but it did. When I joined SIS my colleagues were the finest men in the world. By the time I retired, they had all changed.'

NOTES

[1] West, N. (1997) *The Secret War for the Falklands*, Little, Brown and Company, London.

[2] In my father's day, SIS diplomats with foreign wives were not allowed to serve in their wives' country of birth. This rule appears to have been waived.

[3] My father was meticulous in his recording of SIS gifts and hospitality he received and gave, 1968–78.

[4] Copeland, M. (1969) *The Game of Nations: The Amorality of Power Politics*. Weidenfeld & Nicolson: London.

[5] Aldich, R.J.(2001) *The Hidden Hand*. John Murray: London.

[6] Haines, J. (1977) *The Politics of Power*. Jonathan Cape: London.

[7] Pincher, C. (1981) *Their Trade is Treachery: The Full, Unexpurgated Truth about the Russian Penetration of the Free World's Secret Defences*. Sidwick & Jackson: London

[8] I have always wanted to have the pellets of the 'James Bond' pen analysed to find out what is in them. However, after my father died, I did not trust the No Name who offered to help to return either the pen or pellets to me.

[9] The celebration of 'James Bond' as a 'Secret Agent' subliminally serves to glorify British civil servants at the expense of real spies, i.e. civilians who are not portrayed in the novels. 'James Bond' is, of course, an English civil servant with naval rank.

29

ESPIONAGE IS A STRANGE UPBRINGING

I do not know what sort of person I would have been had my father not been a spy. Espionage is a strange upbringing. It is not the extremes that are so scarring but, relatively speaking, the mildest of the moral confusions. I grew up with a principled father who, because of his job, sometimes deliberately set out to get people drunk to loosen their tongue (he drank olive oil beforehand, so that he remained sober).

Then there were all the lies. I could not get away from them. For example, a friend of mine had a fling with a much older SIS City 'friend' of an SIS diplomat well-known to my family. Nothing could have prepared any of the respective parties for the coincidence of his latest love knowing me, far less that I would be invited by his girlfriend to his dinner table, when he had so recently been a visitor in my father's house. I knew she would be dumped immediately, which she was. I was left to console her, knowing that I was the cause of her disappointment.

Another friend temped during a vacation for the foreign editor of a national newspaper. Writing a story on the Middle East, the journalist wanted to speak to someone 'well-informed' about the area. As a result, my friend suggested my father, not least because the editor lived close by. With the assistance of the Crown, my father courteously got rid of him. However, as always, it was left to me to fudge things with my friend. I also got a bollocking from my father's case officer for drawing attention to my father, when I had not done so.

I found some of the burdens of an espionage-childhood crushing. I was not even allowed to participate in an 'A' level history debate – 'Do you think Philip of Spain's spies in Elizabethan England have parallels today? Is espionage necessary in the modern world?' – in case I put my foot in it. (I found the argument informative – it was the first time that I had heard the word 'spook' in relation to espionage rather than, for example, 'Casper the Friendly Ghost' but, prevented from contributing to the discussion, I felt that I had been stripped of a significant part of who I was.)

As a teenager, I particularly resented the prevailing sense of paranoia in the home, as well as all the safety precautions. I grew up unable to chose my own company, or mix with members of my family. I was constantly alert to the possibility of attack on my father, or kidnap of myself in order to put pressure on him.

In the civilian world, my parents were not who they said they were. In consequence, I was raised in a completely parallel universe which nobody knew existed. As a teenage undergraduate, I sat at my desk knowing that my parents were living under an assumed identity, in new clothes, in an apartment they did not own, in another part of town.

Then there were the problems that I had with Alexis Forte, who, I appreciate, is not here to defend himself. So far as I was concerned, he represented little more than functionary, flunky and farce. This, however, denies Forte's earlier years when he was no doubt at his best, when my family did not know him. However good at his job he may once have been, the fall-out from the personality clash between him and my father collapsed the infrastructure of my family's relationship with SIS. (Nobody knows better than I do that my father was also a difficult man and that Forte probably had as many criticisms of my father as the reverse. A spy is never a hero to his daughter – probably because she knows him too well.)

Whatever the causes of the problems, the impact that Forte had on me was enormous. He had lived an incredible life of derring-do. However, some of my SOAS contemporaries were as travelled as he and had had similar adventures. He was stinging in his sarcasm. In my maturity, I realise that he was doing no more than covering up his hurt. (He was deeply wounded because I unfairly suggested that he believed only the upper classes knew how to travel with their lives in their hands.) Retrospectively, I wish that I had managed him better. The young are not always kind, nor indeed polite, to those they consider buffoons or sentimental old fools, who, sometimes, are only doing their best.

The lasting impact of my espionage-childhood had nothing to do with Forte – but everything to do with the burden of what my father did for a living. To this day, I begrudge the fact that I have been forced to steer away from British groups supporting Iraqi or Palestinian causes in case, however unlikely, association with my father could damage them. This duty was forced upon me by my father and his case officers and still rankles. Yet again, it felt as if I was being denied my identity. Such incidents, trivial though they may seem, meant a lot to me.

The only one who recognised such problems was 'Mrs Geoffrey Kingsmill'. She was always anxious about the impact of espionage on children and, in the teeth of ridicule, was bold enough to state her reservations. When I last spoke to her in the early 1990s, she continued to articulate her anxieties. I admire her for it. She was always years ahead of SIS pastoral staff.

'Mrs Geoffrey Kingsmill' also faced ridicule when she suggested that SIS should take responsibility for those whose mental health collapsed because of their work. Her husband was particularly cold about this issue, and denied SIS had any such responsibilities because 'SIS does not hide the risks'.

'Geoffrey Kingsmill' was right. SIS did not hide the risks. Only everything else.

Knowledge of this is another legacy of an espionage-childhood. What upset me the most was the discovery that SIS had no respect for its spies. I first noticed it when Sir Anthony Blunt's treachery was exposed in 1979. It formed my abiding opinion of SIS.

Sir Anthony served in a different field to my father, and at a different time. However, the product and relationship could have been the same. Every death overseas Blunt could have caused, could have been my father's. The disgrace was not just that the Crown protected Sir Anthony, although it did; not just that SIS sought to minimise Sir Anthony's crimes, although it did; but that it failed to apologise to past, present and future spies, and their families, for their protection of him once his treachery had been discovered.

I have never forgiven my father's employers. All that the Crown did, belatedly, was strip Sir Anthony of his knighthood. Principally, however, it used its considerable resources, paid by the taxpayer, to organise a damage-limitation exercise designed, solely, to protect the eminent.

My family felt this oversight acutely, not least because my father was, at this time, suffering another severe bout of SIS intimidation. I was 24 and did not know that so much worse was to come. Incredulous, I heard that the Crown had embraced a traitor, while criminally harassing my father and bewildered mother, who were patriots.

Over the years, I have watched the Crown, with all the arrogance of its type, set about, little by little, seeking to restore Sir Anthony's reputation by encouraging others to excuse/minimise his treachery. It did not ask espionage-families to comment. Revisionism has powerful friends, especially in the media.

'Revisionism' and espionage, of course, have always been compatible.

This brings me to the final legacy of my espionage-childhood – the knowledge that the 'incompatible' is ruthlessly airbrushed. Including men like my father.

I have never expected people to 'like' him or his profession – being 'liked' was not something that weighed heavily with him, and when it did, he believed this to be a necessary sacrifice for our country. However, I looked to the Crown to acknowledge his work and that of those like him. Over 20 years later, I am still waiting.

Today, his political views date him. He was a monarchist but not an Iraqi monarchist. He wanted the Queen to be head of the Iraqi Republic and wanted Iraq to be part of the British Commonwealth. He believed – passionately – that

Iraq and Britain had everything to gain from each other. He admired Britain and what it represented to the world; but he also admired the Iraqis, especially their commitment to education and family. He was proud that although thousands of Iraqis were in exile across the globe, they had maintained close family bonds and upheld their values and way of life.

He did the job he did because he believed it to be right.

When he retired from SIS, he was crushed by the nightmare of Iraq as it unfolded before his eyes. Today, we know that the Foreign Office rejoiced in the destruction of Iraq's middle classes, and did not displace Saddam Hussein because this would have meant hosting Iraq's transition to democracy and all the good this could have meant for the Middle East. My family knew this from the '70s.

My father's distress was indescribable as his SIS colleagues deemed his mother's people – Iraqis and Kurds – to be valueless. Meantime, my mother wept as the beauty of her Christian faith was defiled by a 'Christian' Crown which considered Muslim lives worthless, their torture and rape inconsequential.

By the end of my father's SIS career, it seemed as if my parents had in front of them a jigsaw they refused to put together because they already knew the whole picture. Each piece of it appeared jagged with recrimination, bitterness and denial. I raged at them as I confronted my father with my loathing for some aspects of my childhood. I was no longer their child, but espionage's daughter. I felt sullied by a past from which I had benefited; raged about what was happening in Iraq; and resented the years of harassment we had endured.

I blamed my father. My attack on him – when he was already so anguished – shames me to this day. To have mocked him when he was powerless is about as base an act of cowardice as can be imagined. The one thing that I know now is that when a daughter makes her father weep, she has to work out what to do with her victory.

It took me a lifetime.

THREE

Inheriting Espionage
1980–2001

30

THE LOBBYING INDUSTRY

Shortly after my father's retirement from SIS in 1979, I acquired a mortgage and moved out of my parents' home. My father remained anxious about the No Names and his moods swung from the rational to the irrational. His greatest worry was that SIS 'could influence our daughter against us, now she is no longer under our roof'. In addition, he feared for his own safety and warned us that he 'could meet with an "accident". I have told my two girls this is a definite possibility. SIS are not clean in this regard.' At one time, he was more frightened in his own country than he had ever been when serving overseas.

He was also worried about my choice of career. He said, 'My daughter is working for a firm of parliamentary consultants. I have asked her to decide upon some other profession since I believe it is too political.'

I refused. I agreed, however, that he could contact one of my joint employers, Lieutenant Commander Christopher Powell RN.

Commander Powell, a former head of War Censorship, was the 'father' of the modern British political lobbying industry. He established his company, with his business partner Charles Watney, in 1929. Watney was a former lobby correspondent and political and foreign editor of the *Daily Mail*, then under Lord Northcliffe. He established the country's first parliamentary consultancy when he could no longer work with Northcliffe and brought Christopher Powell in as junior partner. He died in 1948 and Powell carried on as sole proprietor.

Powell was known as 'The Commander' and to his staff as 'CP'.

I was his assistant from 1978 until 1985.

A procedural and parliamentary drafting expert, CP specialised in taking technical private and private members' bills to statute, outside the private members' ballot, for modest commercial fee. The parliamentarians in whose name the bills were piloted were unpaid. Additionally, he was an authority on statutory instruments, otherwise known as delegated legislation.

In order to maintain the myth that democracy is available to all, much of his work has been denied by Westminster. In fact, democracy has a price and because CP was not allowed to advertise his skill, it was only accessible to those who knew him. Such was Westminster's sensitivity, I was prevented from naming the specific private members' bills on which I assisted him on my curriculum vitae.[1]

Despite attempts by some officials at the Palace of Westminster to close him down, CP regarded himself as a public servant. He worked almost exclusively for charities and private-sector representative organisations, some of which 'would not otherwise have had access to Parliament'. He was also the founding secretary of the prestigious Parliamentary and Scientific Committee.

As soon as I started working for CP, my father asked that I be excused from monitoring one of CP's oldest accounts, which CP wished to switch to me. This was the oil company with which my father had been associated for many years. (The politician who entertained my father on behalf of SIS in the House of Commons in the '60s was a close friend of the Commander's.)[2]

My father said, 'I telephoned Christopher Powell and introduced myself. He invited me to Les Ambassadeurs. Over lunch, I mentioned the oil company and the former distinguished MP who was his old friend. Christopher chuckled and we understood each other perfectly.

'I explained I was retired, had previously been in government service and that there had been difficulties. I also explained, however nonsensical I may have sounded, my anxieties about my daughter. I did not want there to be even the slightest possibility that she could be an intelligence target. Even working as a junior parliamentary monitor on an oil account could have been the excuse for such an approach. I also told him why I had never taught my daughter Arabic.

'Christopher believed my worries to be unlikely. However, he proposed that, rather than switching her to the oil account, and, if it pleased me, he train her instead in parliamentary drafting. It pleased me very much indeed. Such work would be of no interest to the intelligence services and would therefore remove my daughter from my employment past. Christopher was unhappy by what had been happening, but commented, "Regrettably, what you say does not surprise me." Apparently, other businessmen had made complaints about the intelligence services. He was reassuring and adamant that "nobody [would] approach your daughter" while she worked for him.

'Apart from her mother and myself, no man could have afforded our daughter greater nor more honourable protection.'

Soon after, the public-relations company which owned the parliamentary consultancy for which I worked was invited to pitch for a significant PR account from an Arab country. The chairman, a respected former senior financial journalist, knowing I was a SOAS graduate, asked if I knew anybody who spoke Arabic. I suggested he contact my father, which he did. Amused, my father said, 'I have been given another good lunch by my daughter's employers!'

My father was very pleased at the way the meeting went, commenting, 'These are men I understand. It was like a breath of fresh air to be circulating again. I explained to my daughter's chairman, without being specific, that I had not been in the best of health. He could not have been kinder.

'I went straight from the lunch table into a meeting with the prospective client. This went exceedingly well. When we came out, my new colleague was cock-a-hoop. He offered me a lucrative consultancy on the spot.

'I was delighted to accept. I made it clear, of course, my daughter must not be moved from the parliamentary division into the PR company handling the account if we won it. For her own reputation, which only another Arab father will understand, I did not want her anywhere near it.

'Her chairman accepted immediately. He was a lovely roly-poly Jew. As I have noted so often in the past, the Muslims trusted him because he was a Jew. He was a shortie, like me and the Arabs, which makes a difference, although we pretend it does not. He had a brilliant, astute mind. One of the men said to me, in Arabic, "He knows more about my country's banking system than I do. And I am the Minister!"

'The Arabs loved him because, although a devoted family man, he was, like them, a terrible womaniser. They said, "A Jew is like us, not like the English who have no interest in sex. The English can go without a woman for weeks on end. We cannot. Neither can the Jews."

'Since I am not a womaniser, the merciless teasing began immediately. I took on the role of "scold" and they loved it. If I had still been active in SIS, I would have tried to recruit my daughter's chairman immediately. Like all Jews, he was cosmopolitan and knew how to mix. He was not frightened of what was foreign but embraced and loved it. This is what the British diplomat does not do.

'It was wonderful to be back in the company of good men again. When a man retires, he does not realise how much he will miss other men's society.'

As the work involved the Middle East, my father, as a courtesy, checked with the Whitehall SIS civil servant Stephen — to whom he had been introduced at the time of his retirement as 'liaison'. The civil servant saw no reason why my father should not accept the consultancy, saying, 'As I understand the situation, "The Firm" wanted you to go back into business anyway.'

However, asking the name of the country concerned, and various other details, the civil servant said he would confirm. He did so within ten minutes. Permission had been refused. It was a bitter blow. No compensation for the lost consultancy was offered. Instead, SIS repeated its suggestion that my father accept translation work from 'The Office'.

He refused.

NOTES

[1] Such is the humbug of Westminster, that even in death the major part of Commander Powell's accomplishment was denied by omission. For example, his *Times* and *Daily*

Telegraph obituaries made no mention of the legislation he took to statute for commercial fee.

2   Nearly 40 years after the politician gave my father lunch, and unaware he was the same man, I wrote to him when I was writing a biography of Christopher Powell. It was not until I saw his signature, which, despite the intervening decades was identical, that I realised he was the same person.

31

CONTACTING A DAUGHTER

My father's fears were realised when I was contacted by the intelligence services in 1980. I was one month short of my 25th birthday. To this day, I do not know which agency approached me. I hold SIS responsible because the details I was given at a later stage could only have come from my father's SIS file.

I was working for two of the lobbying industry's then most senior figures. First, for Commander Powell; second, for Arthur Butler, who, unlike CP, had no knowledge of my father's espionage past. Described by one newspaper as 'the lobbying industry's sandy-haired pacesetter of the 1980s', Butler was a distinguished former political journalist who specialised in sophisticated government relations and the formation of Westminster All Party groups.

I had a life of some professional, social and financial privilege. I had what I considered the best job in London – employment where I was paid to read the newspapers (which I did anyway) and *Hansard*, write reports, and accompany MPs and peers participating in a Westminster All Party group to various industrial plants. I was working as a parliamentary lobbyist for two of the industry's most senior consultants, employed by a well-known public-relations company. I was also assistant secretary to a Westminster All Party group (APG).

Some APGs were junkets. Many, however, were effective, informal fora for debate and networking in Westminster and, today, the European Parliament. The most active APGs travel widely in this country and abroad. I was assistant secretary to the All Party Motor Industry Group (APMIG) from 1979 to 1985.

The APMIG was established in 1978 by my joint employer Arthur Butler, its founding secretary. My joint chairmen were Hal Miller MP (Conservative) and George Park MP (Labour). I travelled with the Group, in this country and on the Continent, for seven years, as well as attending all its meetings at Westminster. I kept a record of all questions posed by the politicians during these meetings, on behalf of the manufacturers' association funding the group.

199

At the time I went to work for Butler and Powell, I was not aware that, as the country's then leading lobbyists, they were controversial figures. Nor did I know that the lobbying industry itself was controversial, not least because lobbyists, at the time, did not officially 'exist'. The 'secrecy' then demanded by the Palace of Westminster of all lobbyists was identical to those in espionage.

It is a supreme irony that the world I was born into (espionage) and subsequently worked in (lobbying) were, in those days, equally 'invisible'. It was therefore bad luck that my own occupation (which could never have been anticipated when my father signed up to Crown service, and which sits on every fault line of the British psyche, as does espionage) made me fair game. I was certainly not aware of the long connection between espionage and parts of the lobbying/public-affairs industry. I believe that but for this fluke – I only became a lobbyist because I was an out-of-work graduate, who joined, in common with many other young people, a public-relations company – I would not have become prey to the intelligence services.

My two employers were very different: the Commander an establishment man; Arthur Butler, a former Gaitskellite, quite the reverse. I reaped the benefit. I had the opportunity to train under the two who, at the time, knew most about the lobbying industry. A further bonus was that, as they were so busy, I was given considerable autonomy to run my own clients, especially an American pharmaceutical account and a major Japanese trading company.

My work for the Japanese company – particularly my monthly report – was of particular interest to SIS. This was compiled from publicly available sources. It was in two parts. The second, written by a colleague, was on legislative developments in the European Union. We met the client every month, in order to go through the report. The civil servant, Stephen —, whom I met at my father's house, was interested in this. Also of interest to SIS was the sophisticated assistance given by my employers to a right-wing union during the passage of a controversial piece of defence-industry legislation. SIS's scrutiny of it was intense – for example Stephen — presented me with a copy of my own minutes of a meeting that could only have been taken from my office desk. I stopped working on the account although I continued to supply the client with a monitoring service.

Of my two employers, I was closest to the Commander because, given his advancing years, he relied on me more. Politically, however, I was attuned to Arthur Butler's socialism. This became more marked as I travelled and came to know the members of the APMIG. Eventually, although I did not join a political party, I moved from the heavy Toryism of my family, supporting, first, the Social Democrats and finally the Labour Party. I was particularly influenced by my Labour APMIG chairman, George Park MP. I was not close to my Conservative chairman, Hal Miller MP.

In addition to Stephen, I was approached by a No Name when I was standing next to Commander Powell in the Central Lobby of Parliament.

I felt a tap on my shoulder. We both turned around – there had been no attempt to hide the approach – and saw a man so personable our instinct was to smile. He was a Palace of Westminster official, a tall coolie of the couloirs, whose eyebrows were raised seamlessly into the ornate Pugin ceiling above our heads. Our smiles froze on our faces as he delivered his message – 'You are causing embarrassment' – and evaporated. I looked at the Commander in amazement. He shrugged and resumed pointing out the beauty of the room.

A few moments later, sending me off into a select committee, CP strolled into the House of Lords to, as he put it, 'Find out who is being so tiresome.' He was well used to whispered accusations concerning his work, which, apparently, could 'bring the whole thing tumbling down'. He was annoyed, however, that his assistant had been targeted.

I was next approached when I was on my own. I had become a member of the National Union of Journalists (NUJ) and was deemed to be left wing for joining. The comment was made in my parents' house by a No Name. The accusation was as much an insult to the left wing as it was wrong about me. The NUJ in those days were not happy some lobbyists fulfilled NUJ membership criteria and accused those of us who did of 'entryism'. Therefore, those like me were hit from both sides.

The approach came on the steps of St Stephen's Hall, inside the Palace of Westminster, before the sophisticated policing of today, and shortly before I was to take a party of MPs and peers on a visit to an industrial plant with union/management problems. The man who came up to me was much younger than the first man I had encountered. Equally personable, with a warm smile, he was far less lofty and intimidating.

He made a specific request for information about the Labour MPs participating in the trip to the plant and those from the shop-floor they were to meet on the visit. He detained me within full view of the Palace of Westminster police, whom I knew – the Commander was so well known that all those who worked for him needed to say to the Palace police to gain access around Westminster was, 'I am one of Commander Powell's ladies' – and I got the distinct impression that my acceptance of the request was assumed to be no more than a formality. I refused.

The look of astonishment that greeted my refusal was genuine. However, the No Name was polite. Apologising for having briefly delayed me, he left via St Stephen's Hall. I asked the policeman if he knew him. The policeman did not but believed that he worked for 'a Conservative peer'.

With the exception of the first two approaches, every subsequent one was unpleasant, not least because it was usually signalled in advance by intimidation of my father. The years that followed were little more than a record of harassment, strange telephone calls and ringing doorbells. My father was so frightened that at one stage he telephoned 'Geoffrey Kingsmill' and other Whitehall civil servants 'to beg for their forgiveness if, for whatever reason, I have offended them'.[1]

To begin with, requests for information were mild. Also, everything possible was done to win my confidence, although not always successfully. For example, one of the No Names who contacted me said that he remembered my family going to a particular cinema in Iraq. This was a surprising factual error since the Baghdadi middle classes, and all Westerners, only saw movies in the private clubs. He, therefore, knew very little, if anything, about Iraq.

In due course, mildness gave way to pressure. The impact on my father was catastrophic, and his mental health became increasingly fragile. This also changed his relationship with the Commander whom, to my great regret, he no longer trusted. The collapse in confidence caused the Commander immense grief.

The whole business was less destructive of me, since I had youth on my side. I was a confident young woman about town, determined to enjoy myself. I defied my father's request to resign from CP's employment and found it easy to lead a life amidst it all. The harassment went on for so long that I got used to it. It certainly did not prevent me from having fun and making the mistakes that all young people make.

At a later stage, however, it stopped me from moving overseas. I was unwilling to leave my parents on their own, not least because, by this time, my father believed: 'My own daughter is working against me. She is working for British Intelligence to destroy me.'

I cannot begin to describe the descent into madness, as he determined it would be better to 'take' my mother and I 'with him'. Those who have never seen the possibility of such violence, when a loving husband and father has been driven to think of harming those he loves, as well as himself, cannot begin to understand the particular strain on all concerned. He was so distraught that he pulled out all the tulips in his garden because he believed their festival of colours mocked him. Denied the appropriate medical care because of the Official Secrets Act, my father was wholly without medical attention. To his credit, he eventually came out the other side. Until he did, my mother bore the brunt of his trauma with reassuring love.[2]

The whole episode was beyond a sadness I can articulate.

In due course, lofty Westminster coolies of the couloirs gave way to urbane flunkies of fear. Two of the No Names, at different times, contacted me by telephone or by means of a casual meeting, using the name of a distinguished SIS Whitehall civil servant who had been a family friend and for whose children I used to baby-sit. When I refused to help, they referred to my mixed-race parentage – 'You're not English, are you?' – as if my mixed race was the cause of what they perceived to be the problem.

Soon came the first mention of my British passport and how it had been obtained, and the realisation that my nationality was an issue. This came as a shock, since, although I knew how my passport had been acquired, I considered myself British by virtue of my personal allegiance, English mother, Commonwealth father, his service and my education.

A short while later, it was suggested to my father that I had 'dual allegiance' and hence was 'born untrustworthy'. This, in fact, had a good outcome, because it restored balance to our relationship, not least because it was a re-run of a row he had had with Alexis Forte. He still wished me to resign my job, but accepted with good grace that I wanted to continue.

Next, I was faced with a test of my so-called 'dual allegiance'. Raised in what we regarded as a 'Service family', I was not to know that pride in my mixed race 'proved' that I was unworthy of my passport. I was saddened that I was expected to deny my father's origins if I wished 'to prove' that I was British.

I believe SIS was genuinely, albeit mistakenly, confused about my loyalty. For example, during the Falklands War, even a colleague remarked I seemed 'detached' by events and put this down to my foreign background.

I had two reasons for my detachment. First, at the time of the war, I had dinner with a young parliamentary private secretary who trusted me and who mentioned a couple of things that were probably not widely known outside of Westminster. More importantly, also at the time of the Falklands, my father was informed by a No Name that Alexis Forte, then counsellor at the British embassy in Paris, was closely involved in the war effort. For both these reasons, I always steered clear of discussion of the Falklands. However, it is also fair to say that my family were not comfortable with the Conservative government's decision to go to war over the Falklands, supporting the Foreign Office original line that the islands belonged to Argentina.

To this day, I remain absolutely mystified as to why the harassment happened. All these years later, not even the benefit of hindsight provides the answer. It was like bashing a budgie. I believe that it was because Britain was cluttered with unco-ordinated intelligence and policing agencies and, somehow or other, these had intersected in my life without actually touching via a type of 'spaghetti junction'. With no 'crash barriers' to break my fall, I tumbled from one layer to the next.

Back at Westminster, I was asked to secure a research assistant's pass, so that I could move around Parliament more effectively. I refused, and believe I am the only lobbyist to have run a busy parliamentary All Party group without one. Then came requests, similarly refused, for recommendations on PR and lobbying personnel, especially those specialising in Europe. The extent of SIS ignorance of the Westminster and European parliaments, as well as the European Commission, was astounding.

Because of this, I suggested that my father's former colleagues become bona fide public-affairs clients of the PR company which employed me, on a fee basis, so that they could receive the necessary instruction/induction on Westminster and European legislatures. The No Names turned down the suggestion. I was required to continue to work for them, in my own time, and without remuneration. I refused.

The No Names had no political insight, nor any understanding of wider international relations. They did not even recognise the initials of some of the then Palestinian factions. They also did not know how the private sector functioned. I was condemned for 'working for the Japs' – my employer's client – at a time when the Conservative government was particularly welcoming Japanese inward investment.

Next, I was asked to 'report' on Labour and 'Wet' Conservative APMIG members, as well as on the APMIG programme. Of particular interest was a visit to a car plant on the Continent, when members of the APMIG additionally met representatives of a European Communist-dominated union.[3]

Finally, I was told that the work I was doing for the Commander was against the law. He was, by this time, nearly 80 years old and would not have been able to sustain a lengthy investigation. Needless to say, at no time did he break the law. Nor would he have thought of doing so, let alone involve his assistant in any wrong-doing. In the No Names' world, 'old' men (the Commander) retired; 'immigrants' (my father) were grateful; and 'daughters' behaved.

NOTES

[1] Dame Stella Rimington told the *Guardian*, 8 September 2001, about the 'deliberate and heavy attempt to deter, scare and humiliate her', prior to the publication of her autobiography. As a result, she 'thinks she understands better what people outside feel when they're trying to deal with the state, or particularly the secret state . . .'

Dame Stella's ordeal lasted but 18 months. My family's endured for years. I do not think, therefore, that she can begin to understand what we went through. If the leadership of our intelligence services did not know what was going on, they should be stripped of their pensions. If they did know, and did nothing, they should be held accountable under criminal law.

[2] Under the threat of the Official Secrets Act, my mother and I were not allowed to discuss my father's state with our family's trusted NHS (as opposed to SIS's private) doctor. Subsequently, SIS offered medical support with an SIS doctor which we declined.

[3] I understand that there was an agreement between the intelligence services and Parliament that prevented the former from spying at Westminster. I do not accept, as it was later put to me, that the APGs, because many of their activities are outside Westminster, do not fall within this agreement.

Many years later, by then a recognised specialist on the APGs, I gave evidence on them to Lord Justice Neill's Committee on Standards in Public Life (1999). However, advised by a parliamentary ally that I would not be called as a witness if I raised espionage issues, I did not bring up any. Nevertheless, in my written evidence, I documented my anxieties that young APG staff could become espionage targets.

32

THE CHIVALRY OF A LEFT-WING MP

The No Names' demands grew increasingly nasty. These included wanting information on a young Conservative MP, who was a member of the APMIG and a personal friend, who died in tragic circumstances; and other information about another Conservative MP well connected with the Arab world whom I did not know but who married one of my colleagues.

The approaches were always accompanied by comments about a family tragedy, the details of which could only have come from our SIS files and a steady stream of incidents against my father which varied in their intensity and anguish caused. The resulting bewilderment and fear was indescribable. Throughout, my father and I were accused of causing 'embarrassment'. More importantly, he was threatened with the cancellation of his pension because his daughter's 'conduct' could impact on him and his former employment.

The final defining moment came when my confused and sick father was humiliated in front of me and I was forced to write a specific parliamentary report. Had I not written the report, he would have been stripped of his pension because he 'did not exist'. It was the only time I agreed to co-operate.

The demand followed a request that I accept the invitation of a *Tribune* MP, then joint chairman of an All Party country group, that I act as its *pro bono* secretary. The MP was a friend who accepted that I was not a Tribunite but was wholly sympathetic to some of *Tribune*'s overseas causes. I turned down the wholly innocent politician, giving as my reason my existing heavy workload.

Two days later, I was asked to contact the MP to say that I had changed my mind. 'He is a bit of an emotional fool but of interest,' said the No Name. 'You can use the All Party group as a cover to get to know him.' Again, I refused. I required no cover to get to know the MP, since I already knew him. I found even the thought of spying on him, let alone actually doing so, repugnant. I was flabbergasted, however, that SIS had known of the politician's request, let alone, given the sensitivity of my father's former specialist area, that it would demand I act for the All Party country group concerned, in order to get alongside him.

My background, I was told, far from being a drawback, 'was a plus'. Once more my nationality was brought up, this time with specific reference to what I 'owed' the Crown.

When my father complained to a new SIS civil servant now responsible for 'liaison', he was told, 'Your daughter has nothing to do with us. Go to the police if you have proof of such harassment.' In addition, and throughout it all, my father received what he described as 'pin-prick' phone calls from the No Names asking about the family's welfare and forcefully emphasising that his former SIS diplomat and Whitehall colleagues were so senior, or retired, that they could not become involved 'with other people's personal problems'.

An evening of unbearable sorrow followed, the recollection of which night remains scorched in my memory. The following day, under the guise of 'poor pay and conditions', I resigned the job I had held for seven years, giving my employers the six months' notice I was legally contracted to offer. I left the company in May 1985. CP was devastated. I had withstood the pressure for four and a half years.

I wrote the parliamentary report demanded in longhand. My father sat broken-hearted in his armchair, my ballet-slippers on his lap. He had picked these up off the floor where I had dropped them after returning to my parents home for dinner following an after-work ballet class. Endlessly, he wound the pink satin ribbon of one of my slippers around his fingers. The No Name waited patiently for me to finish. He even made me coffee. My father signed off my report on my behalf. It was the only chivalry he was allowed to offer.

I believe the pressure was turned up because I had started to collate the commercial interests of some MPs and peers participating in the new select committees and some All Party groups. I used *Who's Who* as my source document, to compile lists of various parliamentarians and their directorships. (In those days, a sophisticated *Register of Members Interests* did not exist.) I have no doubt that it was this work, which I did in my own time, that led to the accusation I was 'an embarrassment to HMG'.[1]

As a result, I was forced out of a job where my continued and senior advancement had been assured. (I presume, had I agreed to work for the No Names, I could have been assured of similar promotion.) I had to leave a company where I had been supremely happy, working with colleagues and friends I adored, and for two employers whom I liked and respected.

I did not understand then, any more than I do now, why it was so important to destroy my career. I believe that the answer lies in no more than petty vindictiveness towards those who refuse to spy on those who trust them – in my case, my colleagues, employers, their clients, and the politicians with whom, inevitably, I mixed.

I would make the same decision today – it was one of the easiest I have ever had to take. What was difficult, however, was coping with the sense of injustice that, although I had done nothing wrong, I had been penalised. As it happened, my father was diagnosed with terminal cancer soon after, so I would have given up work anyway to assist my mother in his nursing. This, however, was hardly the point.

Conditioned by long years of secrecy and a sense of shame at what had happened, my family told no one of our problems. Throughout it all, however, I had the support of Commander Powell, who did all he could to prop me up. I was also the lucky recipient of many acts of kindness from my friends. (An example would be the invitation from a colleague, married to a lawyer who sang in the Westminster Abbey Choir, who invited my parents to listen to the St Matthew Passion. Noting that my father, who broke down and wept in the Abbey, was 'a deeply troubled man', she did not leave his side.)

At times it was surreal. I had complete normality in the office and in my own apartment. However, at my parents' home or on the road, things were anything but normal. For example, it was put to me that my father had been 'making a nuisance of himself' – he had been seen at his local high-street bank in a 'dishevelled' condition, when he was not in the best of health.

In May 1985 my father was diagnosed with lung cancer – hardly surprising, given his one-time four-packet-a-day habit. As any reader who has been involved with watching someone they love come to terms with terminal illness will know, it is a time when people go into overdrive as they try and find out as much as possible about the medical condition, and the specialist consultants, in the hope that they can delay the future. Everything else becomes irrelevant and, in a strange way, there is far greater equilibrium. Certainly, this is what happened in my family as soon as my father's illness was diagnosed.

SIS simply could not hurt us any more. It is not that the No Names lost power nor that we despised them less. Merely that, for the first time, we could see them clearly.

As I took turns with my mother to nurse my sick father through long days and nights, I coped as best I could with a growing sense of fury at the evil of what had happened. The contrast could not have been clearer. My father's dignity and will to live, gratitude for our care of him, fears for our future, and the tenderness with which, even in his final days, he enveloped us, compared with the No Names, who had no moral reference point, and who had tried, and almost succeeded, in violating my family.

What made things so much worse were their impeccable manners. On one occasion my telephone calls were raised as a subject because these were 'new'. At the time, I was trying to obtain information on lung cancer, including from the United States, because of my father's illness. An immediate apology for the inquiry was given. On another occasion, the No Name was waiting for me at my apartment when I returned late at night, having been nursing my father. He approached in the dark when I parked my car. I refused to speak to him and he was distraught and contrite that he had frightened me.

My father died the following year, in October 1986, leaving – through no fault of his own – my mother and I in a state of espionage 'intestacy' and all the chaos this implied.

Unaware of this, 'Geoffrey Kingsmill' and his wife visited my mother six weeks after my father's death. I was also present.

I had not seen them for several years. Following my father's retirement, I had declined their two invitations to accompany my parents to dinner at their home. I believed 'Kingsmill' had not shown the same loyalty to my father as the reverse; he had abandoned him to Alexis Forte, whom, today, I think was bordering on insanity;[2] 'Kingsmill' had also distanced himself ruthlessly from the criminal harassment of the No Names. I had no desire to be in the same room as him.

The meeting was awkward. Conversation was stilted and formal. Eventually, discussion about family records came up. 'Kingsmill' adored archives and was unhappy to learn that my father had destroyed most of his papers before he died and my mother and I were destroying much of what was left. Referring to my father's long years of service, 'Kingsmill' remarked hesitantly, 'It is a shame it all went wrong.' He seemed genuinely mystified as to why it had. My mother ignored the comment.[3]

A year later, in 1987, still infuriated by what had happened to my family, I approached Bob Cryer, a former MEP and Labour Minister. He had just returned to the Commons after a four-year absence. He had made his name, originally, on lobbying issues, when I had first been in touch with him. He was particularly concerned about MPs who did not declare their commercial interests, as well as, subsequently, the All Party groups. He was vehemently opposed to the APGs because he believed they were anti-democratic and provided a vehicle for commercial lobbyists to influence the system not available to others. I was a supporter of the APGs but wanted them regulated. Some, although not all, of Cryer's conclusions I later shared.

Our relationship was a restricted one, not least because I came from the twin worlds he loathed and worked for Commander Powell, whom he detested, and for whom I had the deepest affection. A lesser man, unable to overcome his prejudices, would have walked away. He did not do so. Instead, he recognised that anger could be a fickle gift, and made it clear he would not hold it against me if, at whatever stage, I wished to break off contact. He was particularly informed about the problems faced by Tribunite MPs and the conduct of the press. He was pragmatic at the negative response I had from a then senior member of the parliamentary press when I approached him about my concerns on lobbying issues.

So far as I could tell, Bob Cryer knew little about espionage, not least because he was 'far too busy' to be 'worried' about the subject. However, I have since been told that the impression he gave me was misleading, and I understand that in 1979 he was one of the first MPs to table questions to Prime Minister Thatcher about Sir Anthony Blunt.

Although a man of the hard left, he was not blind to the cares of those from the right, and was especially saddened at the treatment of my mother. He accepted that those from 'the war generation', especially if, like my mother, they were from a modest background, believed loyalty and service to the Crown was what honourable people offered.

He was also the first to recognise how exposed I was in approaching him in the first place: the intelligence services were suspicious of any left-wing MP or MEP. They also did not regard former Labour Ministers as 'Ministers of the Crown'. Therefore, when I contacted Cryer – who was Parliament's only independent specialist on the lobbying industry – who had been all of these, I was aware, but did not accept, the sensitivities.

Cryer was particularly anxious to protect me because of the work on the commercial interests of MPs and peers that I had been doing privately, which I passed to him. More importantly, he accepted my reservations that I did not become a tool of the hard left, pursuing an agenda I did not share. The result was that we respected each other's limits, and did not press beyond them.

Crucially, he gave me permission to give the No Names his telephone numbers and deal with him directly. As a result, he ensured my mother's SIS pension would be respected; argued successfully that the UK had no bonded workforce: i.e. a parent's previous employment did not bind his or her children; guaranteed that I could not be prosecuted for consulting him; and, as importantly, that my mother and I would be free from further reprisal.

He also introduced me to an investigative journalist with Granada Television's award-winning *World in Action*, Mark Hollingsworth, who subsequently acted as conduit on lobbying issues. Although Hollingsworth was not initially aware of the reasons behind the introduction, his detached personality was a bonus. For example, he had a more balanced approach to the work of Commander Powell than did Bob Cryer.[4]

So far as I know, I am the only commercial lobbyist with whom Cryer was prepared to liaise. He was so protective of me that, on several occasions, he did not use my information in case it inadvertently exposed me as his source to the wider lobbying industry. He did, however, make it clear to the No Names where it had come from, on the basis that they 'would not dare' take him on. The No Names were absolutely panic-stricken and melted away.

He was a shining example of all that is best in a parliamentarian. He did not frighten, and was scrupulous and even-handed. I asked for help. He gave it. I became particularly dependent on him after Commander Powell retired, and later died (1989). Knowing how much CP had meant to me, Cryer offered quiet condolences. I will always be grateful.

At no time, despite his countless invitations, did I meet him. Although disappointed, he was always understanding about my reasons. (I had been straightforward with my former employers about contacting Cryer. However, out of respect for them – Commander Powell was particularly upset – I did not meet him.)

I was in close touch with Cryer immediately before his death in 1994. He had tabled yet more parliamentary questions, in which I had assisted, on the conduct of the commercial lobbying companies. In addition, at my suggestion, he was due to address a seminar organised by a friend of mine on his second great interest, the film industry.

He was thrilled with the invitation and was pleased Mark Hollingsworth and I would be in the audience. In long years, it was the only 'thank you' he was prepared to accept. We looked forward to meeting for the first time. Regrettably, he was killed in a motor accident only days before the appointment.

NOTES

1   At one stage, some years after my father's death, I was so intimidated by the No Names' suggestion that I was 'causing embarrassment to HMG' that I refused a credit in a book on the lobbying industry. This was written by Mark Hollingsworth, the journalist to whom Cryer had introduced me. (*MPs for Hire: The Secret World of Political Lobbying*, published by Bloomsbury, 1991.)

Today, Mark Hollingsworth is *Baghdad's Spy*'s editor. I have paid tribute to him in my acknowledgements.

2   For the best account of the mental health of public servants, see 'Mood Swings', in *Ailing Leaders in Power 1914–94* by Hugh L'Etang, published by Royal Society of Medicine Press in 1995.

3   In the early '90s, I spoke to 'Mrs Geoffrey Kingsmill' again. She was sweet enough to say, 'Your father was a great man.' She was the only person to express appreciation for his work after his death. I thanked her for her kind comment, and passed it to my mother with much pleasure. Such are life's coincidences, I last heard of 'Kingsmill', long into his retirement, when he hired a young person known to a friend of mine, to work for his international relations consultancy.

4   It would be difficult to find three more different people. However, what Cryer, Hollingsworth and I shared was a view, and knowledge, that Parliament was corrupt institutionally, in part because of individuals playing the system in the houses of Lords and Commons. The extent of corruption was censored/withheld from the public and remains one of this country's biggest scandals of parliamentary democracy.

33

AN INTELLIGENCE BLUNDER

Back in 1986, shortly before my father died, he gave clear, authoritative instructions to SIS about a matter which he precisely anticipated arising after his death. For future ease of reference, he recycled the original codeword. In addition, he instructed that I be provided with a crucial, direct Whitehall telephone number so that, when the time came, I could act as the conduit on this matter. Because of his seniority his demands were met.

I agreed with the arrangement. However, I also requested that I be allowed to report to a senior military civil servant, Colonel —, the father of one of my oldest friends. Although the Colonel had no knowledge of my background, I have no doubt that he would have accepted my call. He would also have been able to progress political and military intelligence at the highest and appropriate level. SIS refused the request on the grounds he had been 'in a different organisation'. As a result, the matter was left in the hands of the No Names and there was failure.

Prior to the Gulf War, the crucial direct Whitehall telephone line with which I had been provided was disconnected. I subsequently found out that the colonel whom SIS had prevented me from contacting was a personal friend of the future Gulf War Commander, General Sir Peter de la Billiere.

During the Gulf War I met a former colleague – the lady who had been so kind to my father in Westminster Abbey – in the Central Lobby of Parliament. She was by then the research assistant to a prominent MP and former Conservative Minister. Her son, whom I had known since his childhood, was now a young captain in the Queens Dragoons fighting in the desert.

As young men and women wore the Crown's uniform, a British Chief of Staff responsible for the lives of those same young people discharged his duties by entertaining his mistress, herself the wife of a former Conservative Defence Minister, at a grand London hotel. Meantime, I was aware of chronic SIS failure.

My friend's son returned and is today a husband and father. The young captain did not know that during the Gulf War his mother wept, as all women weep for their sons, whatever the army, whatever the nationality, as she read his letter to me. Nor did he know that as his mother cried, I knew that the Crown, and its constituent offices, had failed its young soldiers as profoundly as it had failed the citizens of Iraq.

I can still see the No Name's look of disbelief and horror, as the extent of the SIS blunder dawned. In a panic, he tried to blame his subordinate. This was a No Name I had met only once, many years before, and who had no responsibility for, or knowledge of, his superior's negligence. I have paid tribute to this No Name in the acknowledgements.

To further protect himself, the more senior No Name arranged for me to receive my first letter from SIS, using a PO box address. This was signed by yet another No Name, pretending that SIS had not been in touch for a number of years, and was apparently only inquiring about the welfare of my widowed mother. (If this had indeed been the motive, he did not explain why SIS had waited four years to find out.)

The letter also cited the name of the SIS civil servant known to me, in whose name the No Names had first contacted me many years previously. (Another letter from an SIS PO box implied that I had met another No Name. Since I did not recognise the alias, I assume SIS inadvertently gave me the wrong one.)

My mother and I were so appalled by SIS's attempt to bluff things out that, on my mother's instructions, I ignored the letter. Some months later, an identical one arrived by registered post, to which I responded. I discreetly pointed out that there had been a serious operational mistake. SIS did not reply.

The following year, came another letter. This time I responded in detail. In addition, I asked that SIS never contact myself or my mother again. This request was ignored.

Next came a Christmas card. In recognition of the illness that killed my father, and presumably in an attempt to be sensitive, the card was sold in aid of a lung-cancer charity. Again, we ignored it. A short while later, now aware, no doubt, of the extent of the blunder, the No Names turned up again.

One morning, immediately after I had left for the office, leaving my mother alone, there was a dreaded knock on the door. The No Names, for the first time represented by a woman, were back. My mother refused to let her in. In some distress, she telephoned me at my office.

I contacted Bob Cryer to explain what had happened. Stunned, he instructed me to explain my late father's history and the operational blunder to someone of seniority whom I trusted and who had the appropriate contacts in the Conservative government's party. He explained that the intermediary would have to introduce me to a politician, who would, unlike himself, be regarded by SIS as a crown servant.

After we rang off, I sat down in a daze. The intermediary whom Cryer and I agreed was the best one for me to approach had known me for years. However, during all that time I had never mentioned my background. Now, out of the blue, I was to plunge him, unprepared, into my espionage inheritance . . .

34

THE RT HON. THE LORD COLNBROOK KCMG

I followed Bob Cryer's instructions. As has so often been the case, although the intermediary whom I approached was surprised – having no connection with espionage himself – he reacted with immediate gallantry and concern.

As a result, under a covering letter which I did not see, I was introduced to the Rt Hon. the Lord Colnbrook, better known as Humphrey Atkins MP, former Conservative Secretary of State for Northern Ireland. He invited me and the kind intermediary who introduced us to an initial meeting in the House of Lords.

The assistance Lord Colnbrook subsequently gave, although for a far more limited period than Bob Cryer's, was similarly helpful. He was surprised at the extent of Bob Cryer's involvement, but concluded that he was '[. . .] sanguine. I have always said that some on the Left are merely misguided. Not my sort of men. But doubtless, I am not their's either.'

However, Colnbrook refused to table parliamentary questions that I had drafted about my allegations, insisting I confine any comments to my mother's well-being and my father's early years of service.

A competent and amusing man, he was straightforward about what he would or would not do. (He was also irreverently politically incorrect, inquiring brightly, as the waiter in the House of Lords took our order, 'Shall we have crumpet for tea?')[1]

As a result of Lord Colnbrook's intervention, I received a qualified apology, via a letter from Downing Street dated 13 April 1994, stating:

> SIS wish to apologise for the distress they seem to have caused Miss Souza's mother. This had certainly not been their intention. SIS are deeply committed to the welfare and well being of their former agents and families and seek to maintain contact and, where appropriate, to offer help and advice [. . .]

The letter continued: 'SIS are unable to trace the letter which Miss Souza sent in February 1992; because they did not know of it, they continued to try to keep in touch with her.'

The significance of the missing letter was that, in it, I had referred to SIS's blunder prior to the Gulf War. To their credit, the SIS No Names subsequently admitted that, although they had been unable to find my February 1992 letter, they had discovered another I had written which also, specifically, referred to the war.

SIS was at its most disingenuous when Downing Street claimed:

> [. . .] Files so far examined do not record the telephone number with which Miss Souza was issued and SIS therefore cannot comment on whether that number has been disconnected. If Miss Souza still has a record of the number and would let SIS have it, it would help them identify it [. . .]

The telephone number that SIS suggested via Downing Street I contact it on was the one that it had disconnected.

SIS had reconnected it.

In addition, a meeting with the then SIS staff counsellor, Sir Philip Woodfield, was suggested. Lord Colnbrook, who knew the staff counsellor well – Sir Philip had been Permanent Secretary at the Northern Ireland Office when Lord Colnbrook was Secretary of State – spoke warmly of him.

Lord Colnbrook was punctilious in writing, stressing that Sir Philip would be happy to see me. However, he made it clear in private that he did not want me bothering Sir Philip unless it was 'really necessary'. Taking the hint, I declined the invitation. Lord Colnbrook was also candid about his patronage – it was conditional upon me confining my comments to administrative and pension matters pertaining to my mother.

In a letter dated 19 May 1994, he wrote:

> I note that you say that your reply [to SIS] is likely to be 'fairly severe'. I am bound to tell you that I thought the Private Secretary's letter was really very helpful. He passes on the apologies of the SIS for the distress they seem to have caused your mother; they offer to discuss the details of her pension and tax position following your father's death; they suggest that you should discuss this either with a representative of the SIS or with the Intelligence Services staff counsellor, whichever you prefer, and they promise not to seek to make further contact with your mother.
>
> It must be, of course, entirely up to you to decide in what terms you reply to this letter but I am bound to say that I cannot see that a 'fairly severe' reply is likely to be particularly helpful to you and your mother.

There followed a cordial meeting with two other No Names on 28 July 1994, who, for the first time, were referred to on government stationery. Also for the first time, I was given permission to have a person of my choice present. I declined, because, following Lord Colnbrook's intervention, I believed it was now in the Foreign Office's interests to be seen to be offering this. I was subsequently informed in a Foreign Office letter that the No Names were 'legal advisers'. Had I been told in advance that they would be lawyers, I would not have met them on my own.

The meeting, which took place at my request in my home, revolved around the No Names' position – and SIS's excuse – that 'perceptions have changed'. In fact, these have not changed to this day, although the Crown's obligations have.

Next, the No Names tried to challenge my father's status. (SIS does not readily admit to having full-time, dual-career civilian spies who, in my father's day at least, also had available, if they chose, a career path and diplomatic and/or military rank.[2])

Backing off quickly, they then tried to claim, 'You were not there.' When this did not work either, they asked me – in some desperation – why I had not made my complaints directly 'to The Chief', the late Sir David Spedding. They followed it up with a query as to why I had not taken SIS through the law courts when I was nursing my terminally ill father. Apart from the absurdity of the suggestion – I was not given permission to have a lawyer until after the meeting, which was eight years after my father's death – the question was so surreal, all I could do was stare at them.

Shortly before the meeting ended, one of the No Names drew my attention to a well-thumbed copy of the Official Secrets Act. The threat was evident.

After the meeting, I changed my mind about consulting the SIS staff counsellor Sir Philip Woodfield. However, when I wrote to the Prime Minister's private secretary at 10 Downing Street, my request was ignored even though I had respected the limits set by Lord Colnbrook.[3] In my letter, I confirmed that I would in due course wish to give evidence to the Parliamentary Intelligence and Security Committee, then being established.[4]

My mother and I had an alternative to Lord Colnbrook as intermediary, namely the former chairman of the *International Herald Tribune*, Sidney Gruson. This came about because his daughter Sheila, a school friend, to whom this book is dedicated, stayed with us for brief periods in the early 1990s. As a result, Sheila was conscious of some of the stress under which my mother and I were living.

Espionage-aware, and raging on our behalf, she was anxious we allow her well-connected father, who had retired into a distinguished American merchant bank, to help. Alternatively, she suggested the assistance of her mother, Flora Lewis, the former Paris bureau chief of *The New York Times*. We declined, selecting the route offered by Lord Colnbrook.

My mother and I did not go, as Sheila put it 'the American way', for two reasons. First, because to go to the Americans would have embarrassed my father's memory. He lived and died a Crown servant. Second, because it could have similarly embarrassed the family of a mutual friend whose parents were close friends of the Gruson family. The father, Colonel —, was the senior British military civil servant, to whom I referred earlier.

Having been preoccupied with the past for many years, I believe it was a mistake for my mother and I to have been so 'well-behaved'. I would recommend anyone in a similar position, if they are fortunate enough to have the contacts, to use them. I believe that, following the Gulf War blunder, had we asked for the chivalry of Sheila's father, or the colonel, they would have given it. I have no doubt that their efforts and prestige, on either side of the Atlantic, would have released my mother and myself from SIS's crass stupidity and intimidation.

I can only assume that the reason for the harassment was to protect Sir David Spedding's reputation and that of his officers in the light of the Gulf War blunder. Sir David became SIS Chief in 1994, the same year Lord Colnbrook raised matters on my behalf. My father's unchallenged authority on Iraq would have been a further embarrassment to Sir David.

A minor bout of harassment followed, including entry into my house and the placing of a stranger's credit card Switch receipt from an IKEA store in my handbag. This was drawn on the same day that I was having lunch in France, and found the same night, on my return. As my Visa statement proves the date and time of my lunch in France, I could not have been anywhere near IKEA at the time of the Switch receipt. Soon after, came interference with my telephone and mail. In addition, various incidents occurred which may or may not have been SIS-inspired. For example, I sent a friend through the post a chapter of a novel I was writing, in which there was discussion of the British honours system. Part of the action took place in a town in Germany. A few days later I received a telephone call at my office, on a heavily echoing telephone line, from a stranger wanting to discuss the German town and, in particular, the British honours system. The telephone call was a nonsense. The man to whom I was speaking got into a hopeless muddle – I ran rings around him – and he eventually put down the receiver.

I recognise coincidences can, and do, happen. Therefore, I am more than prepared to accept that these events could have been coincidence. For example, a journalist asked about my knowledge of a retired senior SIS civil servant who was a potential source for a television programme. I had never mentioned the SIS civil servant, whom I knew, to the journalist. Fearing a set-up, I immediately contacted the civil servant's wife. It later turned out that the civil servant himself had contacted the television programme on another issue. The timing was wholly coincidental.

However, so far as I can tell, there were no explanations for the coincidences mentioned above and others that I have not detailed. I believe that the sole aim of one of the No Names put forward by the Foreign Office to assist me was to subvert the law. His title was (something similar to[5]) 'Head of SIS Pastoral Care'. As a result, there was not only an inherent conflict of interests in his role, but he was also responsible for setting in train the final round of authorised intimidation of me.[6]

Nevertheless, eight years after my father's death, the Crown, finally, on 26 August 1994, wrote to me in detail and officially.

NOTES

[1] Those seeking to establish a paper-chain with patrons from the House of Lords could remember that some peers do not always sign-in their guests with the House of Lords police. Women, therefore, may have to put up with the polite giggles of the Palace of Westminster police, particularly if the peer has a 'reputation'. The way around the problem is to send a letter confirming the meeting beforehand, copied to the Palace police.

[2] Dame Stella Rimington stated in the *Guardian*, 10 September 2001, '[. . .] in the British system agents are never employees of the intelligence services [. . .]'

This may well be the case today. It was not so when my father served the Crown. In addition, although I am not a lawyer, Dame Stella's comment appears to deny the 1996 Employment Rights Act definition of a 'worker'.

[3] I do not know whether, having changed my mind, the request to meet the SIS staff counsellor was ignored as a result of SIS incompetence, or because espionage-families do not fall within the staff counsellor's remit.

In April 2002, the intelligence services announced that staff will have their rights looked after by the First Division Association (FDA), a trade union for senior civil servants. It was not made clear whether the FDA would also take responsibility for espionage-families. Nor was there clarification of the staff counsellor's role.

[4] Although many hopes were raised, the Parliamentary Intelligence and Security Committee is not universally respected. However, I found it interesting to note the extreme nervousness in the eyes of the No Names when I mentioned it. I also noted that they were petrified of the Labour Party.

[5] The No Name did not give me his business card, therefore I cannot remember his precise title.

[6] As I have already stated, the Foreign Office subsequently described the two No Names as 'legal advisers'. If this is the case, I believe that the senior No Name present should have been reprimanded by the Law Society.

35

A LETTER FROM THE FOREIGN OFFICE

Perhaps naively, I was hoping for a more respectful letter. One, for example, paying tribute to my father's work and excellence that my mother could have read with pride. It was not to be. Disappointed, I told her not to look at it since it would only upset her. However, I was grateful to have it because, for the first time, SIS:

- Responded on official Foreign Office notepaper;
- Gave me permission to have a lawyer.

I read its 'legal' paragraph several times to see if there were any conditions. There were none. SIS were stating clearly: '[. . .] You are free to obtain independent legal advice and will not be in breach of your obligations under the Official Secrets Act (OSA) in discussing with your solicitors matters which are relevant [. . .]'.

The relief was enormous – I had first asked for this right in 1984, two years before my father died. The only thing SIS appeared to be saying additionally was something that I knew anyway, i.e. the granting of such permission meant that the Crown, by implication, was saying that I did have OSA obligations, which it was now waiving, even though I had never been a Crown employee.

I did not instruct lawyers for several reasons. First, because I knew the harassment would continue if I did. Second, because I did not have the money to do so. Third, because I would have been gagged if lawyers, acting on my behalf, had taken on the state. However, those I spoke to, especially one in the House of Lords, were so incensed by SIS's conduct that they wanted to act on my behalf for free.

All agreed – including a civil servant predisposed to support the Crown – that SIS had, throughout the years, 'been in error' in using the OSA to gag me. (According to the No Names, any reference to my family life – whether the anguish at being forced to give up access to aunts, uncles and cousins, or mention of specific details of my father's career – could have been considered a contravention of the Act, with possible criminal charges.)

SIS also, for the first time, acknowledged my letter. In this, I had confirmed my father's rank (full colonel) and set out my allegations. These were what I perceived to be SIS's two-tier employment system, racism, blackmail, intimidation, incompetence, blunder prior to the Gulf War and, finally, salary and pension issues.

SIS ignored every point I made bar one – it set out its version of the financial arrangements with my father. It said that:

> [. . .] the terms of the oral contract are documented by your father's case officers [. . .] There is no record of your father challenging the terms of his agreement with SIS; neither his fee arrangements nor his pension terms were the subject of complaint from him.

Particularly striking was SIS's piety about money. This, as it was designed to be, was insulting. For example, SIS stated: 'Your father worked voluntarily for SIS in return for monetary reward. He was not staff [. . .]'

The obvious riposte is that civil servants and diplomats – the staff – similarly work 'voluntarily' for SIS for 'monetary reward'. Moreover, as my father's career proved, the word 'voluntary' was only accurate up to a point. SIS was 'voluntary' when he joined; but he was prevented, by intimidation, from resigning.

Next came a blatant lie on the 'fees' that SIS paid him. It stated: '[. . .] The contract varied in respect of the regular fees received by your father and the amount and type of work he agreed to do [. . .]'

SIS's use of the word 'fees' implied that my father was not a full-time dual career civilian Crown servant, but a contract or part-time worker – not that a spy can lose his life on a contract or part-time basis!

In fact, my father was not paid 'fees' but a 'salary'. I have a full set of his SIS bank statements to prove it. These show that his salary was paid by monthly remittance, from an SIS bank account, into his SIS bank account, on the same day, for the same amount, rising annually on the basis of his pay-rises. Moreover, after he retired, SIS wanted him to become a 'part-time' SIS translator – meaning he was 'full-time' before his retirement.

The Crown spoke in terms of 'fees' rather than 'salary' because SIS, via a letter from Downing Street on 13 April 1994, had been trying to claim that my father's pension, and by extrapolation, my mother's widow's pension, was at its discretion: 'The payment of pensions to former agents is not standard practice in SIS, who are not obliged to make such payments. They did so in the case of your father in recognition of his years of loyal service . . .'

SIS's reiteration that it had no legal obligation to pay my father a pension, was reminiscent of the blackmail I had encountered ten years earlier. In fact, my father was eligible because pensions were automatically included in 'salaries' and, despite what the No Names said, neither my father, nor subsequently his widow, could have been denied it.

I will always be sad that SIS's sole written acknowledgement of my father's years of courage had to be forced out of it; and that, once bounced, it sullied his memory by lies and boiling things down to money.

DOCUMENTS

Letter from the Prime Minister's Private Secretary William Chapman, 13 April 1994
Letter from the Rt Hon. the Lord Colnbrook KCMG, 19 May 1994
Letter from the Foreign Office, on behalf of SIS, 26 August 1994

10 DOWNING STREET
LONDON SW1A 2AA

From the Private Secretary

13 April 1994

Dear Lord Colnbrook,

The Prime Minister has asked me to thank you for your letter of 24 March on behalf of Miss Corinne de Souza of ███████████████ ████ with which you enclosed a copy of Miss de Souza's letter of 17 March to him.

SIS wish to apologise to Miss de Souza for the distress they seem to have caused her mother. This had certainly not been their intention. SIS are deeply committed to the welfare and well being of their former agents and families and seek to maintain contact and, where appropriate, to offer help and advice. In addition they are responsible for the correct discharge of funds from the Secret Vote. SIS are unable to trace the letter which Miss de Souza sent in February 1992; because they did not know of it, they continued to try to keep in touch with her.

In recognition of his services to HMG, Miss de Souza's father was offered either a lump sum payment or an index-linked pension. The basis on which the sums had been calculated was clearly set out. After some reflection he decided to opt for the pension, understanding that his widow would receive 50 per cent of that amount if he died. The payment of pensions to former agents is not standard practice in SIS, who are not obliged to make such payments. They did so in the case of Miss de Souza's father in recognition of his years of loyal service.

The SIS file indicates that when Miss de Souza queried details of the pension and tax position in November 1986, following her father's death, she was content with the arrangements as set out to her. SIS recognises that matters may have changed since then. They wonder whether Miss de Souza would find it helpful to discuss with a representative of SIS the detailed points she raises. If she would like to pursue this, SIS will, without prior commitment, revie[w]

- 2 -

level of her mother's pension, if she is suffering financial hardship. SIS would, of course, be very happy for you to be present, if Miss de Souza wishes. Equally, they would be happy to arrange for her to meet an officer in the presence of the Intelligence Services Staff Counsellor, Sir Philip Woodfield.

I am afraid that files so far examined do not record the telephone number with which Miss de Souza was issued and SIS therefore cannot comment on whether that number has been disconnected. If Miss de Souza still has a record of the number and would let SIS have it, perhaps through you, it would help them identify it.

If either you or Miss de Souza would like to telephone David Ackonson on ███████████ he would be pleased to make the arrangements. Despite her wish to have no further contact with SIS, I think the points she has raised are probably best dealt with in discussion. I hope she will feel able to take this up. Should she prefer not to, then I can assure you that SIS will not seek to make further contact with either Miss de Souza or her mother. The pension will of course continue to be paid, as at present.

Yours sincerely,
William Chapman

WILLIAM CHAPMAN

The Right Honourable The Lord Colnbrook KCMG

The Rt Hon The Lord Colnbrook KCMG

19 May 1994

Dear Miss de Souza,

    Thank you for your letter of 17 May, in reply to the one I sent you on 19 April, enclosing the one I had received from the Prime Minister's Private Secretary.

    I note that you would like to respond and ask if I would be willing to forward your letter. Since I initiated this correspondence on your behalf, I would be happy to continue it. So, if you would like to send me your letter, I will pass it on.

    I note that you say that your reply is likely to be "fairly severe". I am bound to tell you that I thought the Private Secretary's letter was really very helpful. He passes on the apologies of the SIS for the distress they seem to have caused your mother; they offer to discuss the details of her pension and tax position following your father's death; they suggest that you should discuss this either with a representative of the SIS or with the Intelligence Services Staff Counsellor, whichever you prefer, and they promise not to seek to make further contact with your mother.

    It must be, of course, entirely up to you to decide in what terms you reply to this letter but I am bound to say that I cannot see that a "fairly severe" reply is likely to be particularly helpful to you and your mother.

    I look forward to hearing from you.

Yours sincerely

Humphrey Colnbrook

Dear Miss De Souza

This to confirm in writing the legal position regarding your late father's contractual arrangements with SIS and his subsequent pension, as outlined by one of our legal advisers at the meeting on 28 July 1994. We also acknowledge receipt of your letter of 10 August 1994, sent on to us by the Prime Minister's Office.

Your father voluntarily provided services to SIS in return for monetary reward. He was not a member of staff and the terms of his contract for services with SIS were unique to him and varied throughout his 17 1/2 years of service according to the circumstances. There was no written contract between your father and SIS; the terms of the oral contract, however, are documented by your father's case officers in the many write-ups of their meetings. Prior to 1971 your father had been paid annual fees based on the amount of work he was doing for the service. The amount fluctuated, with the agreement of both parties.

In 1971, your father was offered and accepted pension terms which would come into operation upon his retirement. This constituted a variation of the former contract, which did not include a pension. The record shows that your father never asked for an increase in his fees nor requested to be given pensionable terms. These were offered by the Service and accepted by him.

At the time, no details of the pension calculation were given to your father but our records show that he accepted the principle 'with delight'. Subsequently, the contract varied only in respect of the regular fees received by your father and the amount and type of work he agreed to do. Upon retirement, in addition to the agreed pension, your father was given 3 months paid notice and 3 months pay in lieu of notice. This was not contractual but an _ex gratia_ provision which SIS gave in recognition of your father's long and valued service.

/When ...

- 2 -

When the time came for your father to retire in 1978, he was receiving a fee of £5,000 per annum. The pension he was offered was calculated on the standard basis of one eightieth of the final year's fees per year of service, and was index-linked. The terms of the pension were clearly explained, with the figures identified as £1,094 per annum with a lump sum of £4,898, half of which could be forgone as a contribution towards a widow's pension at half the rate of your father's. As an alternative he was given the option of a one-off lump sum payment of £31,000 which would have been a direct commutation of the pension. The records show that your father considered the options carefully and in October 1978 decided to take the £31,000. In December 1978, upon reconsideration of his accounts, your father decided to opt for the pension scheme which allowed for a half-rate widow's pension. There is no indication on file that any pressure was exerted to persuade him to take one course or the other. The decision was entirely his own.

The pension was duly paid throughout the remainder of your father's lifetime and the half-rate widow's pension continues to be paid to your mother. The Service has fulfilled and continues to fulfil its legal obligations arising out of its contract with your father including its continuing obligation to pay your mother the pension in accordance with the terms agreed. The value of this pension is no longer open to negotiation, but the Service operates an ex-gratia welfare scheme to assist the families of former agents who are suffering hardship. If you feel that your mother would be deemed a hardship case upon examination of her current circumstances, please put forward a case.

The above represents a summary of the legal position between the Service and your family. You are free to obtain independent legal advice and will not be in breach of your obligations under the Official Secrets Act in discussing with your solicitors matters which are relevant to this. We should point out that there is no record of your father challenging the terms of his agreement with SIS; neither his fee arrangements nor his pension terms were the subject of complaint from him.

I hope this meets your requirements for a summary of the legal position prepared by our legal advisers.

In answer to the enquiry in your letter to the Prime Minister's office as to where your solicitors should address correspondence, they may write to me at the above address.

Yours sincerely

D.W. Clayton

36

A SPY'S DAUGHTER SETS HER AGENDA

The problem with the Crown's letter was that, in describing what it called the 'contract' between my father and SIS, it had ignored the years of intimidation my family had suffered. It was confining me to one issue (and was even lying about this), as well as denying me access to the SIS Staff Counsellor and intimidating me into silence about all the rest. Because of this, I did not want the Crown to have 'the last word'.

Therefore, I set my own agenda. I could not bring individual SIS staff to justice. I could expose them collectively and hope that I have done so. I have not pursued things lightly – I knew that those taking on the State, at the end of it, are not the same people they were when they started.

A bit like espionage, really.

However, I could not walk away. I thought that it would be a betrayal of my passport, for which so much had been sacrificed, if I did not confront the Crown with its past. I was not 'only' half English, but a citizen who is as proud of her English blood as she is of her mixed-race parentage, and carries her British passport with more pride than the Crown will ever know. To have accepted the Crown's conduct would have been to condone it. For these reasons, and others I will not commit to paper, I chose my direction.

I took advice, of course, and considered it a triumph when a kindly meant member of the House of Lords cautioned, 'My dear, you will not be pretty forever. There is nothing more unbecoming than a woman with a cause, her good looks behind her.' (I was thrilled with the comment – in espionage, there are some lines you do not forget. That was one of them.)

I never once wavered from my objective. Supposing that there were other espionage-families which had suffered similarly – or worse – I thought that I might be better placed than they to try to tackle espionage-grievances which are only acknowledged privately. This was because I had, ever since I was a teenager, a detailed knowledge of SIS's coercive methods; a modest financial safety net, as I had inherited a small amount of money from my father – which would have lasted longer had I taken fewer holidays – and a few social connections. By virtue of my own career, I also had a sophisticated knowledge of Whitehall, government and the EU. However, these are not the same as power. They give the edge because you know what you are up against but not the wherewithal to fight your corner.

For this reason, it has taken me eight years to achieve what little I could. To do this, I lined up my strengths. These were: vanity – a desire for my father's name to have meant something to his employers; continuity – those who represent the Crown change while espionage-families do not; morality – it is immoral to harass the sick (my father) or blackmail a spy's daughter (myself).

Luckily, one gift of an espionage-childhood is that I play chess.[1] Therefore, I was able to visualise my battle and work out the best way to proceed. This is because – in chess – the goal is to protect the king, i.e. the Crown. However, the king can only move one square at a time and is dependent on the powerful pieces, as well as the humblest pawn, to protect him. His knights are able to strike from an angle outside the immediate field of vision and his queen has the greatest ability to move across the field, and therefore is the key to the king's protection.

By seeing things in this way, I worked out that the Crown has many knights but no queen. It is wholly dependent on other branches of the establishment, all of whose movements are inflexible, to defend it according to a predetermined pattern. While I had no knights, at least I knew what I was up against.

In addition, I had a queen – my mother – whose life had been given over to her husband and his service to the Crown. Therefore, with my queen and knowledge of the Crown's knights, I knew that if I moved sideways, I could go forward; if I acted outside the patterns, I could make my presence felt; and, better still, that the Crown would not notice until it was too late. Those considering a similar route should know their subject well but never worry about mistakes and have a sufficient knowledge of Whitehall and the political system to set worlds in collision with each other.

I could not campaign in the traditional way because the Crown did not wish me to and Parliament had no jurisdiction. To support my efforts, however, I could write a book to bring to the public's attention – with, I hope, the gallantry of our media – the Crown's treatment of our country's spies. In this way, I hoped to raise awareness of some espionage issues which might not otherwise be considered by our politicians and civil servants. For me to write a book that would interest my target groups, I had to establish name recognition within Westminster and parts of the media.

I did so by publishing the first exposé of the lobbying industry; submitting detailed research papers to the Committee on Standards in Public Life on the Westminster All Party groups; and compiling the first directory of lobbying consultancies. All of these, for a variety of reasons including fast turnarounds, had manifest imperfections but contributed to the creation of my specialist profile. In addition, I was fortunate to become a contributor to the country's leading specialist espionage magazine *Lobster*, which completed the process. I have paid tribute to its editor, Robin Ramsay, in my acknowledgements.

As a result of this preparatory work, I believe that I have done all I can to create an environment where some of my arguments may be considered. I do not claim this book will make a difference. I do believe that it may contribute to raising the profile of our country's spies and the Crown's treatment of them; and, for the first time, place in the public domain knowledge of the impact that SIS can have on a spy's family and children.[2]

Inevitably, throughout the eight years that I have been pursuing my objective there have been various incidents which I assume – perhaps erroneously – were inspired by our intelligence services. These were unpleasant but strengthened my resolve. They included an attempt to intimidate me at a lobbying industry cocktail party when I thought that I was among friends. (My first book gave specific advice to those in the lobbying industry considering working for the intelligence services. As a result, one senior espionage-aware lobbyist recognised that I had an alternative agenda and queried it at a meeting of one of the lobbying industry's regulatory bodies.)

The incident that hurt me the most was when the wife of a senior civil servant dropped my mother from her bridge circle. The mandarin's wife, part Memsahib and part Mignonette, delivered her snub with exemplary sophistication. My mother dealt with it with equal aplomb – she placed me opposite the mandarin's wife as her partner. A spy's widow is seldom intimidated by the wives of mandarins. In addition, she has a particular aptitude for charade.

There have also been countless privileges. These include friendships dating back to my school days which have stood the test of time; much kindness from individuals within the media, including the specialist press; and much appreciated goodwill of former colleagues in the lobbying industry or involved in the political process.

Surprisingly, there have been a couple of good jokes too. The best was when I received a letter in 'green ink' posted in Switzerland from a former senior Conservative politician. ('Green ink' can be a sign of a communication from the intelligence services because SIS's first Chief, Sir Mansfield Cumming, wrote only in green ink.[3])

When the letter arrived, I took it to a friend in the House of Lords. He studied it, put it down and got in another round of drinks. Finally he remarked, 'You should set up the "Green Ink Totty Society". GITS for short. Westminster could do with a few laughs.'

We do well to remember that jokes are the first and last weapon of a democracy, while being the only refuge of the reverse.

NOTES

1 Spy-children were always encouraged to play games. When I was growing up, the card game 'Brag' was considered good for bluff; 'Racing Demon' for alertness; chess for strategy and discipline; and 'Bridge' to improve memory.

All spies, although this could have changed today, also played games. 'Bridge' was a particular favourite since it allowed spies, accompanied by their necessarily bridge-playing spouse (usually a wife), to circulate without attracting attention. Other wives, when overseas, were encouraged to play Mah-jong, knowledge of which, in some parts of the world, often produced invitations to the Mah-jong parties of the wives/mothers of important men.

In addition, spies like my father were encouraged to frequent exclusive casinos. Others played dominoes and backgammon to enable them to mix in, say, backstreet coffee shops. (Despite backgammon's fashionable status in Europe, it was not a socially acceptable game in the Middle East.)

2 To go the distance, you will have to sacrifice many things, including your career, without any promise of success. If you fail, do not whinge.

Those raising espionage-family issues may find it difficult to establish a media profile. In addition, it can be difficult to challenge what sometimes appears to be a media espionage-cartel. Those coming across this problem could consider the 'back door' method. The one that became available to me, for which I will always be grateful, was *Lobster* magazine.

(Those prepared to make the compromises could have an easier journey if they make a direct appeal for support from some of those on the right, or some of those on the left. I did not, although it was tempting, because some on the right still extol the virtues of a free market, including an espionage one, which I refused to endorse; while some on the left expected me to deny my pride in my father, which I was not prepared to do.

Those who are hard-line perform an idiotic *pas-de-deux* while missing simple truths.)

3 I grew up with the knowledge that 'I must not write in green ink'. However, I cannot remember if it was my father who told me not to, or one of his colleagues.

The last piece of advice I offer to those considering exposing SIS is that they must be mindful of the safety of those connected with their parents' careers. (In addition, so far as it is possible, ringfence personal friends so that they are not exposed to SIS intimidation. The latter is particularly important if, say, they have City jobs since any association, however inadvertent, with those who challenge the State can impact negatively on their careers.)

Finally, you must protect those friends working overseas – if necessary drop them – in case their innocent assocation with a spy's family could endanger them.

37

SOURCES AND SORROW

Arriving home from the House of Lords, I settled down to pull my story, and what I knew of my parents, together. It took two years.

The first problem I stumbled upon was deciding what to put in, and what to leave out. I had dozens and dozens of documents, commercial files, notebooks and diaries to go through. For example, I discovered some notes that my father had written after he retired from SIS. Parts referred to gossip about various Arab Ministers chasing after the wives of some Western journalists attached to news agencies in the Middle East.

Another batch referred to speculation surrounding the private life of an employee of an overseas international agency. (Romance – and human nature – is always of interest to spies. Even retired ones.) All of this information bothered my father because, if true, it had security implications. Specific names were detailed and so were other matters. ('Pillow talk' is an acknowledged part of espionage and can be illuminating – one reason why reliance on technology and spy satellite intelligence has always been ridiculous.)

For obvious reasons, I destroyed the notes. Nor have I referred to any of the incidents or people mentioned. I also destroyed other records.

I decided not to write up the notes myself by disguising the individuals because I was anxious not to make a mistake – errors, including minor ones, can be more informative than accuracy. (I knew this because, reading a well-researched bestselling spy novel, I noticed that the author, in an effort to give an authentic background to a sensitive area I knew well, had made an inadvertent error – some errors are deliberate – in part of the text. This told me more about the author's overseas source than was prudent.)

Therefore I knew that I had to avoid making the same mistake and hope that I have done so. However, I would have liked to have retained some of the material so that it could have been archived for future historians of espionage. I regret that the Crown – despite a lot of huff and puff – offers no acceptable assistance. Of my own volition, I have self-censored and erred on the side of caution. For this reason, having first shown supporting documentation to my publisher and editor, some of it unique, I have not included it.

Mindful of security implications, by far the greatest frustration in writing the book has been not being able to do justice to who my father was. For obvious reasons, I could not name those with whom he circulated, and usually recruited. Even flicking through a magazine last year, 15 years after his death, struck a chord when I spotted a photograph of a high-ranking overseas diplomat whom I knew when he was young, and whose history, relatives and friends were known to me because of my father's work.

I also knew that I had to respect the privacy and safety of all my father's former sources, their families and/or heirs. Therefore I could not put in any of the atmosphere of espionage which is determined by the participants. In particular, I could not identify my father's sources pertaining to Iraq or Kurdistan, who have, at various times, opposed the regime in Baghdad.

This is a pity because while today many Iraqis and Kurds with whom our country has liaised for many years rightly stand condemned for factionalism or corruption – as well as much worse – I would have liked to recognise the honourable intentions of some of these men in youth, especially their courage and ideals. Not being able to write about the people associated with my father's career, meant that I had to deny the honour and integrity of the best. There are whole areas I have not even touched upon.

In many ways, my mother 'handicapped' me the most. She was too modest to talk about her own daring; too disciplined to reveal her knowledge; and too dignified to condemn the Crown.

My final source is my memory. This goes so deep that espionage will be my skeleton. As a result, long into my maturity, I still see with child's eyes. I remember the wonderful picnics in the desert with Iraqi friends in the 1960s; the lies that I was told when I was later prevented from playing with their children; just as I see the fear in their father's eyes when he scuttled across an airport lounge to get away from me after we bumped into each other at an international airport in the 1990s. It was the fear of a man who knew that I knew that he had sold his own people for the price of an apartment in London; and my father had recruited and paid him. It was wrong then. It would be wrong today. I cannot bring myself to talk in terms of 'corruption' to which my father, on behalf of the Crown, was a willing party and accessory. But this is what it sometimes was. They all failed Iraq.

There were some who did not. For this reason, I remember also the freemasons and Communists of Iraq who were patriots and paid the price with their lives. In particular, I recall one of my parents' friends, a handsome Iraqi army officer. He should have been allowed to grow old, with his books and his football, his music and his singing; with a wife to love, and with a thousand children and grandchildren. He did not deserve what happened to him.

Time does not dim the past. It forces transparent acknowledgement.

I did not choose to be my own source. It is the final legacy of my espionage childhood. This has caused my mother Julia extra sorrow. My single-minded pursuit to force the Crown to acknowledge its mistakes and, in consequence, the life that I chose was not the one my parents would have wished for me. Sources and memories translated into book-form sometimes condemn the dead even if you loved them.

However, they can also bond the living. Richard – to whom I have been a selfish partner – changed his aspirations to accommodate mine, and did so without a single reproach when he was entitled to so many. No memory will ever be more precious than our flaws, the mistakes we made and the solutions we found.

To my mother and Richard, my gratitude and heart.

As for the Crown, my sources are the letter of condolence it never wrote, the wreath it never sent and the apology it never made.

Conclusion

OPEN LETTER TO SIR RICHARD DEARLOVE

Director General
'The Chief'
SECRET INTELLIGENCE SERVICES

London,
20 October 2002

Dear Sir Richard,

The absence of effective spies with the appropriate seniority, and their necessity, was brought home to us by the tragedy of 11 September 2001.

I have not a shadow of doubt that, had my father been alive, he would have heard the rumours concerning what was about to happen to the World Trade Centre; had the linguistic and cultural skills to sort out fact from fiction; had the contacts within al-Qaeda, the Islamic world in general, as well as key law enforcement agencies overseas, to ascertain precise details; had the authority to ensure that the Americans were warned at government-to-government level and the forcefulness to guarantee that his warnings were acted upon.

As a result, lives would not only have been saved in the United States but in other parts of the world. As a spy, this would have been his job and he would have done it well.

I hope my book explains some of the reasons why the SIS failed to nurture a new generation of spies with the appropriate skill-sets to replace him; and, in consequence, on 10 September, was unable to honour its responsibilities to one of its principal allies.

I turn now to other issues. You will agree, I am sure, that part of SIS's problems are due to its poor recruitment policies, administration and personnel management. The latter two were certainly the case when I was dealing with the Foreign Office in 1994. For this reason, I was disappointed to learn from your

232

entry in *Who's Who* that you were Director of SIS Personnel and Administration 1993–94. I appreciate that by the time Lord Colnbrook was raising pastoral issues on my behalf, you had moved on to become Director of Operations.

Nevertheless, in view of the fact that 'personnel' was, at one time, your responsibility, I hope that you will be interested in why I believe things went wrong for me.

I think it was for two reasons.

First, because in 1994, and at my request, Lord Colnbrook referred to the Gulf War blunder. This could have embarrassed the outgoing Director of Operations and newly appointed 'Chief', Sir David Spedding, who had been responsible for Gulf War intelligence. Therefore, I think the attempts to silence me were due to a cover-up at subordinate level in order to protect Sir David's reputation.

Second, I was naive to inform your organisation that I wanted to give evidence to the Parliamentary Intelligence and Security Committee (ISC) then being established and up-and-running by autumn 1994. At the time (and before my profound disillusionment with the ISC set in), I thought it would be interested to have an informed opinion of the pastoral care SIS offers its espionage-families.

I believe that the decision as to whether or not I be called as a witness ought to have rested with the ISC. At the time, much was expected of it. For this reason, Sir Percy Cradock's comments are informative. In his book *In Pursuit of British Interests*,[1] Sir Percy, Foreign Policy Adviser to prime ministers Thatcher and Major, and chairman of the Joint Intelligence Committee from 1984 to 1992, writes: 'I was not in favour of it [the ISC] but accept that in its present form it may give public reassurance that the intelligence services are working as they should be.'

His view has been supported by a sort of Cradock cumulus of mandarins. I believe that the problem I unwittingly presented was that I knew the SIS had not been 'working as it should be'; wanted to say so to the ISC; and, since I was not a former Crown employee, did not require the Crown's permission to do so. As a result, I had to be silenced.

If my beliefs are correct, it says a lot about your subordinates.

This, however, belongs to the past. What is important is the future – my anxiety is that I do not see how you can recruit men and women to replace people like my father, unless, first, you can confirm the morality of the Crown's ambitions, and second, demonstrate that it will take care of them and their families.

Spies move from, for example, the elegance of the Opera House to the terrors of a politically unstable Middle Eastern country, to the backstreets of the capitals of Europe. Much of the time they work in isolation, against professional and hideous enemies, with only their fears as companion. What keeps them going is not pecuniary interest – as the Crown seeks to imply – but service to our citizens and those of other countries. The least these men and women deserve – in the field and in retirement – is an appropriate level of succour and support.

Those of us who have witnessed their courage – bearing in mind that our spies are civilians, ordinary people with human failings the righteous condemn – never forget it. We are humbled by the experience and know we can never be that fearless ourselves. It should not have been a spy's daughter who sang her father's praises, but the Crown as his proud employer.

With these comments in mind, you will recall my opening letter and four objectives. These require no repetition. I also expressed the wish that you ask Her Majesty the Queen to consider a memorial to our spies.

I made clear that I had a second request.

This is it: given the standing of my witnesses, you will probably be aware that I could have sued SIS for damages. Instead, in lieu of any compensation for myself, and with the public's permission, I hope that you will use taxpayers' money to provide an appropriate donation, in my father's name, to widows of Commonwealth agents to top up their existing and very limited SIS pensions. Some of these, I understand, are living in penury. They are in their 80s and 90s and deserve better.

In 1994 your colleagues asked me what I wanted. You have my answer.

As for the tragedy of Iraq, no spy could have prevented the heinous decades. The Crown could have done.

Instead, the staff, including those in the oil industry, sustained evil. This is all the more shameful because as a result of venality, the right and honourable candidate to lead Iraq step-by-step into social justice was wilfully thwarted. Had the staff not connived in such thwarting, the dignified, highly educated and joyous Iraqi and Kurdish people would have been spared untold suffering.

My father was SIS's foremost authority on Iraq and knew or recruited many of the personalities involved, including those he advised be discarded who were subsequently picked up by the CIA. Because of the oil industry and the nature of Iraqi and Kurdish society, much of his work and advice have remained germane. It should not have done.

I hope that the Crown drinks the oil it covets. It has shamed the British people in whose name it has plundered and destroyed Iraq and Kurdistan.

Yours sincerely,

Corinne

NOTES

1 Cradock, P (1997) *In Pursuit of British Interests: Reflections of Foreign Policy Under Margaret Thatcher and John Major*. John Murray: London

DEDICATION

Sheila Gruson

IN MEMORY

Sheila was one of those rare people who could bring the spirit of America to a small part of England. No daughter of the United States could have been more loved. An alumnus of one of America's finest universities, she was a scholar, artist, carpenter, musician, writer, linguist, mathematician, translator, European, internationalist, New Yorker and American patriot.

Divorced and a single mother, she loved newspapers, idiom, narrative and adventure.

Born to glittering parents, Sheila was a mix of arrogance and humility; astonishing wealth and hand-to-mouth existence. She brought chaos into the lives of her friends because she expected us to change the world with her.

When the Berlin Wall came down, she flew to Germany to welcome others to freedom.

When the tanks rolled over students in China, she joined protest marches in London and Paris.

When atrocity happened in the Middle East, she lit candles for the children of all.

When she knew she was dying, she flew to South Africa with her beloved only daughter, so that they could dance in the ocean.

As Colonel —, the father of one of her dearest friends, says, 'We miss her chaos now.'

During her divorce, I commissioned Sheila to make me a 'small' jewellery box. Eighteen months later, she turned up with it. It was so large, she had had to hire a van to transport it.

Only Sheila's imagination could turn it into an adult-sized rocking horse, based on the Chinese dragons of Brighton Pavilion. The jewellery box was hidden in the seat. Presenting it, she said gleefully, 'You will never want to leave your father's house now. How would you find another one large enough to fit your jewellery box in?'

Sheila was right. Richard and I, with my widowed mother, have never left my father's house. As ever, she got the last word. She always did.

She died on my birthday in 1999.